THE PHENOMENON OF LIFE

Northwestern University
Studies in Phenomenology
and
Existential Philosophy

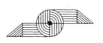

THE PHENOMENON OF LIFE

Toward a Philosophical Biology

Hans Jonas

With a foreword by Lawrence Vogel

Northwestern University Press
Evanston, Illinois

Northwestern University Press
Evanston, Illinois 60208-4170

Originally published in 1966 by Harper & Row, Publishers, Inc., New York.
Copyright © 1966 by Hans Jonas. Northwestern University Press paperback edition published 2001 by arrangement with Eleanore Jonas. Foreword by Lawrence Vogel copyright © 2001 by Northwestern University Press. All rights reserved.

Printed in the United States of America

10 9 8 7 6 5 4 3 2

ISBN 0-8101-1749-5

Library of Congress Cataloging-in-Publication Data

Jonas, Hans, 1903–
    The phenomenon of life : toward a philosophical biology / Hans Jonas ; with a foreword by Lawrence Vogel.
        p. cm. — (Northwestern University studies in phenomenology and existential philosophy)
    Originally published: New York : Harper & Row, 1966.
    Includes bibliographical references and index.
    ISBN 0-8101-1749-5 (pbk. : alk. paper)
    1. Life. 2. Existentialism. I. Title. II. Northwestern University studies in phenomenology & existential philosophy.

B3279.J663 P48 2000
113'.8—dc21

                                                                00-064570

The paper used in this publication meets the minimum requirements of the American National Standard for Information Sciences—Permanence of Paper for Printed Library Materials, ANSI Z.39.48-1992

For my wife,
whose belief
that I had something to say
made me say it

Contents

Foreword

I

Hans Jonas's *The Phenomenon of Life* is the pivotal book of Jonas's intellectual career. Along with Hannah Arendt's *The Human Condition,* Hans-Georg Gadamer's *Truth and Method,* and Emmanuel Levinas's *Totality and Infinity, The Phenomenon of Life* is one of the texts produced by former students of Heidegger that continues to reward careful study in the twenty-first century.[1] It articulates the core of Jonas's philosophy: an "existential interpretation of biological facts." But it also reminds us of the long road he travels to get there: in particular, his debt to, and break with, Heidegger. Finally, it foreshadows the two key developments of Jonas's philosophy to come: his ontological grounding of an imperative of ethical responsibility and his post-Holocaust Jewish theology. My aim is to show how *The Phenomenon of Life* comprises the center around which all of Hans Jonas's work orbits.

Born in 1903 in Mönchengladbach, Germany, to a Conservative Jewish family, Jonas migrated to Berlin to study religion, and in particular Torah, but then decided in 1921 to pursue philosophy at the University of Freiburg. There, he came under the tutelage of Husserl but worried about phenomenology's "restrictive emphasis on pure consciousness." Drawn by Heidegger's use of phenomenology to explore existential issues, Jonas transferred to Marburg and experienced the publication of *Being and Time* in 1927 as an "earthquake affecting the philosophy of our century" by "shatter[ing] the entire quasi-optical model of a primarily *cognitive* consciousness, focusing instead on the willful, striving, feeble, and mortal ego."[2]

Under the guidance of Heidegger and Rudolf Bultmann, Jonas used existential categories to interpret Gnosticism: a variety of religious teachings in the Hellenized Near East of the first three centuries A.D.

which shared a radically dualistic metaphysics. According to Gnostic theology, God utterly transcends the material world, which is under the sway of an evil demiurge. A person's task is to attain *gnosis,* or knowledge, allowing his soul after death to be freed of all worldly substance and to reunite with God. The *pneumaticos,* or spiritual person, liberates himself, through sacramental and magical preparations, from mundane norms—both natural and moral—for laws are rules of the demiurge's game. Jonas labels this dualistic attitude "anthropological acosmism" and sees in it the roots of nihilism.

> As the totally other, alien, and unknown, the Gnostic God has more of the *nihil* than of the *ens* in his concept. For all the purposes of man's relation to the reality that surrounds him, this hidden God is a negative term; no law emanates from him—none for nature, and thus none for human action as part of the natural order. His only relation to the world is the negative one of saving from the world. Antinomianism follows naturally, even if not inevitably, from these premises.[3]

Jonas's classic in the history of ideas, *The Gnostic Religion,* was begun in the late 1920s but only completed in the mid-1950s after his participation in both World War II and the Israeli War of Independence.[4]

Having completed the first volume of *The Gnostic Religion* in 1933, Jonas found out that the German Association for the Blind had expelled its Jewish members. He bore witness to the Nazis' "betrayal of the solidarity of a common fate" by abandoning the homeland where he had hoped to pursue an academic career.[5] And upon hearing of Heidegger's "shameful" decision in 1933 to assume the rectorship at Freiburg, Jonas was forced to decipher the "hidden" meaning of *Being and Time.* How, asked Jonas, could Heidegger's account of authenticity have allowed him to interpret Nazism as Germany's authentic destiny? His question became unavoidable after Jonas, having spent six years fighting for the Jewish Brigade of the Eighth British Army, returned to Palestine, only to discover that his mother, trapped in Germany, had been murdered at Auschwitz.

In the ninth essay of *The Phenomenon of Life,* "Gnosticism, Existentialism, and Nihilism," which should be read as a prologue to the rest of this book, Jonas describes the epiphany that enabled him to move from being a historian of ideas to a creative philosopher in his own right. While existential categories allowed him to enter the Gnostic world, his study of Gnosticism in turn provided a clue to a dualistic and hence nihilistic pattern at the heart of modern philosophy, and in particular Heidegger's "existentialism." Gnosticism and existentialism, movements so distant in time, share two fundamental premises: 1) the denial that the cosmos is ordered for the good; and 2) a belief in the transcendence of the acosmic self. Like the Gnostic *pneumaticos,* "the authentic individual" of existentialism stands above any moral law, or *nomos.* Without belief in a moral law rooted in nature, Jonas insists, the authentic individual is free to create values from his own perspective "beyond good and evil"—with an eye toward the open future but no orientation toward an eternal measure to stabilize the present.

While acknowledging *Being and Time* as the "most profound and . . . important manifesto of existential philosophy,"[6] Jonas traces Heidegger's "leap" into the arms of the Nazis to "the absolute formalism of his philosophy of decision," in which "not *for* what or *against* what one resolves oneself, but *that* one resolves oneself becomes the signature of authentic Dasein."[7] The root of this nihilism lies, according to Jonas, in Heidegger's uncritical acceptance of the "spiritual denudation [of the concept of nature] at the hands of physical science" since the Copernican revolution.[8] No longer believing that humanity belongs to a sacred order of creation or "an objective order of essences in the totality of nature," moderns have lost not only the grounds for cosmic piety but also a stable image of human nature—even the conviction that we have a nature. Jonas laments:

> That nature does not care, one way or the other, is the true abyss. That only man cares, in his finitude facing nothing but death, alone with his contingency and the objective meaninglessness of his projecting meanings, is a truly unprecedented situation. . . .Will replaces vision; temporality of the act ousts the eternity of the "good-in-itself." . . . As the product of the indifferent, his being, too, must be indifferent. Then the facing of his mortality would simply warrant the reaction "Let us eat and drink for tomorrow we die." There is no point in caring for what has no sanction behind it in any creative intention.[9]

In other words, Heidegger's existentialism gives us no good reason to care about humanity as a whole or the long-term fate of planet Earth.

But existentialism, on Jonas's diagnosis, is no idiosyncrasy within modern thought; it is instead the most complete expression of the "ethical vacuum" caused by two key assumptions of the modern credo: 1) that the idea of obligation is a human invention, not a discovery based on the objective reality of the Good-in-itself; and 2) that the rest of Being is indifferent to our experience of obligation.[10] Hans Jonas's whole philosophy aims at explaining, in a manner consistent with modern science, why human destiny makes a real, objective difference— because living nature is essentially good, is worth being cared for, and even intends that we care for her so that we, her most sublime creation, can continue to be.

II

Jonas's recovery of the meaning of Being unfolds in three stages: 1) existential, 2) ontological, and 3) theological. First, in *The Phenomenon of Life,* Jonas offers "an 'existential' interpretation of biological facts," arguing that purposive existence is not a special attribute of human beings but is present throughout living nature. Second, in *The Imperative of Responsibility: In Search of an Ethics for the Technological Age,* he provides an ontological grounding of our ethical obligations to nature and to ourselves as special products of its evolutionary labors.[11] These two stages are moments of his naturalistic project. But the third stage, represented by essays collected in his last book, *Mortality and Morality: A Search for the Good after Auschwitz,* finds Jonas proposing a Judaic theology of divine creation that he takes to be consistent with, though not necessitated by, his naturalistic existentialism and ontology. *The Phenomenon of Life,* however, already adumbrates the ontological and theological arguments that Jonas will develop in his later works.

1. The first through seventh essays of this book—and the transition that summarizes them—comprise the first stage of Jonas's reply to nihilism. Jonas uses Heidegger's own *existential* categories to undermine the modern credo that human being is the source of all value. Jonas provides "an 'existential' interpretation of biological facts" that lets us see, against Heidegger, how all organisms, not only humans, have "concern for their own being." Value and disvalue are not human creations but are essential to life itself. Every living thing has a share in life's "needful freedom" and "harbors within itself an inner horizon of transcendence," for each organism must reach out to its environment in order to stay alive.

Still, not all forms of life are the same. Plants, animals, and the human animal display an "ascending" development of organic functions and capabilities. Plants are driven by their metabolic needs and stand in an immediate relationship to their environment. In animals, the powers of motility and appetite, feeling and perception are grafted onto metabolism, allowing animals to have a more distanced relationship to their surroundings. "The great secret of animal life," writes Jonas, "lies precisely in the gap which it is able to maintain between immediate concern and mediate satisfaction."[12] Finally, in humans, what Aristotle called the nutritive and sensitive powers of soul can be guided by the "rational" capacities for imagination, thinking, and moral responsibility. These capacities enable us to act from a sense of our place in the world as a whole. But our widened horizon of self-transcendence brings in its wake perils peculiar to human existence: moods like anxiety, guilt, and despair.[13] Against the mechanistic tendency of modern thought, which boils the complex down to its simplest parts, Jonas finds the germ of what is higher in the lower forms from which the higher evolves. "Reality or nature is one," insists Jonas, "and testifies to itself in what it *allows* to come forth from it."[14]

2. The extension of *psyche,* or self-concern, to the entire organic world invites the second, *ontological* stage of Jonas's thought, for it enables him to venture two conjectures that cannot be proved but are consistent with the biological facts existentially interpreted: 1) that matter's feat of organizing itself for life attests to latent organic tendencies in the depths of Being; and 2) that the emergence of the human mind does not mark a great divide within nature but elaborates what is prefigured throughout the life-world. And these two points make room for a third speculation with dramatic ethical consequences: 3) insofar as we see ourselves, with our capacity for reflecting Being in knowledge, as "a 'coming to itself' of original substance," we should understand ourselves as being called by nature, our own source, to be her guardian.[15] By extending the category of "existence" to all organisms, Jonas makes possible a radical conversion of modern thought: "a principle of ethics which is ultimately grounded neither in the autonomy of the self nor in the needs of the community, but in an objective assignment by the nature of things."[16] Jonas announces the prospect of such an ethics in the epilogue to this book, but he only develops the connection between nature and ethics in *The Imperative of Responsibility.*

That all organisms must be able to experience value subjectively in order to avert death implies that value is inherent in nature. Jonas wor-

ries, however, that a "nihilist" may acknowledge the presence of subjective value in Being yet doubt "whether the whole toilsome and terrible drama is worth the trouble."[17] What must be established is the
objective reality of value—a Good-*in-itself*—because only from it can
a binding responsibility to guard Being be derived. On the basis of
"intuitive certainty," Jonas derives "the ontological axiom" that the
goodness of life is not relative to already existing purposes, for "the
very capacity to have purposes at all is a good-in-itself."[18] Through life,
Being says "Yes" to itself. Only humans, however, are able to discern
the ontological truth: that the presence of life in Being is "absolutely
and infinitely" better than its absence. The ethical consequence of this
axiom is that we have an obligation to protect the life-world. But do
all living things have equal ethical status? Jonas resoundingly answers,
"No." The primary object of responsibility within the Good-in-itself of
living nature, he contends, is humanity itself.

> Since in [man] the principle of purposiveness has reached its highest and
> most dangerous peak through the freedom to set himself ends and the power
> to carry them out, he himself becomes, in the name of that principle, the first
> object of his obligation, which we expressed in our "first imperative": not to
> ruin, as he well can do, what nature has achieved in him by the way of his
> using it.[19]

The evolution of the human species marks the transition within nature
from vital goodness to the capacity for moral rightness: from desire to
responsibility. That our primary responsibility is to protect the future
of humanity is no anthropocentric conceit but an objective assignment
by Being to safeguard the natural environment that has allowed us to
come forth from it.

Jonas thinks that unless we can think of nature as being a source of
value, and not a mere resource upon which we project our interests, we
will be unable to believe in the importance of limits to our technological remaking of nature. Such limits are especially urgent given our
increasing power to destroy our habitat and to alter "the human image"
by exerting control over behavior, the process of dying, and even the
genetic makeup of life.

3. Finally, we arrive at the *theological*—and specifically Judaic—
stage of Jonas's thought. Having located the Good-in-itself within
nature, what need is there for belief in God? Jonas concedes that nei-

ther his existential interpretation of the biological facts nor his onto-logical grounding of an imperative of responsibility *demands* that we see living nature as God's creation. But they do not *rule it out* either, according to Jonas, so long as our appreciation of the meaning of Being is *compatible* with faith. Jonas contends that although we can make ethical sense of our place in nature without appealing to religious belief in the transcendent, we can also make sense of nature—and perhaps deepen its meaning—by thinking of it as God's creation.

Jonas unabashedly conceives of God in what Heidegger—and Emmanuel Levinas, too—would decry as an "onto-theological" manner. In "Immortality and the Modern Temper," the eleventh essay herein, Jonas invents "a tentative myth" that shows the compatibility between reason and faith. He imagines that God withdraws from His own creation in order that the world might be "for itself," fraught with risk. God—utterly exhausted by His creative effort and with nothing left to give—pronounces His experiment to be good only with the long-awaited, but not inevitable, emergence of life: of creatures who affirm their own existence. Prior to the advent of knowledge, however, God's cause cannot go wrong because life retains its innocence. Eventually, with the evolution of humanity, life arrives at the highest intensification of its own value, for our capacities for knowledge and freedom represent "transcendence awakened to itself." But there is a price to be paid, for with knowledge and freedom come the power to will and do evil: an unprecedented power in this technological age, given our ability to destroy our species. Still, moral responsibility is the mark of our being made "for" God's image, not "in" it. Among earthly creatures only we can acknowledge the transcendent importance of our deeds: that we are the "mortal trustees of an immortal cause." To God's self-limitation we owe thanks, for this makes room for us to help Him by requiring us to bear responsibility for our own vulnerable affairs. We are called "to mend the world" for the sake of a caring God who is powerless to realize the promise of His creation on His own.

Years after completing "Immortality and the Modern Temper," Jonas concedes that the myth that forms its center "has theological implications that only later unfolded to me."[20] In subsequent theological essays contained in *Mortality and Morality,* Jonas shows how his concept of a self-limiting God is compatible with three dimensions of modern knowledge that our reason cannot deny: 1) the brute reality of evil in the world, ineradicably symbolized by Auschwitz; 2) modern science's exclusion of divine intervention from the explanation of nature; and 3) modern cosmology's evidence that the universe began with "the big bang" and that life is a late, rare, and precarious product of nature's labors. Jonas concludes that Judaic faith in the goodness of a God who created the universe and revealed Himself to uniquely elected individuals remains a genuine option today even for those who refuse to turn their backs on what reason commends to them.

Though Jonas's "imperative of responsibility"—never to let the existence or essence of humanity as a whole be threatened by the hazards of action—follows from Judaism's appreciation of the goodness of life and the special dignity of humanity, he contends that this imperative is available to reasonable people everywhere, even atheists who do not interpret nature as God's creation. The individual's duty to be "the executor of an trust which only he can see, but did not create,"[21] is founded, Jonas insists, on a judgment concerning the value of life "that can be separated from any thesis concerning [the world's] authorship."[22] The presupposition of a Creator would offer us no reason for judging the life-world to be good if this world did not justify our perception of its value in its own right. The person of faith should believe not that creation is good because God created it, but that God created it because He recognized life as a Good-in-itself and morally responsible life as the highest evolution of the Good. But this means that theistic—and in particular Judaic—faith, though compatible with an understanding of nature that commands our responsibility, is not necessary for such an understanding.

III

What troubles Hans Jonas about modern philosophy in general and Heidegger's existentialism in particular is the ontological assumption that there exists a stark divide between human beings and the rest of nature. This dualism diminishes Being by denying that living nature is a Good-in-itself: a meaningful whole to which we belong and which commands our responsibility.[23] Whereas Heidegger tries to persuade us of a silent call of conscience commanding us to be authentic in the face of the nothingness of Being, Jonas alerts us to an ethical imperative emanating from the plenitude of Being. The phenomenon of life itself opens up "a genuine present" because it gives us a future worth caring for: a future that is already present in the integrity of nature, both outside ourselves and within. I have indicated how *The Phenomenon of Life*—by its argument that value is present throughout living nature—comprises the first stage of Jonas's attack on the nihilism epitomized by Heidegger's *Being and Time*. But I also hope to have shown that this book lays the foundation for the ontological and theological arguments that complete Jonas's rejoinder to nihilism: arguments that Jonas elaborates during the last three decades of his life.

In this overview of the structure of Jonas's project, I have not yet mentioned the tenth essay contained herein, "Heidegger and Theology," which contains the words for which Jonas became most famous. Offering the keynote address to a 1964 conference at Drew University on the topic "Non-Objectifying Thinking and Speaking in Contemporary Theology," Jonas, as a former student of Heidegger, might have been expected to dutifully interpret a set of theses that Heidegger himself had sent to the conference. Instead, Jonas used the occasion to lambaste Heidegger's notion that the role of authentic thinkers today is to subordinate objective thinking to the task of listening to "the call of Being." With obvious reference not only to Heidegger's philosophy but also to the moral character expressed by his choices, Jonas confesses:

[I]t is hard to hear man hailed as the shepherd of being when he has just so dismally failed to be his brother's keeper. The latter he is meant to be in the Bible. But the terrible anonymity of Heidegger's "being," illicitly decked out with personal characters, blocks out the personal call. Not by the being of another person am I grasped, but just by "being"! And my responsive thought is being's own event. . . . In this sense indeed also Hitler was a call. *Such calls are drowned in the voice of being to which one cannot say No;* as is also, we are told, the separation of subject from object.[24]

Jonas worries about "the specter of arbitrariness and anarchy" that appears when philosophers are tempted to jettison conceptual rigor for "haunting language"—argument for poetry—for then "the only criterion that remains is authenticity of language."[25] And we have no "yardstick" for assessing whose words most authentically serve to ventriloquize "Being."

It is ironic to conclude with an example that shows the personal courage that Hans Jonas summoned in standing up to Heidegger, for Jonas wanted us most of all to remember his arguments. He was uncomfortable in a culture more inclined to recall biographical anecdotes of a philosopher than the complex movements of his thought. *The Phenomenon of Life* proves that Jonas should be appreciated not only as "the philosopher who took on Heidegger," but, more importantly, as a thinker whose ideas deserve to be taken as seriously as those of his teacher.

Lawrence Vogel
Connecticut College

Notes

1. This book belongs to a family of texts produced about a decade after the end of World War II, including Hannah Arendt, *The Human Condition* (Chicago: University of Chicago Press, 1958); Hans-Georg Gadamer, *Warheit und Methode* (Tubingen: J. B. C. Mohr, 1960); and Emmanuel Levinas, *Totalité et infini: Essai sur l'extériorité,* Phaenomenologica 8 (The Hague and Boston: Nijhoff, 1961).

2. Hans Jonas, "Philosophy at the End of the Century: Retrospect and Prospect," trans. Hunter and Hildegarde Hannum, in the collection of Jonas's later essays, *Morality and Morality: A Search for the Good after Auschwitz,* ed. Lawrence Vogel (Evanston: Northwestern University Press, 1996), p. 44.

3. Hans Jonas, "Gnosticism," in *The Encyclopedia of Philosophy* (New York: Macmillan, 1967), vol. 3, p. 341.

4. Hans Jonas, *The Gnostic Religion: The Message of the Alien God and the Beginnings of Christianity* (Boston: Beacon Press, 1958; enlarged edition, 1963). For Jonas's own story of how he came to study Gnosticism and complete his work on it, see "A Retrospective View," chapter 6 of *On Faith, Reason and Responsibility* (Claremont: Institute for Antiquity and Christianity, 1981).

5. Hans Jonas, "Is Faith Still Possible?: Memories of Rudolf Bultmann and Reflections on the Philosophical Aspects of His Work," chapter 7 of *Mortality and Morality,* p. 146.

6. Hans Jonas, "Gnosticism, Existentialism, and Nihilism," in *The Phenomenon of Life,* p. 229.

7. Hans Jonas, "Heidegger's Resoluteness and Resolve: An Interview," in *Martin Heidegger and National Socialism,* ed. Günther Neske and Emil Kettering (New York: Paragon House, 1990), p. 200.

8. Jonas, "Gnosticism, Existentialism, and Nihilism," p. 232.

9. Ibid., pp. 233, 215, 233–34.

10. For the transition from Jonas's philosophy of nature to his ethics, see "Epilogue: Nature and Ethics," in *The Phenomenon of Life.*

11. Hans Jonas, *The Imperative of Responsibility: In Search of an Ethics for the Technological Age* (Chicago: University of Chicago Press, 1984).

12. Hans Jonas, "To Move and to Feel: On the Animal Soul," in *The Phenomenon of Life,* p. 102.

13. For a compact summary of his argument, see "Evolution and Freedom: On the Continuity among Life-Forms" and "Tool, Image, and Grave: On What Is beyond the Animal in Man," chapters 1 and 2 of *Mortality and Morality.*

14. Jonas, *The Imperative of Responsibility,* p. 69.

15. Jonas, "Epilogue: Nature and Ethics," p. 284.

16. Ibid., p. 283.

17. Jonas, *The Imperative of Responsibility,* p. 49.

18. Ibid., p. 82.

19. Ibid., p. 130.

20. The myth of the self-withdrawing God appears verbatim in one of Jonas's later essays, "The Concept of God after Auschwitz: A Jewish Voice," chapter 6 of *Mortality and Morality.*

21. Jonas, "Epilogue: Nature and Ethics," p. 283.

22. Jonas, *The Imperative of Responsibility,* p. 48.

23. For Jonas's charge that *Being and Time* expresses cosmic impiety, see his seminal essay "Gnosticism, Existentialism, and Nihilism."

24. Hans Jonas, "Heidegger and Theology," in *The Phenomenon of Life,* p. 258; italics in original.

25. Ibid., p. 256.

Preface

Put at its briefest, this volume offers an "existential" interpretation of biological facts. Contemporary existentialism, obsessed with man alone, is in the habit of claiming as his unique privilege and predicament much of what is rooted in organic existence as such: in so doing, it withholds from the organic world the insights to be learned from awareness of self. On its part, scientific biology, by its rules confined to the physical, outward facts, must ignore the dimension of inwardness that belongs to life: in so doing, it submerges the distinction of "animate" and "inanimate." A new reading of the biological record may recover the inner dimension—that which we know best—for the understanding of things organic and so reclaim for the psychophysical unity of life that place in the theoretical scheme which it had lost through the divorce of the material and mental since Descartes.

Accordingly, the following investigations seek to break through the anthropocentric confines of idealist and existentialist philosophy as well as through the materialist confines of natural science. In the mystery of the living body both poles are in fact integrated. The great contradictions which man discovers in himself—freedom and necessity, autonomy and dependence, self and world, relation and isolation, creativity and mortality—have their rudimentary traces in even the most primitive forms of life, each precariously balanced between being and not-being, and each already endowed with an internal horizon of "transcendence." We shall pursue this underlying theme of all life in its development through the ascending order of organic powers and functions: metabolism, moving and desiring, sensing and perceiving, imagination, art, and mind—a progressive scale of freedom and peril, culminating in man, who may understand his uniqueness anew when he no longer sees himself in metaphysical isolation.

The reader will, however, find nothing here of the evolutionary optimism of a Teilhard de Chardin, with life's sure and majestic march toward a sublime consummation. He will find life viewed as an experiment with mounting stakes and risks which in the fateful freedom of man may end in disaster as well as in success. And the difference from de Chardin's as also from other, and better conceived, metaphysical success stories will, I hope, be recognized as one not merely of temperament but of philosophical justness.

Although my tools are, for the most part, critical analysis and phenomenological description, I have not shied away, toward the end, from metaphysical speculation where conjecture on ultimate and undemonstrable (but by no means, therefore, meaningless) matters seemed called for. The departure is clearly marked, and the more positivistically inclined reader is free to draw the line which he will not wish to cross with me. It is not, however, arbitrary choice, but intrinsic in the subject, that its discussion should involve me in theories of being from Plato to Heidegger, and in matters stretching from physics and biology to theology and ethics. The phenomenon of life itself negates the boundaries that customarily divide our disciplines and fields.

Portions of this book were previously published, as articles or parts thereof, in the following journals: *Harvard Theological Review* (55, 1962: copyright 1962 by the President and Fellows of Harvard College); *Journal of the History of Philosophy* (3, 1965: copyright 1965 by the Regents of the University of California); *The Journal of Philosophy* (47, 1950); *Measure* (2, 1951: Henry Regnery Company); *Philosophy and Phenomenological Research* (14, 1953); *The Review of Metaphysics* (18, 1964; 19, 1965); *Social Research* (19, 1952; 20, 1953; 26, 1959; 29, 1962); *University of Toronto Quarterly* (21, 1951). Grateful acknowledgement is made to the editors and publishers of these journals for their permission to use the material in question. Its present adaptation represents various degrees of revision and expansion of those first versions.—No words can match my debt of gratitude to the Center for Advanced Studies of Wesleyan University in Middletown, Connecticut, to its Director, and its staff, for the unique opportunity which a year's residence as a Fellow offered me to bring to a conclusion this labor of many years. My special thanks are due to Mrs. Tanya Senff for her devoted secretarial services throughout that year.

THE PHENOMENON OF LIFE

On the Subjects
of a Philosophy of Life

A philosophy of life comprises the philosophy of the organism and the philosophy of mind. This is itself a first proposition of the philosophy of life, in fact its hypothesis, which it must make good in the course of its execution. For the statement of scope expresses no less than the contention that the organic even in its lowest forms prefigures mind, and that mind even on its highest reaches remains part of the organic. The latter half of the contention, but not the former, is in tune with modern belief; the former, but not the latter, was in tune with ancient belief: that *both* are valid and inseparable is the hypothesis of a philosophy which tries for a stand beyond the quarrel of the ancients and the moderns.

Surveying the vast landscape of life on our planet, the philosopher will not be content with the assumption (fitting as it is as a tool for the scientist) that this sustained and far-flung process, moving through aeons with circuitous consistency, always trying itself in subtler and bolder creations, should have been "blind" in the sense that its dynamics consist in nothing but the mechanical permutation of indifferent elements, depositing its chance results along the way and with them accidentally giving rise to the subjective phenomena that inexplicably adhere to them as a redundant byplay. Rather, since matter gave such account of itself, namely, did in fact organize itself in this manner and with these results, it ought to be given its due, and the possibility for doing what it did should be attributed to it as residing in its primary nature: this genuine potency must then be included in the very concept of physical "substance," just as the purposive dynamics seen at work in its actualizations must be included in the concept of physical causality. The nondogmatic thinker will not suppress the testimony of life; he will accept it today as a call to a revision of the conventional model of reality inherited from a natural science which may well itself be passing beyond it. (That such a revision need not mean a return to Aristotle can be seen in Whitehead's example.)

Independently of the story of its genesis, the manifold of existing life presents itself as an ascending scale in which are placed the sophistications of form, the lure of sense and the spur of desire, the command of limb and powers to act, the reflection of consciousness and the reach for truth. Artistotle read this hierarchy in the given record of the organic realm with no resort to evolution, and his *De anima* is the first treatise in philosophical biology. The terms on which his august example may be resumed in our time will be different from his, but the idea of stratification, of the progressive superposition of levels, with the dependence of each higher on the lower, the retention of all the lower in the higher, will still be found indispensable. One way of interpreting this scale is in terms of scope and distinctness of experience, of rising degrees of world perception which move toward the widest and freest objectification of the sum of being in individual percipients. Another way, concurrent with the grades of perception, is in terms of progressive freedom of action. The correlation and interpenetration of these two aspects—of perceiving and acting, of the variety and adequacy of the one, the range and power of the other—is a constant theme for the empathic study of the many forms of life.

Both scales culminate in the thinking of man and there come under the question: which is for the sake of which? Contemplation for action, or action for contemplation? With this challenge to choice, biology turns into ethics. Whatever the answer, one aspect of the ascending scale is that in its stages the "mirroring" of the world becomes ever more distinct and self-rewarding, beginning with the most obscure sensation somewhere on the lowest rungs of animality, even with the most elementary stimulation of organic irritability as such, in which somehow already otherness, world, and object are germinally "experienced," that is, made subjective, and responded to.

Twice in the preceding statements did we speak of "freedom": in the scale of perception and in that of action. One expects to encounter the term in the area of mind and will, and not before: but if mind is prefigured in the organic from the beginning, then freedom is. And indeed our contention is that even metabolism, the basic level of all organic existence, exhibits it: that it is itself the first form of freedom. These must sound strange words to most readers, and I do not expect it otherwise. For what could be further from freedom, further from will and choice which are required for it by any normal understanding of the word, than the blind automatism of the chemistry carried on in the depths of our bodies? Yet it will be the burden of one part of our discourse to show that it is in the dark stirrings of primeval organic substance that a principle of freedom shines forth for the first time within the vast necessity of the physical universe—a principle foreign to suns, planets, and atoms. Obviously, all consciously "mental" connotations must at first be kept away from the concept when used for so comprehensive a principle: "Freedom" must denote an objectively discernible mode of being, i.e., a manner of executing existence, distinctive of the organic *per se* and thus shared by all members but by no nonmembers of the class: an ontologically descriptive term which can apply to mere physical evidence at first. Yet, even as such it must not be unrelated to the meaning it has in the human sphere whence it is borrowed, else its extended use would be frivolous. For all their physical objectivity, the traits described by it on the primitive level constitute the ontological foundation, and already an adumbration, of those more elevated phenomena that more directly invite and more manifestly qualify for the noble name; and these still remain bound to the humble beginnings as to the condition of their possibility. Thus the first appearance of the principle in its bare, elementary object-form signifies the break-through of being to the indefinite range of possibilities which hence stretches to the farthest reaches of subjective life, and as a whole stands under the sign of "freedom."

Taken in this fundamental sense, the concept of freedom can indeed guide us like Ariadne's thread through the interpretation of Life. As to the mystery of origins—it is closed to us. Most persuasive to

me is the hypothesis that even the transition from inanimate to animate substance, the first feat of matter's organizing itself for life, was
actuated by a tendency in the depth of being toward the very modes
of freedom to which this transition opened the gate. Such a hypothesis affects the entire inorganic substrate on which the structure of
freedom is reared. For our purpose we need not commit ourselves to
this or any hypothesis on first origins, for where we start, the "first
stirrings" have long occurred. But once within the realm of life, whatever its cause, we are no longer reduced to hypothesis: the concept of
freedom is germane there from the outset and called for in the
ontological description of its most elementary dynamics. And it will
stay with us all along the upward road as a descriptive and inter-
pretative tool.

But this is not a success story. The privilege of freedom carries the
burden of need and means precarious being. For the ultimate condition for the privilege lies in the paradoxical fact that living substance,
by some original act of segregation, has taken itself out of the general
integration of things in the physical context, set itself over against the
world, and introduced the tension of "to be or not to be" into the
neutral assuredness of existence. It did so by assuming a position of
hazardous independence from the very matter which is yet indispensable to its being: by divorcing its own identity from that of its
temporary stuff, through which it is yet part of the common physical
world. So poised, the organism has its being on condition and revocable. With this twin aspect of metabolism—its power and its need—
not-being made its appearance in the world as an alternative embodied in the being itself; and thereby being itself first assumes an
emphatic sense: intrinsically qualified by the threat of its negative it
must affirm itself, and existence affirmed is existence as a concern. So
constitutive for life is the possibility of not-being that its very being is
essentially a hovering over this abyss, a skirting of its brink: thus
being itself has become a constant possibility rather than a given
state, ever anew to be laid hold of in opposition to its ever-present
contrary, not-being, which will inevitably engulf it in the end.

The being thus suspended in possibility is through and through a
fact of polarity, and life always exhibits it in these basic respects: the
polarity of being and not-being, of self and world, of form and matter, of freedom and necessity. These, as is easily seen, are forms of
relation: life is essentially relationship; and relation as such implies

"transcendence," a going-beyond-itself on the part of that which entertains the relation. If we can show the presence of such transcendence, and of the polarities that specify it, at the very base of life in whatever pre-mental a form, we have made good the contention that mind is prefigured in organic existence as such.

Of all the polarities mentioned, most basic is that of being and not-being. From it, identity is wrested in a supreme, protracted effort of delay whose end is foredoomed: for not-being has generality, or the equality of all things, on its side. Its defiance by the organism must end in ultimate compliance, in which selfhood vanishes and as this unique one can never be retrieved.

That life is mortal may be its basic self-contradiction, but it belongs to its nature and cannot be separated from it even in thought: life carries death in itself, not in spite of, but because of, its being life, for of such a revocable, unassured kind is the relation of form and matter upon which it rests. Its reality, paradoxical and a constant challenge to mechanical nature, is at bottom continual crisis whose momentary resolution is never safe and only gives rise to crisis renewed.

Committed to itself, put at the mercy of its own performance, life must depend for it on conditions over which it has no control and which may deny themselves at any time. Thus dependent on propitiousness or unpropitiousness of outer reality, it is exposed to the world from which it has seceded, and by means of which it must yet maintain itself. Opposing in its internal autonomy the entropy rule of general causality, it is yet subject to it. Emancipated from the identity with matter, it is yet in need of it: free, yet under the whip of necessity; isolated, yet in indispensable contact; seeking contact, yet in danger of being destroyed by it, and threatened no less by its want: imperiled thus from both sides, by importunity and aloofness of the world, and balanced on the narrow ridge between the two; in its process, which must not cease, liable to interference; in the straining of its temporality always facing the imminent no-more: thus does the living form carry on its separatist existence in matter—paradoxical, unstable, precarious, finite, and in intimate company with death. The fear of death with which the hazard of this existence is charged is a never-ending comment on the audacity of the original venture upon which substance embarked in turning organic.

The huge price of dread which life had to pay from the first, and which steadily mounted with its ascent to more ambitious forms, stirs up the question about the meaning of this venture and, once asked, never lets it come to rest again. In this question, asked at last by man, as presumptuous as it is inevitable—as presumptuous indeed as the attempt of form undertaken by substance at the dawn of life—the initially problematical nature of life has, after aeons of mute insistence, found voice and speech.

With matters like these a philosophy of life must deal. That is, it must deal with the organic facts of life, and also with the self-interpretation of life in man. It must interpret both: it has an existential stake in both. Accordingly, the essays collected here range over the scale of faculties with which organisms meet the challenge of the world—metabolism, sentience, motility, emotion, perception, imagination, mind—and over the ideas with which man in history has met the theoretical challenge of life's nature and his own: the latter theme being inevitably moral and in the end metaphysical. The essays range over these subjects but do not offer a finished theory of them—the goal that guided their conception. Written, with this goal in mind, and partly published from 1950 onward, I believe they do express in various facets one philosophy of organism and life. Its systematic statement, under construction these many years, has yet to reach its final shape; but the looser statement in the form of essays, that is to say, of attempts and experiments, can convey its emergent essence, and at the same time records some steps of the road by which it is being reached.

Life, Death, and the Body
in the Theory of Being

I

When man first began to interpret the nature of things—and this he
did when he began to be man—life was to him everywhere, and being
the same as being alive. Animism was the widespread expression of
this stage, "hylozoism" one of its later, conceptual forms. Soul
flooded the whole of existence and encountered itself in all things.
Bare matter, that is, truly inanimate, "dead" matter, was yet to be
discovered—as indeed its concept, so familiar to us, is anything but
obvious. That the world is alive is really the most natural view, and
largely supported by prima-facie evidence. On the terrestrial scene, in
which experience is reared and contained, life abounds and occupies
the whole foreground exposed to man's immediate view. The proportion of manifestly lifeless matter encountered in this primordial field
is small, since most of what we now know to be inanimate is so
intimately intertwined with the dynamics of life that it seems to share
its nature. Earth, wind, and water—begetting, teeming, nurturing,
destroying—are anything but models of "mere matter." Thus primitive panpsychism, in addition to answering powerful needs of the
soul, was justified by rules of inference and verification within the
available range of experience, continually confirmed as it was by the
actual preponderance of life in the horizon of its earthly home. In-

deed not before the Copernican revolution widened this horizon into the vastness of cosmic space was the proportional place of life in the scheme of things sufficiently dwarfed so that it became possible to disregard it for most of what henceforth was to be the content of the term "nature." But to early man, standing on his earth arched by the dome of its sky, it could never occur that life might be a side issue in the universe, and not its pervading rule. His panvitalism was a perspective truth which only a change of perspective could eventually displace. Unquestioned and convincing at the beginning stands the experience of the omnipresence of life.

In such a world-view, the riddle confronting man is *death:* it is the contradiction to the one intelligible, self-explaining, "natural" condition which is the general life. To the extent that life is accepted as the primary state of things, death looms as the disturbing mystery. Hence the *problem* of death is probably the first to deserve this name in the history of thought. Its emergence as an express problem signifies the awakening of the questioning mind long before a conceptual level of theory is attained. The natural recoil from death takes courage from the "logical" outrage which the fact of mortality inflicts on panvitalistic conviction. Primeval reflection thus grapples with the riddle of death, and in myth, cult, and religious belief endeavors to find a solution to it.

That death, not life, calls for an explanation in the first place, reflects a theoretical situation which lasted long in the history of the race. Before there was wonder at the miracle of life, there was wonder about death and what it might mean. If life is the natural and comprehensible thing, death—its apparent negation—is a thing unnatural and cannot be truly real. The explanation it called for had to be in terms of life as the only understandable thing: death had somehow to be assimilated to life. The question it inspired faces backward and forward: how and why did death come into the world whose essence it contradicts? And whereto is it the transition, since whatever it may lead to must still belong to the total context of life? Early metaphysics attempts to answer these questions; or, despairing of an answer, remonstrates with the incomprehensible law. It is the question of Gilgamesh—the answer of the funeral cult. As early man's practice is embodied in his tools, so his thought is embodied in his tombs which acknowledge and negate death at the same time. Out of the tombs arose pristine metaphysics in the shape of myth and religion. That all is life and that all life is mortal is the basic contradiction it strives to resolve. It meets the profound challenge; and to save the sum of things, death had somehow to be denied.

Any problem is essentially the collision between a comprehensive view (be it hypothesis or belief) and a particular fact which will not fit into it. Primitive panvitalism was the comprehensive view; ever-recurring death, the particular fact: since it seemed to deny the basic truth, it had to be denied itself. To seek for its meaning was to acknowledge its strangeness in the world; to understand it was—in this climate of a universal ontology of life—to negate it by making it a transmutation of life itself. Such a negation is the belief in a survival after death which primeval burial customs express. The cult of the dead and the belief in immortality of whatever shape, and the speculations into which they evolve, are the running argument of the life-creed with death—an argument which could also recoil on the embattled position and eventually lead to its breaking-up. At first, any settling of the contradiction, any solution of the riddle, could only be in favor of life; or the riddle remained, an outcry without answer; or the original position was abandoned and a new stage of thought ushered in. Both the first two alternatives attest the original ontological dominance of life. This is the paradox: precisely the importance of the tombs in the beginnings of mankind, the power of the death motif in the beginnings of human thought, testify to the greater power of the universal life motif as their sustaining ground: being was intelligible only as living; and the divined constancy of being could be understood only as the constancy of life, even beyond death and in defiance of its apparent verdict.

II

Modern thought which began with the Renaissance is placed in exactly the opposite theoretic situation. Death is the natural thing, life the problem. From the physical sciences there spread over the conception of all existence an ontology whose model entity is pure matter, stripped of all features of life. What at the animistic stage was not even discovered has in the meantime conquered the vision of reality, entirely ousting its counterpart. The tremendously enlarged universe of modern cosmology is conceived as a field of inanimate masses and forces which operate according to the laws of inertia and of quantitative distribution in space. This denuded substratum of all reality could only be arrived at through a progressive expurgation of vital features from the physical record and through strict abstention from projecting into its image our own felt aliveness. In the process the ban on anthropomorphism was extended to zoomorphism in general. What remained is the residue of the reduction toward the properties of mere extension which submit to measurement and hence to mathematics. These properties alone satisfy the requirements of what is now called exact knowledge: and representing the only knowable aspect of nature they, by a tempting substitution, came to be regarded as its essential aspect too: and if this, then as the only real in reality. This means that the lifeless has become the knowable par excellence and is for that reason also considered the true and only foundation of reality. It is the "natural" as well as the original state of things. Not only in terms of relative quantity but also in terms of ontological genuineness, nonlife is the rule, life the puzzling exception in physical existence.

Accordingly, it is the existence of life within a mechanical universe which now calls for an explanation, and explanation has to be in terms of the lifeless. Left over as a borderline case in the homogeneous physical world-view, life has to be accounted for by the terms of that view. Quantitatively infinitesimal in the immensity of cosmic matter, qualitatively an exception from the rule of its properties, cognitively the unexplained in the general plainness of physical things, it has become the stumbling block of theory. That there is life at all, and how such a thing is possible in a world of mere matter, is now the problem posed to thought. The very fact that we have nowadays to deal with the theoretical problem of life, instead of the problem of death, testifies to the status of death as the natural and intelligible condition.

Here again, the problem consists in the collision between a comprehensive view and a particular fact: as formerly panvitalism, so now panmechanism is the comprehensive hypothesis; and the rare case of life, realized under the exceptional, perhaps unique conditions of our planet, is the improbable particular that seems to elude the basic law and therefore must be denied its autonomy—that is, must be integrated into the general law. To take life as a problem is here to acknowledge its strangeness in the mechanical world which is *the* world; to explain it is—in this climate of a universal ontology of death—to negate it by making it one of the possible variants of the lifeless. Such a negation is the mechanistic theory of the organism, as the funeral rites of prehistory were a negation of death. *L'homme machine* signifies in the modern scheme what conversely hylozoism signified in the ancient scheme: the usurpation of one, dissembled realm by the other which enjoys an ontological monopoly. Vitalistic monism is replaced by mechanistic monism, in whose rules of evidence the standard of life is exchanged for that of death.

In the new monism, too, one face of the question is turned backward: no longer, how did death, but how did life come into the world, the lifeless one? Life's place in this world has shrunk to that of the organism, a problematical specialty in the configurations of extended substance. In it alone do "extended" and "thinking" being meet, after they had first been sundered into two ontological spheres of which only the first is "world," and the second not even belongs to the world. Their meeting in the organism then becomes an insoluble riddle. But since the organism, as a corporeal thing, is a case of the extended, thus a piece of "world," however particular a configuration of its parts, it cannot be essentially different from the rest of the world, i.e., from the general being of the world.

In itself this argument, of course, cuts both ways: If there is to be homogeneity, then either the general can be seen in the image of the particular (which is first and nearest in experience), or the particular in the image of the general—i.e., either world-nature in the image of the organism, or the organism in the image of world-nature. But what the general nature of the world is, has been decided in advance: mere matter in space. Therefore, since organism represents "life" in the world, the question regarding life now poses itself thus: How does the organism stand in the total context already defined, how is this special order or function of it reducible to its general laws—how, in short, is life reducible to nonlife? To reduce life to the lifeless is nothing else than to resolve the particular into the general, the complex into the simple, and the apparent exception into the accepted rule. Precisely this is the task set to modern biological science by the goal of "science" as such. The degree of approximation

to this goal is the measure of its success; and the unresolved remainder left at any time denotes its provisional limit, to be advanced
in the next move.

The earlier goal, we have seen, was to interpret the apparently
lifeless in the image of life and to extend life into apparent death.
Then, it was the corpse, this primal exhibition of "dead" matter,
which was the limit of all understanding and therefore the first thing
not to be accepted at its face-value. Today the living, feeling, striving
organism has taken over this role and is being unmasked as a
ludibrium materiae, a subtle hoax of matter. Only when a corpse is
the body plainly intelligible: then it returns from its puzzling and
unorthodox behavior of aliveness to the unambiguous, "familiar"
state of a body within the world of bodies, whose general laws provide the canon of all comprehensibility. To approximate the laws of
the organic body to this canon, i.e., to efface in *this* sense the boundaries between life and death, is the direction of modern thought on life
as a physical fact. Our thinking today is under the ontological dominance of death.

One may object here that we speak of "death" when we mean the
mere indifference of matter, which is a neutral character whereas
"dead" has an antithetical meaning applying only to what is (or could
be, or once was) alive. But in fact, though this is forgotten, the
cosmos once *was* alive as perceived by man, and its more recent
lifeless image was built up, or left over, in a continuous process of
critical subtraction from its fuller original content: at least in this
historical sense the mechanistic conception of the universe does contain an antithetic element and is not simply neutral. Moreover, that
"subtraction" was set in motion and for long sustained, not by the
critical understanding, but by dualistic metaphysics which has
demonstrable roots in the experience of mortality. *Dualism* is the link
that historically mediated between the two extremes which so far we
have opposed to each other unhistorically: it was indeed the vehicle
of the movement which carried the mind of man from the vitalistic
monism of early times to the materialistic monism of our own as to
its unpremeditated, even paradoxical result; and it is difficult to
imagine how the one could have been reached from the other without
this gigantic "detour."

III

In more ways than one, the rise and long ascendancy of dualism are among the most decisive events in the mental history of the race. What matters for our context is that, while it held sway, and in an otherwise varied career, dualism continued to drain the spiritual elements off the physical realm—until, when its tide at last receded, it left in its wake a world strangely denuded of such arresting attributes. One clearly recognizable component (there are others) in its origin and motivational history is the death theme. The "unto dust shalt thou return" which every corpse calls out to the living, the finality of the state which its decay opposes to the transience of life, must have first and ever again forced "matter" as bare and lifeless into the reluctant human view, and it never ceased to renew the challenge which panvitalistic creed, in the funeral cult, could appease but not silence. Whether and when this contradiction came to a crisis depended on historical circumstances with which the "death" motif had to ally itself so that at some time it could overwhelm the "life motif." But when this happened, the naïve monism broke up into a dualism, with whose growth the traits of the bewildering sight from which it had started—the sight of the corpse—could progressively spread over the face of the physical All. Death in fact conquered external reality.

Soma—sema, the body—a tomb: this Orphic formula expressed the first dualistic answer to the problem of death—now conceived (as that of life, which only now became a problem too) in terms of the interrelation of two different entities, body and soul. The body as such is the grave of the soul, and bodily death is the latter's resurrection. Life dwells like a stranger in the flesh which by its own nature—the nature of the corporeal—is nothing but corpse, seemingly alive by favor of the soul's passing presence in it. Only in death, relinquished by its alien visitor, does the body return to its original truth, and soul to hers.

The discovery of the "self," made first in earnest (for the West) in the Orphic religion and culminating in the Christian and gnostic conception of an entirely nonmundane inwardness in man, had a curiously polarizing effect on the general picture of reality: the very possibility of the notion of an "inanimate universe" emerged as the counterpart to the increasingly exclusive stress laid on the *human* soul, on its inner life and its incommensurability with anything in nature.[1] The fateful divorce, stretched to the point of a complete foreignness which left nothing in common between the parted members, henceforth qualified them both by this mutual exclusion. As the retreating soul drew about itself all spiritual significance and metaphysical dignity, contracting them and itself alike within its innermost being, it left the world divested of all such claims and, though at first decidedly demonic, in the end indifferent to the very question of value either way.

At the peak of the dualistic development, in Gnosticism, the *soma-sema* simile, in its origin purely human, had come to extend to the physical universe. The whole world is tomb (prison house, place of exile, etc.) to the soul or spirit, that alien injection in what is otherwise unrelated to life. There, one might be tempted to say, the matter rests to this day—with the difference that the tomb has meanwhile become empty. With the critical evaporation of the hypostasized spiritual entity, of the "something" which could be thought of as enclosed in that grave or prison, only the walls remained, but these exceedingly solid. This is, metaphorically speaking, the position of modern materialism, which inherited the estate of a defunct dualism, or what was left of it. Thus the splitting of reality into self and world, inner and outer existence, mind and nature, long sanctioned by religious doctrine, prepared the ground for the postdualistic successors.

---

1. Illuminating in this connection are some of the charges which in the sixth century A.D. Simplicius, one of the last of the Platonists, leveled against his Christian contemporary Johannes Philoponus. He accuses him of blasphemy for likening the light of the heavens to ordinary fire and to glowworms, its color to that of fishscales (*in Arist. de caelo,* p. 88, 28 ff. Heiberg; he also takes him to task for denying, against Aristotle, the eternity of the world, *ibid.,* p. 66, 10). It was a gallant protest of the doomed cosmos-piety against the indignity done to nature under the dispensation of transcendental religion: the submersion of its hierarchy in the common status of mere created things. Almost one thousand years earlier Anaxagoras had been charged by the Athenians with blasphemy for declaring the sun to be a mass of heated metal or stone. Between the two events lie the rise and fall of cosmological religion. The dualistic challenge was more radical than the naturalistic one of the Ionians who were potentially "pantheists." A naturalism, coming after dualism had done its work, was accordingly bound to be more thoroughgoing. (Compare the Ninth Essay, "Gnosticism, Existentialism, and Nihilism").

If dualism was the first great correction of the animistic-monistic one-sideness, materialist monism which remained as its residue is then the no less one-sided, total triumph of the death experience over the life experience. In this sense, the theoretical shock that once issued from the corpse has turned into a constitutive principle, and in a universe formed after the image of the corpse the single, actual corpse has lost its mystery. All the more does the one unresolved remainder clash with the universal norm: the living organism, which seems to resist the dualistic alternative as much as the alternative dualism-monism itself. The quest for its analysis on the terms of general physical law is the running argument with the refractory from the position of the ontology of death—an argument, this too, which may yet turn back on the position itself and cause its exclusive claim to be reappraised. In its heyday, when the new ontology ruled unchallenged, any settling of the contradiction, any solution of the riddle, could only be in favor of death; or the riddle remained, an annoying dualistic rest: either case testifies to the ontological dominance of death. This dominance is the inverted monism with which mankind emerged at the far shore from the waters of dualism which long ago it had entered with the archaic monism of the soul.

But precisely the nakedness of the new monism from which the general life had been banished and which no transcendent pole complemented anymore, exposed to view the particular, finite life in its metaphysically expatriated identity—and left it to be appraised in its "own" terms after it had so long been measured by other ones. Its solely remaining here-and-now, suspended between beginning and end, acquires a prominence which both preceding views had denied to it. The attention to its peculiar nature, belonging to nothing else, has increased in proportion as, in retreat from both the diffusion of animism and the width of dualistic tension, it has become narrower— in proportion, that is, as the locus of life within being has shrunk to the special case of the organism in its conditioning earthly environment. The conditioning, life-enabling character of that environment is in turn an improbable accident of a universe alien to life and indifferent in its material laws. All modern theories of life are to be understood against this backdrop of an ontology of death, from which each single life must coax or bully its lease, only to be swallowed up by it in the end.

The road through dualism here briefly indicated marks the irreversible time-order of the two positions, and dualism itself represents so far the most momentous phase in the history of thought, whose achievement, however overtaken, can never be undone. The discovery of the separate spheres of spirit and matter, which split primeval monism asunder, created forever a new theoretical situation. From the hard-won observation that there can be matter without spirit, dualism inferred the unobserved reverse that spirit can also be without matter. Irrespective of the tenability of the ontological thesis, the essential difference of the two had now come into view, and their dualistic separation inspired the resolute spelling-out of both their natures in their stark otherness, which was never to be confounded again. Every conception of being that can come thereafter is in essence, not merely in time, postdualistic, as the preceding one was essentially predualistic. As in the latter the specificness and difference of the two fundamental dimensions was not yet discovered (so that its monism was naïvely unproblematic, disturbed only by the experience of death and gradually eroded by technology—until intellectually self-conscious dualism spelled the end of this and all naïveté), so has any postdualistic theory of being inescapably to deal with the two pieces which dualism left behind and concerning which it can be monistic only at the price of choosing between them, i.e., of opting for one of them: at least so long as the dualistic heritage still enforces the recognition of its alternative. With this alternative at its point of departure, any postdualistic monism includes a decision which it has made for one or the other side; that is to say, it is itself of an alternative and thus partial nature, having its opposite as the excluded possibility with it.

It follows that in the postdualistic situation there are, on principle, not one but two possibilities of monism, represented by modern materialism and modern idealism respectively: they both presuppose the ontological polarization which dualism had generated, and either takes its stand in one of the two poles, to comprehend from this vantage point the whole of reality. They are thus in their origin, though certainly not in their intention, partial monisms, unlike the integral monism of prehistory in which the two sides were still fused undifferentiated. There is no returning to this: dualism had not been an arbitrary invention, for the two-ness which it asserts is grounded in reality itself. A new, integral, i.e., philosophical monism cannot undo the polarity: it must absorb it into a higher unity of existence from which the opposites issue as faces of its being or phases of its becoming. It must take up the problem which originally gave rise to dualism.

IV

The problem is still the same: the existence of feeling life in an unfeeling world of matter which in death triumphs over it. If its dualistic solution is theoretically unsatisfactory, the two partial monisms—materialism and idealism—at bottom evade it, each in its own manner of one-sidedness. Their means of unification, i.e., of reduction to the chosen denominator, is the distinction of primary and secondary reality: of substance and function (or "epiphenomenon") in the case of materialism, of consciousness and appearance in the case of idealism. As an ontological position, i.e., as serious monism, either standpoint claims totality for itself and thus excludes the other. But since the point of departure in either case is partial with respect to integral reality, they severally embody the internal contradiction of a partial monism—a contradiction which betrays itself in the failure of their reduction of one element to the other. In the case of materialism, this failure happens in relation to consciousness, in that of idealism—in relation to the thing-in-itself.

Both standpoints, it is true, can dissemble their monistic, i.e., ontological character and, rather than for total views of being, try to pass for a division of labor in the cultivation of two separate fields of reality—their own separateness thus resting first on the difference of their subjects, which naturally also demands different methods. We then would have a phenomenology of consciousness and a physics of extension, and the method of one discipline would be as necessarily idealistic as that of the other materialistic. Their separation would then be not ontological, according to alternative concepts of being, but "ontic," according to subject matter. Here the mutual relation of the two seems to be that, not of alternative, but of complementation: "sciences of nature—sciences of mind." But this peaceful coexistence presupposes that the two "fields" are in fact separate, and can be isolated from each other. Precisely this is not the case. The fact of life, as the psychophysical unity which the organism exhibits, renders the separation illusory. The actual coincidence of inwardness and outwardness in the *body* compels the two ways of knowledge to define their relation otherwise than by separate subjects. Otherwise also than as complementary descriptions of the same subject from different "sides" which can eschew the question of how those abstract aspects concretely cohere in being. For such a descriptive abstention, which is to insure metaphysical neutrality, could be maintained only on condition that the two fields of phenomena are closed in themselves at least *qua* phenomena and do not transcend themselves by their own contents: that either one, thus, can be described entire without drawing in the other. Yet precisely our living body constitutes that very self-transcendence in either direction and thereby makes the methodological *epochē* founder on its rock. It must be described as extended and inert, but equally as feeling and willing—and neither of the two descriptions can be carried to its end without trespass into the sphere of the other and without prejudging it. The physical-outward description cannot be carried to its end without compromising the freedom and thus the genuine reality of the mind; the vitalistic-inward description not without compromising the total determination and autarky of the "extended" realm.

Dualism, when its work was done, had left behind the "extended" as the lifeless and unfeeling, and the body undeniably is a part of this extended: either, then, it is essentially the same as the extended in general—then its being alive is not understood; or it is *sui generis*— then the exception claimed for it is not to be understood and calls into question the whole rule, i.e., the materialist interpretation of substance as such along the pure properties of indifferent extension. The same goes, *mutatis mutandis,* for the other side, that of idealist consciousness. Dualism had left it behind as the uncorporeal absolutely, the unextended and purely inward *per se,* and the "body" as the sensible field of feeling and volition belongs to this inwardness itself: either, then, as part of the total phenomenal extension it is but one among the "external ideas" ("cogitations") of consciousness— then its being the body *of* this consciousness, its being *my* body, my extended I and my share in the world of extension, is not understood; or life and inwardness are really extended through it ("to the tips of my fingers"), it really is "I"—then it is, even though phenomenally extended, not an *idea* of consciousness but the actual outward extent of its own inner spatiality which itself occupies space in the world: and therewith it calls into question the whole idealist interpretation of consciousness as opposed to the entire world of extension.

Thus the organic body signifies the latent crisis of every known ontology and the criterion of "any future one which will be able to come forward as a science." As it was first the body on which, in the fact of *death,* that antithesis of life and nonlife became manifest whose relentless pressure on thought destroyed primitive panvitalism and caused the image of being to split, so it is conversely the concrete unity manifest in its *life* on which in turn the dualism of the two substances founders, and again this bi-unity which also brings to grief both alternatives branching off from dualism, whenever they—as they cannot help doing—enlarge themselves into total ontologies. Indeed, it is this very bi-unity which compels them thus to enlarge themselves, i.e., to transgress their boundaries, and prevents them from sheltering in the seeming neutrality of mere part areas or part aspects. The living body that can die, that has world and itself belongs to the world, that feels and itself can be felt, whose outward form is organism and causality, and whose inward form is selfhood and finality: this body is the memento of the still unsolved question of ontology, "What is being?" and must be the canon of coming attempts to solve it. These attempts must move beyond the partial abstractions ("body and soul," "extension and thought," and the like) toward the hidden ground of their unity and thus strive for an integral monism on a plane above the solidified alternatives.

V

The problem of life, centered in the problem of the body, is thus a cardinal theme for ontology and the constant disturbance of its latter-day antithetical positions in materialism and idealism alike. It is characteristic of the postdualistic situation that the problem poses itself today as that of life and not of death: this inversion is the end result of that contraction of life from the whole of nature into its distinct singularity which began with the first dawn of dualistic lightening of the indistinctness. Against the enormous boundary transgression of primordial monism which made life coextensive with being, discrimination could only mean, first, discovery of lifeless matter as such, and then, ever-increasing expansion of the extent of the lifeless —until this in turn became coextensive with being. Now obviously, as expression of this postdualistic theoretical situation, materialism is the more interesting and more serious variant of modern ontology than idealism. For among the totality of its objects—bodies in general—materialism lets itself in earnest also encounter the living body; and since it is bound to subject it, too, to its principles it exposes itself to the real ontological test and with it to the risk of failure: it gives itself the opportunity of knocking against its limit—and there against the ontological problem. Idealism is able to evade it: it can always from the secure standpoint of pure consciousness, artificial as it is, interpret "the body," like all other bodies, as external "idea" or "phenomenon" in its intentional horizon and can thus disown the corporeality of the self: by this means it saves itself the problem of life as well as of death. This was the reason why at the outset we have chosen materialism as the representative of postdualistic ontology (the "ontology of death") and as the true counterpart to the predualistic ontology of panvitalism. Materialism is the real ontology of our world since the Renaissance, the real heir to dualism, i.e., to its residual estate, and with it must be our discourse. Only with a "realist" standpoint can there be fruitful discourse anyway, whereas an idealistic one can slip through its fingers.

Moreover, it can be shown that the idealism of the philosophy of consciousness is itself but a complementarity, an epiphenomenon as it were, of materialism and thus in the strict sense also one face of the ontology of death. This shall here be indicated in just one respect. Only a world objectified to pure extensive outwardness, as materialism conceived it, leaves opposite itself a pure consciousness which has no share in it, in its dimension and its function—which no longer acts but merely beholds. And vice versa, it is this bodyless, merely beholding consciousness for which reality must turn into series of points juxtaposed in space and succeeding in time: points of extensity necessarily as external to one another as they all together are to consciousness, and therefore offering no other rules of order than those of extraneous collocation and sequence. Indeed, without the body by which we are ourselves an actual part of the world and experience the nature of force and action in self-performance, our knowledge—a merely "perceptive," beholding knowledge—of the world (in that case truly "external world" with no real transition from myself to it) would really be reduced to Hume's model, viz., to sequences of contents external and indifferent to one another, regarding which there could not even arise the suspicion of an inner connection, of any relation other than the spatio-temporal ones, nor the least justification for postulating it. Causality here becomes a fiction—on a psychological basis left groundless itself.

At this agnostic resignation modern physics has arrived from its own end, i.e., from its materialist premises which by the road of absolute externalization must lead to the same skeptical framing of the concept of causality as the theory of consciousness must by its road of absolute internalization. Neither can do otherwise, and both from the same cause: pure consciousness is as little alive as the pure matter confronting it. Accordingly, the one can as little generate the aliveness of active connection in its understanding as the other can present it to perception. Both are fission products of the ontology of death to which the dualistic anatomy of being had led. Note that this renders them helpless, not just in dealing with life, but already on the subject of general causality. In the latter field, that of mechanical law, transcendental and materialist theory alike had claimed their principal triumph, for which to forgo the knowledge of organic teleology seemed not too high a price to pay. However, it seems that in the long run no part of a whole can profit from what that whole loses in another part, and in the end even general causality loses in intelligibility what the elimination of life was meant to secure for it in terms of scientific knowledge. The fate of the causality problem in idealist epistemology on the one hand and in materialist physics on the other bespeaks the fact that both positions, considered ontologically, are fragmentary, residual products of dualism, and both are merely consistent when they, each by its own kind of skepsis, acknowledge the inevitable outcome of their isolation, to wit: the inexplicability of that which through the sundering has become inexplicable. The artificial sundering of *res cogitans* and *res extensa* in the heritage of dualism, with the extrusion between them of "life": this double-faced ontology of death creates problems which it has rendered unsolvable from the start.

But is there not here a contradiction? Has not the discrimination of the lifeless and the living first made possible the distinct articulation of what is peculiar to life? And has this not benefited the "spirit,"

which as it were drew to itself what there was of life in the universe
and concentrated it within itself as "consciousness"? If matter was
left dead on one side, then surely consciousness, brought into relief
against it on the other side and becoming heir to all animistic vitality,
should be the repository, even the distillate of life? But life does not
bear distillation; it is somewhere between the purified aspects—in
their concretion. The abstractions themselves do not live. In truth, we
repeat, the pure consciousness is as little alive as the pure matter
standing over against it—and, by the same token, as little, mortal. It
lives as departed spirits live and cannot understand the world anymore. To it the world is dead as it is dead to the world. The dualistic
antithesis leads not to a heightening of the features of life through
their concentration on one side, but to a deadening of both sides
through their separation from the living middle. This deadening ex-
acts its revenge in the fact that—not to speak of the riddle of life—
even for the interpretation of the external regularity in the movements
of matter, the image of a causality by active force no longer finds
legitimation in any admitted firsthand givenness.

V I

Here we recall Kant's answer to Hume's skeptical challenge which
claimed to supply just that legitimation, not indeed in a "given," but
in an a priori structure of the mind. However, the transcendental
solution of the problem which heroically undertakes to ground causality and its objective meaning in the pure consciousness alone, does
not escape the truth that you cannot derive the concreteness from one
of its abstractions. The success of Kant's attempted solution depends,
inter alia, essentially on the proof that "causation" is indeed a concept of the pure understanding (after that, on showing why it should
be valid objectively). But an unprejudiced examination will find that
not the pure understanding but only the concrete bodily life, in the
actual interplay of its self-feeling powers with the world, can be the
source of the "idea" of force and thus of cause. The understanding as
such knows merely of reason and consequence, not of cause and
effect: the latter denote a connection of reality, by means of force,
not of ideality, by means of form. The experience of living force,
one's own namely, in the acting of the body, is the experiential basis
for the abstractions of the general concepts of action and causation;

and the "schematism" of directed bodily *movement,* not of neutrally receptive intuition, mediates between the formality of the understanding and the dynamics of the real.

Causality is thus not an a priori basis of experience, but itself a basic experience. That experience has its seat in the *effort* I must make to overcome the resistance of worldly matter in my acting and to resist the impact of worldly matter upon myself. This happens through and with my body, with its extensive outwardness and its intensive inwardness at once, which both are genuine aspects of myself. And advancing from my body, nay, myself advancing bodily, I build up in the image of its basic experience the dynamic image of the world—a world of force and resistance, action and inertia, cause and effect. Thus causality is not the a priori of experience in the understanding but the universal extrapolation from propriobodily prime experience into the whole of reality. It is rooted in just the point of actual, live "transcendence" of the self, the point where inwardness actively transcends itself into the outward and continues itself into it with its actions. This point is the intensive-extensive body in which the self exists, at once, for itself (intensive) and in the midst of the world (extensive).

Causality is primarily a finding of the practical, not of the theoretical, self, of its activity, not of its perception—an experience of the one, not a law of the other. (Regarding the problem of causality in this context, see Appendix 1 to this Essay.)

Admittedly, whether the universal extrapolation which in fact, and irresistibly, we do make from propriobodily experience is also rationally justified, is a question of philosophical critique which we must here leave open. It is, however, in the first place an ontological and not an epistemological question. Into ontology also belongs the problem of anthropomorphism in the widest sense which at this point raises its head. The anathema on any kind of anthropomorphism, even of zoomorphism, in connection with nature—this in its absoluteness specifically dualistic and postdualistic prohibition, may well turn out to be, in this extreme form, a prejudice. (See Appendix 2 to this Essay.) Perhaps, rightly understood, man *is* after all the measure of all things—not indeed through the legislation of his reason but through the exemplar of his psychophysical totality which represents the maximum of concrete ontological completeness known to us: a completeness *from which,* reductively, the species of being may have to be determined by way of progressive ontological subtraction down to the minimum of bare elementary matter (instead of the complete being constructed from this basis by cumulative addition). The question is still open whether life is a quantitative complexification in the arrangement of matter, and its freedom and purposiveness nothing but an apparent blurring of its simple, unambiguous determinacy through the massed complexity as such (a fact of our bafflement rather than of its own nature)—or whether, contrariwise, "dead" matter, as one extreme of a spectrum, represents a limiting mode of the properties revealed by feeling life, their privative reduction to the near-dwindling point of inchoateness: in which case its bare, inertial determination would be dormant, as yet unawakened freedom. The ontological justification for this question lies in the fact that the living body is the archetype of the concrete, and being *my* body it is, in its immediacy of inwardness and outwardness in one, the *only* fully given concrete of experience in general. Its actual, concrete fullness teaches us that matter in space, otherwise experienced only from without, may have an inner horizon too and that, therefore, its extended being need not be its whole being. Seen from the only true concreteness furnished to us, both pure "extension" and pure "thought" may well appear to be mere abstractions.

Independently, however, of this metaphysical question of a unity of being and the propositions derivable from it if granted, independently also, therefore, of the question concerning the *right* of the de facto extrapolation from our corporeality, there is the plain fact that *without* the body and its elementary self-experience, without this "whence" of our most general, all-encompassing extrapolation into the whole of reality, there could be no idea whatever of force and action in the world and thus of a dynamic connection of all things: no idea, in short, of any "nature" at all. Idealism—in that respect the faithful mirror image of materialism—by ranging the body entirely among the external objects, thus understanding it as an object of experience and not its source, as datum for the subject and not as active-passive reality of the subject, has deprived itself of the possibility to go beyond a rule of external orders of sequences and grasp a real connection of things rooted in their own nature—be it in the form of efficient, be it of final causation (on this, the transcendental standpoint has no say anyway, whatever its historical preference).

But whichever causality it be, on this point Hume's critique was right that it is not met with in any perception, and that the nexus between the data is not a datum itself—not a perceived content. Force indeed is not a datum, but an "actum" humanly present in effort. And effort is surely not a percept, even less a form of the synthesis of percepts. But objectifying thought is wedded to perception ("intuition"="presentational immediacy") and thus cannot encounter what is not contained therein.

VII

Thus it appears that waiving the intelligibility of life—the price which modern knowledge was willing to pay for its title to the greater part of reality—renders the world unintelligible as well. And the reduction of teleological to mechanical causality, great as its advantages are for analytical description, has gained nothing in the matter of comprehending the nexus itself: the one is no less mysterious than the other.

Our reflections were intended to show in what sense the problem of life, and with it that of the body, ought to stand in the center of ontology and, to some extent, also of epistemology. Life means material life, i.e., living body, i.e., organic being. In the body, the knot of being is tied which dualism does not unravel but cut. Materialism and idealism, each from its end, try to smooth it out but get caught in it. The central position of the problem of life means not only that it must be accorded a decisive voice in judging any given ontology but also that any treatment of itself must summon the whole of ontology. To this whole belong the hitherto, in its history, realized possibilities of ontology, even if they happen to teach more on posing than on solving the problem. Our considerations have shown that not even "animism," i.e., the panvitalism of the dawn, is to be excluded from the ontological evidence that has to be weighed: the principle of the interpretation of being which it, however preconceptually, represents is not really done with even from the perspective of modern knowledge.[2] Yet the decisive phase in the unfolding of the problem, so we

---

2. We may refer to the panpsychism of a Teilhard de Chardin, or (on a considerably higher philosophical plane) of Whitehead's theory of all actuality as "feeling."

found, was dualism, which also in other respects represents the most pregnant chapter in the history of man's interpretation of being and himself. At its hands, the paradox of life received its most pointed antithetical articulation and, on its expiration, was left behind in its most irreconcilable form. Lastly, we found that of the postdualistic positions which divided the dualistic legacy between them, materialism has an advantage over idealism as a meeting ground with the problem of life, since it can be less easily evaded there. One sign of this is that materialism, herein more faithful to the dualistic bequest, knows of death whereas idealism has forgotten it. Also, the thinker himself is here less easily bribed. In materialism, he looks his own negation in the eye; but since he at the same time, in what he does by thinking, exemplifies the very case to which his thought denies a place, he is here less in danger to forget one side of the question than is the follower of idealism, which with the primacy of thought, so flattering to the thinker, has in advance taken his side.

APPENDIX 1 (p. 23)
Causality and Perception

Hume has shown that "causation" is not found among the contents of sense perception. This is incontrovertible so long as "perception" is understood, with Hume, as mere *receptivity* that registers the incoming data of sensation. This also is how Kant understood it when he accepted Hume's negative finding. And if, again, such passive perception is held, with both Hume and Kant, to be the *only* mode in which the outer world is originally "given"—so that even of our own bodily activity we only know by our receptivity, whose sequential data have then to be *interpreted* in terms of action—then indeed causality must be some *mental addition* to the raw material of prime givenness; and the difference of doctrine concerns only the source and nature of that addition. Hume saw it in the habit of association (itself passive on the part of the subject), Kant in the structuring by the understanding ("active" to be sure, but in strict mental immanence).

Now, both these positive doctrines fail to supply the deficiency which the success of the negative argument has created. Unchallenged as Hume's contention stands that causation is not a "given" in perception, i.e., an appearance among appearances that are nontransitive by definition, his account of its bastard birth from the unsupervised liaisons (mutual attractions) between our ideas, which in their own interrelations are allowed the very dynamics they deny to the things in their portrayal of them, does not stand scrutiny.[1] Neither does Kant's alternative, replacing psychological with "transcendental" origin, since reason by itself no more yields the notion of action and influence than does the sense perception of Hume's description: even if it yields—a different matter altogether—the formal notion of "necessary rule" where the associative mechanism yielded the concrete feeling of constraint on the imagination.[2]

But whether felt constraint on imagination or conceived necessity for thought, whether psychological or rational rule—neither has much to do with the compelling thrust of things, in which we have a share outside the sanctuary of our minds. Both doctrines wish to substitute internal for external dynamics, spurious for genuine origin: both on the assumption, born of the silence of "perception" under the seclusion of the cognitive monopoly thrust upon it, that there is no firsthand knowledge of force,

---

1. A *post hoc* company-formation among the ideas, whatever its effect otherwise, cannot restore to the atomic and intrinsically static record the character their representation withheld from it to begin with. And although psychological compulsion or suggestion, such as their automatism may engender, can indeed mislead thought into making wrong connections, as well as accidentally prompt the right ones, the "original" of such connection must be available from its own source *before* either proper or improper use can be made of it under any prompting. Only on this condition is the misreading of mental for physical dynamics at least psychologically plausible—viz., as a *secondary* fact, the primary being the acquaintance with physical dynamics as such: then the confounding of one with the other becomes possible. Also we can distinguish, as belonging to different spheres, between even the strongest drift of imagination and the faintest testimony of things, and correct the former in the light of the latter: vividness of mental impress has no say in the matter—no more than rhetoric has in an argument, the efficacy of either notwithstanding. Finally, the "force of habit" acting in the association of ideas may well, for its own explanation, require to call on physical causes (e.g., brain mechanisms), that is, on the very reality of that which it merely seemed to fake.

2. A necessary, general rule of connection requires that of which it is to be the rule and which it cannot provide itself but must find originally exemplified in those actual instances of determinative connection where the "necessitating" *force* of the transition from A to B has been practically (i.e., with *myself* one of the relata) experienced—which is something entirely different from the "necessity" of the *rule* to which such instances "must" (a priori—else: are found to) universally conform. The rule merely says that *some* necessitating link or other (its original paradigm in direct experience being only one kind) operates in *every*

transitivity, and the dynamic bonds of things. Both burden their choice with an impossible task. Both, in short, forget the body.

Now, perhaps the real problem lies in the very fact which Hume and Kant accepted as ultimate: the causal muteness of percepts. If this itself is taken as a matter for wonder and explanation, as it should, an interesting inversion of Hume's problem suggests itself: Considering what is known about the causality involved in the genesis of sense perception itself, its indeed decausalized content presents its own riddle which sharpens Hume's more general riddle into the *paradox* that a *specific causal* nexus —affection of the senses—should terminate in its own presentational *suppression* as part of its specific performance. This disowning of its genesis by the perceptual mode, i.e., the terminal obliteration of its own causal character, forms an essential feature of what Whitehead calls "presentational immediacy," and is the condition of its objective function which is thus bought at a price.

The inversion of the problem here proposed implies an independent and

---

change, even where not experienced by either agent or percipient; that there is a uniform measure for all changes, or, all individual necessities are part of a general necessity; and that *this in turn is "necessary,"* but in a new sense: not from the nature of necessitation itself (let alone the kind experientially involving myself), but from the nature of nature "as a whole," viz., if it is to be an intelligible unity—of being or of "experience." The difference is obvious. Yet this transparent equivocation of the term "necessity" bedevils much of Kant's argument: when I tell of having been swept away, in a desperate struggle, by a torrent too strong for me to resist, I obviously speak of "necessity" of a different, uncategorial kind from the categorial "necessity" I predicate of the holding of a universal *law* of causality. In the second case I speak of a necessity of necessity— an abstract necessity of concrete necessities, i.e., of there obtaining some necessity=necessitation (transitive) in every case, and of all these necessitations together forming one homogeneous system. Kant's argument concerns exclusively this second-level (nontransitive) necessity and has no bearing whatsoever, not even by implication, on the question of our authentic experience of causation as such. His denial of the latter antecedes his argument on Humean premises, i.e., on the traditional (ultimately Cartesian) view of perception as a procession of neutral "ideas"= representations=images. But I don't think that this (erroneous) presupposition is vital to the essence of the Kantian argument. Its essence, I take it, is to ground, not the factuality and contingent (single) experience of causation, but the validity of a universal *law* of causality for experience as such: what must be examined then (but is none of our concern here) is whether it does *this* validly. Whatever the answer, a law *of* experience can never substitute for the primary experience itself.

legitimate source of causal knowledge whose deliverance is not affected by the negative findings of perception; on the contrary, it has to be drawn upon for the explanation of perception itself no less than for the supplementation of its findings.

Whitehead's distinction of "causal efficacy" and "presentational immediacy" as belonging to two modes of perception offers an important clue with respect to Hume's problem, but beyond its statement no sufficient explanation of itself (in fact, the term "immediacy" is apt to mislead). Following up this clue, we propose to show: (a) how it is that the several senses, in differing degrees, eliminate the imprint of their own causal constitution from the integration of their imagery; (b) why the sacrifice of the causal element extends from the self-presentation of the actual perceiving mode to its general object picture, coinciding with the range of "objectivity" as such, which is thus reality denatured (deactivated) but would not be possible otherwise; (c) why the objectifying modes so constituted have of necessity come to monopolize the concept of knowledge, and their object type that of reality, thereby creating problems peculiar to this self-curtailment (*inter alia* the problem of "necessary connection").

(a) How do the senses come to deliver a decausalized content? A complete answer involves an analysis of the senses at once genetic and phenomenological: to confine oneself to the latter alone would be to commit oneself from the outset to the face value of perceptional testimony and thus not to escape from the magic circle of Hume's argument. As this is not the time for a detailed analysis,[3] a few remarks shall here indicate the line of reasoning.

The smallness (in dimension, time rate, and energy) of the unit-actions and reactions involved in affection of the senses, i.e., their minute scale relative to the organism, permits their mass-integration into one continuous and homogeneous effect (impression) in which not only the single impulses are absorbed, but the character of impulse as such is largely canceled and replaced by that of detached image. Where qualities are perceived, the raw material is action: impacts, hustlings, clashes on a molecular scale. Organisms not far exceeding that scale can therefore have no perception, but the collision experience only. Theirs would be a world not of presences but of incidences, or, not of existences but of forces. To the large-scale organism, on the other hand, when it does have the force-experience in interaction on its own scale, this always comes already superimposed on the becalmed continuum made up of the per-

---

3. See, for parts of such an analysis, Sixth Essay and Seventh Essay, sect. III.

ceptual transcripts of the small-scale influences that all along engage
sensitivity but in the transcription loose the character of influence: as
continual and effortless presence of deactivated content, they seem to
offer that neutral substratum of being to which the force-experience then
happens to be added on particular occasions, and from which indeed it
stands out as a particular phenomenon. This result: the apparent priority
of enduring entity over occasional activity—the cognitive child of perception—is an inversion of the originative ontological order, and the
root of a theoretical problem of causality later on.

The degree to which the dynamical relationship is, or is not, perceptible
and represented in the perception itself, and the degree to which sequence
of happening is translated into simultaneity of a statical presence, can
serve to classify the senses with respect to their objectifying function.[4]
From a comparative analysis, sight emerges as the sense with the most
complete neutralizing of dynamic content and the most unambiguous
distancing of its object from the perceptive function. In degrees, the self-
effacement of causal efficacy takes place in all sense perception: where
violence of the stimulus forces the threshold and causality floods sensation, there sense perception is ousted by the experience of impact or by
pain, i.e., it ceases to be perception proper. Especially in touch, the
transition from apprehension of quality to experience of pressure and
thence to exercise of power is a matter of traceable degrees. Or to ex-
emplify from another sense: in the case of a detonation nearby, the force
acting on our receptor may exceed the acoustic limits, and instead of
just hearing a sound of particular quality and intensity we feel assaulted
by power, to be endured and resisted by power. And as noise can deafen,
so light can blind when it exceeds the limits of sensuous assimilation.
Thus the world, instead of presenting itself, can intrude dynamically into
its testimony, its causality overwhelming perception. The latter is therefore constitutionally bound to the former's exclusion from the record—at
least in relation to itself—and fulfills its specific task by performing just
this feat. In the case of vision, the feat is made possible to perfection by
the dynamical properties of light and the relative orders of magnitude
involved. The seeming inactivity and self-containedness of the seen object
correspond to the seeming inactivity and self-containedness of the spectator; yet both characters are the purified result of a particular set of
connecting activity. Its total elimination from the presentational result,
which gains by losing but loses nevertheless, introduces an element of
abstraction—the abstraction of image—into the very constitution of sense
perception, hence into object knowledge as such.

(b) The suppression of object-subject causality in perception entails

_____

4. See Sixth Essay on "The Nobility of Sight."

that of object-object causality there as well—or that of causality pure and simple within the "theoretical" domain when this is fashioned in the perceptional analogy alone. For then it does not admit into its evidence the testimony of the *acting* subject—that seemingly inalienable, "inside" knowledge of subject-object causality of which man *qua* agent is possessed in his practical intercourse with things: only after having itself been subjected to perceptual objectification, its contents transformed into serial data—i.e., after the active quality has been leached from it—is its testimony admitted into theory. By the rejection of this evidence in its pristine terms (a rejection with a long history in the growth of the theoretical ideal), understanding deprives itself of the one nonperceptual source, the force-experience of my own body in action, which could by analogy still supply the dynamical links in the sequence of observed events: these, having become objects by disconnection from the reality of the observer, stand thereby stripped of that character which would explain also their connectedness among themselves. The detachment of objectification left them detached from one another as well. The character generally suppressed is *force* which, being not a "datum" but an "actum," cannot be "seen," i.e., objectified, but only experienced from within when exerted or suffered. The primary neutralization of this character by perception, which changes actualities into data, is bequeathed to the concepts of the understanding, which rises from this very basis of objectification. Understanding by itself, when left to deal with the stripped percepts alone, cannot restore that character, nor compensate for it by its own means of connection (here Hume was right—and Kant wrong). But enjoying the advantages of disconnection in the subject-object relation, namely, the freedom of theory, it has to accept its disadvantages as regards object-object relation.

(c) Abscondence of causal efficacy is the price by which presentation of being in itself, and consequently objectivity, are gained. On the credit side, effacement of causality means disengagement from it. Perception as such, and vision particularly, secure that standing back from causal involvement which frees the experient for observation and opens a horizon for elective attention. The object, staying in its bounds, faces the subject across the gap which the evanescence of the force context has created. From the onrush and impact of reality, out of the insistent clamor of its proximity, the distance of appearance (*phenomenon*) is won: image, in the place of effect, can be looked at and compared, in memory retained and recalled, in imagination varied and freely composed. This separation of contained appearance from intrusive reality, the original feat of perception, gives rise to the separableness of essence from existence that underlies the higher freedoms of theory. It is but the basic freedom of vision, and the element of abstraction inherent in image, which are carried further in conceptual thought; and from perception, concept and idea inherit that ontological pattern of objectivity it has primarily created. The stillness of object, aloof from the turmoil of forces, recurs enhanced in the stableness and permanent availability of "idea": it is in the last analysis at the bottom of "theory" as such.

It follows that the dominance, in epistemology, of the cognitive modes derived from perception—a dominance pushed historically to the point of excluding other modes of acquaintance with reality—is intimately bound up with the possibility of knowledge as such: so is the corresponding dominance in ontology of their object pattern. The exclusiveness, however, has its penalty.

On the debit side, the same gap between subject and object which provides the dimension of freedom for theory, and which is found duplicated in the gap between object and object, provides in both respects also the breeding ground for a class of problems that beset the history of knowledge—unavoidable because rooted in its very conditions, and by the same token insolvable within those conditions. As regards object-object relation, an epistemological case in point is Hume's problem of necessary connection as a pale substitute for real causality (and in this devitalized form taken over by Kant). In its ontological version, the problem of *relation* revolves around the classical concept of self-contained, inactive substance—"that which requires nothing but itself in order to exist" (Descartes)—which is by no means an historical freak, but the conceptual framing of perceptual truth: "substance" conceived on that model admits of external relations only and by definition excludes all self-transitiveness. To release "being" from this imprisonment in "substance" is among the major preoccupations of contemporary ontology. Further, the homelessness of "force" in the system (just one aspect of that imprisonment) raises the issue of "anthropomorphism," whose banishment from exterior knowledge is far too much taken for granted as the proper thing in scientific epistemology (see Appendix 2).

As regards subject-object relation, the gulf opened by perceptual objectification in sole command is partly responsible for those puzzles of the consciousness-external word dualism which parallelism, occasionalism, idealism, have in vain attempted to solve. For without the self-transcendence of the ego in *action,* i.e., in its physical dealings with the environment and in the attendant vulnerability of its being, the closure of the mental order is logically unassailable, and solipsism can appear as rational discretion instead of as madness.[5] In fact one can say, with utter brevity,

---

5. Not that anyone but a madman has ever taken solipsism *seriously:* arguing for it, except in soliloquy, is to acknowledge the "other" whose

that denial of causality leads straight to solipsism—and is consequently never made in complete earnest.

This is but a bare catalogue of the problems originating in the perceptive situation and made over to the reflection of theory. In all of them, an original freedom of animal life, perception—itself an offshoot of the more basic freedom of organic being as such—presents the bill for its privileges to the yet higher freedom of thought.

Conclusions. Reverting to Hume's issue we find: that his result, the nongivenness of causation among percepts, is only what is to be expected from the nature and meaning of perception itself; that the result, in being confirmed, is at the same time limited to its proper field and thereby divested of its skeptical implications; that what calls for explanation in the first place is not how, from the causal vacuum of perception, we still come to the idea of causation, but how it is that perception, and just perception, does *not* exhibit it, i.e., contrives to conceal it—its absence there and not its presence among our ideas being the puzzling fact; that the primary aspect of causality is not regular connection, not even necessary connection, but force and influence; that these are themselves original contents of experience and not interpolations between contents of experience (= percepts) by a synthetic function, be it association or reason; that the source of this experience is, indeed, not sense perception, but our body exerting itself in action—the source which Hume summarily dismisses under the head of "animal nisus"; that, lastly, the right of extrapolation from this source beyond its immediate range of deliverance is a question to be studied, without fear of the blame of anthropomorphism, by an organic philosophy.

APPENDIX 2 (p. 23)

Note on Anthropomorphism

In any account of what the scientific attitude, as such, postulates in, and what it excludes from, its objects, foremost among the exclusions will stand that of teleology, i.e., of final causes. On this point the spokesmen of science from its inception in the seventeenth century have been particularly emphatic, and so much has it become an unquestioned article of the scientific creed that the blunt question "Why must final causes be excluded?" will nowadays find many scientists unprepared with a satisfactory answer. A restatement of the reasons will do away with the air of

---

consensus is sought. The argument is then frivolous, *qua* dialogue, while the absolute monologue is the madman's privilege. Neither can claim the virtue of critical austerity with which solipsism pleads its cause.

obviousness which the maxim has acquired through sheer undisputed possession and refer it to the conditions which qualify its validity.

First, the maxim concerns teleology as a causal mode of nature itelf, or immanent teleology, and not transcendent teleology such as might have been exercised by the creator of the existing system of nature in once creating it as it is: any design on his part in the initial arrangement of universal matter would be well compatible with the strictly mechanical operation of that matter, which would in this very way fulfill the design.[1] If only spoken of as unknown and on principle unknowable, and therefore not an object for scientific inquiry, the general admission of such a design is inoffensive to the scientific world-concept. Insofar as the rising science dealt at all with this aspect of teleology, it was to reject its crudely anthropocentric version of a nature devised for the benefit of man. Apart from that, the conception of a divine engineer (of supreme skill but inscrutable ends) was actually a requisite for the mechanistic world-concept itself during its most vigorous phase of growth.

The real problem was with final causes as *modi operandi* of and in nature itself. Historically their rejection was part of the great struggle with Aristotelianism which marked the birth of modern science, and in this setting it was closely connected with the attack on "substantial forms." Regarding final causes, we must observe that their rejection is a methodo-logical principle guiding inquiry rather than a statement of ascertained fact issuing from inquiry. There is not first a record of persistent failure to detect them in nature—which would anyway not warrant the *axiom* that they can on principle not be expected there and must indeed on no account be sought for. The mere search for them was quite suddenly, with the inauguration of modern science, held to be at variance with the scientific attitude, deflecting the searcher from the quest for true causes. It is only then, in the exercise of that attitude, that the negative record is accumulated, viz., by the success of doing without final causes. To repeat, the exclusion of teleology is not an inductive result but an a priori prohibition of modern science. This it can only be if teleology contradicts the very type of being presupposed in possible objects of natural science and thus also the concept of cause proper to such objects.

Yet it has never been argued that final cause is a far-fetched or abstruse

---

1. The parallel is the teleology of a man-made machine: in its design it embodies a final cause which guided its constructor, and its working is by efficient causes alone whose mode of efficacy was foreseen in the design. In other words, finalism is transmitted to the machine not as such, but translated into efficient causation to which the achievement of the end is hence entrusted.

or even "unnatural" concept—on the contrary, nothing is more cognate to the human mind and more familiar to the basic experience of man: and this was precisely what in the new scientific attitude counted against it. Our very proneness to final explanation makes it suspect. Bacon lists it among the "idols of the tribe," the prejudices innate in human nature. "And then it is that in struggling towards that which is further off, [human understanding] falls back upon that which is more nigh at hand—namely on final causes, which have relation clearly to the nature of man rather than to the nature of the universe, and from this source have strangely defiled philosophy."[2] Even at this early date the issue itself—the inhospitality of nature to final causes—is taken as settled and in no need of argument. But it is significant that the one reminder deemed sufficient to compromise teleology for the intelligent reader is that final causes have relation to the nature of man rather than to the nature of the universe—implying that no inference must be drawn from the former to the latter, which again implies a basic difference of being between the two. This is a fundamental assumption, not so much of modern science itself as of modern metaphysics in the interest of science. In the generation following Bacon's the assumption was raised by Descartes to the rank of a systematic principle. Exterior reality, under the title of *res extensa* entirely detached from the interior reality of thought, henceforth constituted a self-contained field for the universal application of mathematical and mechanical analysis: the very idea of "object" was transformed by the dualistic expurgation. Intimately connected with this process is the epistemological monopoly accorded to the perceptional mode of cognition, i.e., to outside knowledge mainly on the visual model, in consequence of which "objectivity" becomes essentially the elaboration of exterior sense-data on the lines of their extensional properties. (See Appendix 1.) Other possible modes of relation to reality, such as the communication between life and life, or the experience of the impact and resistance of things in bodily effort, fell short of the ideal of exact knowledge and ceased to count. This dominance of "distancing" and objectifying perception concurred with the dualistic rift between subject and object, considered as two heterogeneous domains, in putting a severe ban on any transference of features of internal experience into the interpretation of the external world (though later the reverse encroachment in materialistic psychology proved to be much less taboo). Anthropomorphism at all events, and even zoomorphism in general, became scientific high treason. In this dualistic setting we meet the "nature of man" as a source

---

2. Francis Bacon, *Novum Organum* I, 48.

of defilement for "philosophy" (natural science), and the objection to "final" explanation is that it is anthropomorphic.

Thus the struggle against teleology is a stage in the struggle against anthropomorphism which by itself is as old as Western science. The criticism that started with the Ionian rejection of mythological personification had now come, under the new stimulus of scientific dualism, to discover the taint in the much subtler form of Aristotelian finalism. But the argument once under way did not stop there: it overtook even the efficient causation in whose favor final causes had been ousted. According to Hume, the idea of force and necessary connection, alien to the record of things, arises from certain internal impressions of the mind regarding its own working: reading them into the record of things is therefore another case of that transference of traits from human self-experience into nature which had become anathema to objective science. Even if Hume's particular account of the origin of these ideas is not accepted, it is certainly true that the concepts of force and cause spring from a type of experience which involves "impressions of reflection" in addition to those of "sensation"; i.e., they involve the subject's awareness of his own inward mode of affectedness (such as the proprioceptive awareness of muscular effort) as an integral part-content of the object-experience itself. This "subjective" element is sufficient to bring the insinuation of those concepts into the realm of mere objects under the general verdict of anthropomorphism.

Science followed the skeptical lead of philosophy. Discarding the explanatory concept of force as anthropomorphic, and as unverifiable by a mere measuring account of extensity, science restricted its claim to that of registering sequences of positions in a space-time system of coordinates and of formulating quantitative regularities in such sequences as "the laws of nature." Explanation has thus been forsaken for mere description, which, by attaching quantitative values to the positions and positional changes in extensity and letting these values stand for the entities themselves, becomes pure mathematical description. The search for motive springs has been as completely abandoned as that for substantial forms, that is, causal explanation has followed final explanation into limbo; and indeed the very idea of explanation has evaporated with the completion of the anti-anthropomorphic movement in epistemology. A profound dialectic, therefore, is revealed in this movement. Mythical personification, and later impersonal teleology, were discarded to clear the ground for a "true explanation" of external nature: this explanation, in terms of efficient cause, itself still depended on one remnant of despised animism, namely, on the universal interpolation of the images of force and causation into the picture of the world, an interpolation whereby these elements of the personal effort-motion experience became available as the connective tissue between perceived natural events. With the complete elimination of "animism," science cut out from under its feet that same ground it had earlier, by a *partial* suppression of animism, wrested from it for rational explanation. The long road from pristine panpsychism via dualism to postdualistic materialism ends in an agnostic renunciation of the idea of knowledge as an understanding of its objects. Ironically, this happened when with the abdication of dualism the *metaphysical* necessity for a strictly devitalized model of nature had ceased to exist.

The importance of the last remark for the question of teleology is this. As with other "anthropomorphic" features, it is evident that the justification for the a priori exclusion of final causes from external reality lay in a dualistic metaphysics which, in the act of exclusion, also saved the truth of the excluded trait in its own native realm. Finalism must have its legitimate seat somewhere whence the idea of it could be derived, and in the dualistic division the essence of man or of life which provides this seat is not yet disowned; it is only dissociated from that of the *res extensa*. But dualism proved untenable in the face of organic experience. Occasionalism and psychophysical parallelism were desperate attempts to save the consistency of the new ontology of science. With their failure, scientific materialism was left in sole but uneasy possession, no longer sheltered by the dualistic alibi, and burdened with a task from which the former division of labor had kept it free. For when dualism departs and the *res cogitans* in its organic foundation becomes itself part and product of unitary nature, Bacon's reference of final causes to the "nature of man" ceases to have the extrusive effect it had in the dualistic setting; and finally the doctrine of evolution, now inseparable from modern monism, obliterates any vestige of the dividing line on which the whole argument of contrasting "nature" and "man" rests.

Thus in a monistic ontology the case against anthropomorphism in its extreme form becomes problematical and is on principle reopened. It then seems to issue in this choice of monistic alternatives: either to take the presence of purposive inwardness in one part of the physical order, viz., in man, as a valid testimony to the nature of that wider reality that lets it emerge, and to accept what it reveals in itself as part of the general evidence; or to extend the prerogatives of mechanical matter to the very heart of the seemingly heterogeneous class of phenomena and oust teleology even from the "nature of man," whence it had tainted the "nature of the universe"—that is, to alienate man from himself and deny genuineness to the self-experience of life.

Philosophical Aspects of Darwinism

I

The mechanistic model of nature which the seventeenth century brought forth concerned itself at first with existing structures, be it solar system or animal organisms, without committing the thinker on the question of their genesis. Each structure as found was conceived as a functioning mechanism whose analysis into elementary components of matter and motion was to explain its actual functioning by a uniform standard: how it had come to be in a past history of nature was no part as yet of the scientific agenda, if sometimes the subject for summary speculation. This temporary avoidance of a question fraught with theological dangers protected the infancy of modern science. For a century or so its founders were spared the problem of origins by their theistic beliefs. Even when the infant had grown in strength, eighteenth-century deism still supplied the tenuous theological setting for the new scientific cosmology. Against the idea of the Cosmos as a living self-created whole to which pantheists clung, deism accepted the idea of a vast machine which, once set up, follows its course automatically. But it had to be set up in the first place: the continual creator became the constructor (the "clockmaker") active but once; and the place of the unmoved mover who draws the world into his eternal present was taken by the initial mover who had imparted a fixed momentum in the past. By a curious irony of fate, the Biblical concept of an extramundane Creator, and of creation as a circumscribed act in the beginning, had helped to prepare the ground for this jejune picture. *"Was wär ein Gott, der nur von aussen stiesse?"* protested Goethe. However, the idea of the ready-made mechanism was for the scientific mind itself a temporary expedient only. The first things in explanation must inevitably also become the first things in time, and the present configuration must become the latest member of a time-series connecting it with those first things. If these are the utterly primitive ones of matter and motion unplanned, and the series leading to the present condition can be constructed from their premises alone, creation becomes supererogatory.

Questions of origin have been inherent in any comprehensive inquiry into the nature of things since the beginnings of human speculation, and mechanistic philosophy is no exception. Its principles initiated of themselves two trains of investigation with regard to every physical entity, of which the second was taken up as soon as the maturation of the first allowed science to emerge from the shelter of deism. The first, as we said, was the analysis of given physical systems, that is, the explanation of their observed functioning in terms of the general principles of mechanics; the second was the reconstruction of the possible generation of such systems from antecedent states and ultimately from some primordial state of matter which, by the operation of the same general principles of mechanics and without the intervention of an intelligent design, would in due course transform itself into the stable system under consideration as simply a necessary stage in its causal history. The two sides are exemplified on the one hand by Newton's theory of the solar system as an existing mechanism, on the other, by the Kant-Laplace nebular hypothesis of the origination of this system.[1] The point in modern physics is that the answer to both these questions must employ the same principles, that is to say, that origin and resulting existence do not differ except in the sense of antecedent and subsequent states of an identical substratum: the producing reality is of the same order as the product, being merely differently located in the infinite time-series of cause and

---

1. Both sides were already articulated in Hobbes' genetic derivation and functional analysis of the "body politic": the same primitive dynamic, fear of violent death, determines the unordered "state of nature," the transition from this to the commonwealth, and the mechanics of the latter.

effect. This implies that any given entity can be treated at the same time as a product and as itself productive of the future state which will result from it.[2] The only qualitative difference admitted between origins in general and their late consequences (if the former are to be more self-explaining than the latter and thus suitable as a relative starting-point for explanation) is that the origins must, in the absence of an intelligent design at the beginning of things, represent a simpler state of matter such as can plausibly be assumed on random conditions. With this sole difference, earliest origins and latest results are of the same nature. And since it is nothing but disequilibrium that provides the dynamics of change, any state of organization attained is a measure of equilibrium resulting from the instability of an earlier distribution. Thus the place of transcending, constructive creation is taken by the total series in its infinite continuation itself. The metaphysical secret of this new approach lies in the radically temporal conception of being, or in its identification with action and process. The central position which motion assumes in the ontological scheme, in replacement of any *ens realissimum* envisaged in former speculation, denotes this shift.

In this new meaning of "origins" we observe a complete reversal of the older conception concerning the superiority of the originating principle over its effects. It had mostly been assumed that there must be not only more power but also more perfection in the cause than in the effect. The originating agency must possess more reality than the things originated by it. It must also be superior in formal essence, to account for the degree of form that the derivative things

---

2. The view is illustrated by Laplace's hypothetical "divine Calculator," to whose analysis the present state of the universe, instead of representing a lasting machine once constructed, is but a passing configuration of matter in the continual shift of configurations which compose the world's existence in limitless time. *All these configurations are equivalent* as temporal sections through a constant quantity of matter and motion. Thus any choice of a point for the beginning is as arbitrary as that of one for an ending, and indeed as the choice of the existing state for representing the design of the creator. Each instant of time is alike qualified to provide in its data of bodies, positions, and forces the basis from which to construct backward and forward the states at each and any other instant of time. To the limitless analytical intellect, one instant contains the whole history of the world in past and future. The world is conceived as the *history of matter* rather than as a particular order of matter.

may enjoy. At the very least the cause must possess of these things "as much as," "not less than," the things springing from it.[3] Obviously this pattern is completely reversed in the kind of genetic deduction which modern theory inaugurated. If the most elementary situations can of themselves give rise to all diversification and order, and if the latter are explained by the dynamics of the former, then, paradoxically speaking, the antecedent cause is here inferior to the effect, in terms of structural articulation though not in terms of quantity, which is constant. Thus genetically as well as functionally, the primitive is called upon to account for the more articulated, the unstable for the stable, disorder for order, becoming for being.

I I

Of all provinces of reality the living kingdom longest defied the application of this idea of origins, and it was only in the nineteenth century that the theory of *evolution* succeeded in subjugating it in this respect to the general scheme. What were the particular difficulties? To Descartes, animal bodies were machines constructed to function as they do, and though there is neither intelligence nor purposiveness in their functioning itself, this being automatic, their construction *toward* such functioning seemed to call for precisely those qualities. If then the constructive task assumedly devolves upon matter itself, the very success of the scientific analysis of organisms—unlike that of the majestically crude cosmic structure—stands in the way of making the assumption good in *their* case. For the more admirably they revealed themselves to be constructed, the less possible it seemed to conceive of the genesis of such patterns other than by design, and at

---

3. It was characteristic of the classical attitude to understand the lower, i.e., more elementary, in the light of its being a "less" of the higher, to that extent as lacking in reality, and as subservient to the higher realization. As the first principle of explanation was taken from the highest kind of being, which is also ontologically "first," explanation was typically from the top of the scale downward, the lower orders being derived from the higher by way of privation. The realm of passion, for example, is characterized by the absence of reason, but in order to exist it must still participate in the principle of being, though it does so to a lesser degree than does reason. Plotinus furnishes the extreme example of this direction of explanation from higher to lower, where the bottom of the scale is the last to be accounted for.

that by a design as far superior to the design of human ingenuity as the natural machines proved superior in construction to man-made ones. If design or teleological direction were ruled out, the odds against a mere chance production would seem no less overwhelming than those against the famous monkeys' randomly hammering out world literature on their typewriters in the aeons at their disposal. The comparison holds so long as the fixity of species, and consequently separate origination of each, is assumed.

The problem is complicated by the fact that in the case of these mechanical structures, i.e., organisms, unlike the more enduring cosmic ones, we constantly witness their coming-to-be in the individual instances. If anywhere, then here genesis does belong to the complete picture of the entity itself; but the genesis in question points distinctly away from the mechanistic pattern. For in the ever-repeated origination of highly organized individuals from an infinitesimal germ, the working-out of a prearranged *plan* of growth and development seems obvious. Thus the very idea of "development" which the facts of *reproduction* suggested stood in the way of applying to the living kingdom the same categories of genesis that were applied on mechanistic principles to reality at large. Indeed, the term "evolution" denoted originally just this phenomenon of individual genesis, and by no means the genesis of species. On the contrary, "evolution" in its literal sense presupposes the existence of the species, because it is precisely this which, in the persons of the parent individuals, provides the prearranged plan to be "evolved" in every given case of generation. What evolves is not the model itself but its re-embodiment in each generation from germ to maturity: what evolves was involved in the germ, its potency there derived from its act in the progenitor. In terms of cause-effect relation, then, the parent accounts not only for its offspring's existence but also for its offspring's *form* by its own possession of this selfsame form. This is a pattern very different from the mechanistic chain of cause and effect and strongly suggests the operation of a *causa formalis* in addition to a *causa efficiens*, or the existence of substantial forms, which were otherwise banned from the whole system of natural explanation. In short, the very concept of *dévelopement* was opposed to that of mechanics and still implied some version or other of classical ontology.

When, therefore, the question of origin was at last extended to those permanently self-repeating plans of growth themselves, a venture of prime ontological importance was initiated, whose success on the terms of natural science was bound to complete the anti-Platonic movement of the modern mind. On the premise of the noneternity of our earth, which followed from the scientific cosmology, first representatives in the chains of generation were still called for (as they were in the doctrine of creation), but they no longer would have to be representatives of the existing patterns, if these are regarded as the temporal outcome rather than as the timeless determinants of the life-process. The probability-problem indicated by the example of the monkeys would then be split up into two divisions, that of the spontaneous generation of the first forms and that of the descent from them of the present ones, and this splitting-up held the secret of success in that it overcame the monstrous improbability embodied in that example.

"Evolution" in the modern sense made it possible to credit unaided matter more plausibly with the production of the living kingdom, and thus to advance the materialistic monism of science by a decisive step. It did so by *abandoning* the original meaning of the term "evolution," derived from the growth process of individual organisms: the idea of preformation and unfolding was abandoned and replaced by the quasi-mechanical picture of an unplanned, undirected, yet progressive sequence whose beginnings, unlike the germ, adumbrate nothing of the outcome or of the successive steps. If the living forms are descended from one another and have not each arisen independently, the stumbling block of spontaneous generation is pushed back to the very first instance of life as such, where its magnitude and therefore its theoretical inconvenience are reduced in proportion to the minimum of organization assumed in these first beginnings. Immeasurably consequential as was the first step, the transition from inorganic to organic, it can hypothetically be made small enough not to overstrain the probabilities of chance combination. All further variegation is then left to the dynamics of this initial something, and for the whole doctrine to be a scientific one it is essential that the dynamics invoked do not contain any element of teleology, of preformative disposition or aspiration toward the higher forms to come, but that they "evolve" those higher forms without their being in any sense "involved" in the initial stage. Everything therefore depends on a conception of these dynamics which both is causally satisfactory and does not burden the primitive with any mysterious content anticipatory of the more advanced: the operative causality, while accounting for the emergence of the advanced in succession from the primitive, must let the latter be as unambiguously primitive as it is. Then, while each throw of the dice is still blind, the probability-situation is yet decisively changed: the first and simplest form of life once given, all further shaking of the dice occurs in confined dice-boxes with selected dice and defined ways for them to be cast, so that the game of chance is vastly narrowed down. Also each "throw" is bound by the sum of the previous ones, adding to their result and not starting over again. In other words, life, once existing, progressively sets its own conditions for the mechanical play of variations; and the probabilities do look better than for the monkeys, who at each moment start anew, their action undetermined by their past performance.

Thus *heredity,* which at first seemed the strongest argument for the doctrine of immutable species, becomes an instrument for their very derivation by way of change: transmitted in reproduction, the effects of mutation can accumulate within one strain, superadded one upon the other, and the small steps of chance are allowed to grow into vast and complex patterns. In addition to this cumulative functioning of mutation through heredity, the working of *natural selection* on its results seems to fill admirably the place of a directing principle vacated by teleology. Indeed it was the Darwinian theory of evolution, with its combination of chance variation and natural selection, which completed the extrusion of teleology from nature. Having become redundant even in the story of life, purpose retired wholly into subjectivity.

Like every major theory, the contemporary theory of evolution and genetics is an intricate combination of fact, hypothesis, and deduction. In the category of established fact belongs evolution as such: that species do change, have emerged in series of changes from ancestral forms, and in their entirety form a branching family system of common descent in which the simple precedes the complex, and transitions are gradual. Also an ascertained fact is the occurrence of mutations; but not their nature or cause. Natural selection is a logical deduction from the two premises of competition and of differences in the competitors, which themselves are facts. The chance-character of mutations is a hypothesis: the inducement of some of them by external forces, such as radiation, is a fact of laboratory experience, but the claim that these are representative for all of them and for their underlying dynamics is a mere trial with Occam's razor; and the sufficiency of this kind of variability for the emergence of the major plans of organization is, so far, more a metaphysical contention (or, more soberly, a methodological postulate) than a scientific hypothesis—if "hypothesis" implies the construction of at least a mentally workable model. All these aspects raise philosophical issues, some of which we shall indicate.

III

The mere factual discovery of evolution had a profound significance for the very concept of life, quite apart from the special issue of the descent of man. In Descartes' conception of animal nature, the point of departure is some definite mechanical structure—a given type of organism—and the life of the animal in question is the function of that structure, the performance of the machine. Here structure unilaterally determines function and explains it; its analysis therefore answers all the questions which can reasonably be asked with respect to a living thing. Evolutionism, however, regards this given type of structure, the condition for a specific performance of life, as itself a product of life, the outcome and temporary stopping-place of a continuous dynamism which itself must be termed "life." Thus life appears in its very means, that is, in its structural equipment for living, as its own achievement, or at least result, instead of being simply endowed with its means and faculties. This is one of the most far-reaching discoveries ever made with regard to the nature of life. Among other things, it completes the liquidation of immutable essences, and thus signifies the final victory of nominalism over realism, which had had its last bulwark in the idea of natural species. This is a major philosophical event in that it powerfully confirms the anti-Platonism of the modern mind. If we add to this the absence of any teleological directedness, the evolutionary process presents itself as a sheer adventure with an entirely unforeseeable course. This specifically modern idea of the unplanned, open-ended adventurousness of life, the corollary to the absence of immutable essence, is again a major philosophical consequence of the scientific doctrine of evolution.

As on the physical scene at large, so in the history of life *conditions* take the place of essence as the originating principle. In the shape of "environment," condition becomes so much a necessary correlative to the concept of organism that it enters into the very derivation of its being. The constitutive function of environment is common to Lamarckism and Darwinism. Organism is seen as primarily determined by the conditions of its existence, and life is understood in terms of the organism-environment situation rather than in terms of the exercise of an autonomous nature.

Organism and environment together form a system, and this henceforth determines the basic concept of life. Living, then, is the behavior induced by this bipolar system in one of its poles; and the typical patterns of living, the relative stability and specificness of behavior in any given species, represent the equilibrium achieved between the two factors that make up the situation. But so does organic structure itself: this too, not only its current behavior, represents an equilibrium relative to the long-term generic situation, being the outcome of the previous working of that situation on the substratum of life. In other words, the nonfixity of species, added to the principle of environment, divests the subject of life to an unprecedented degree of original and inherent determinations. In the unplanned transactions of the biological situation, and with the formative role of environment whose effects accumulate over the generations, life's own created and immutable essence contracts toward a minimum, while the import of the total situation, with its demands and selective criteria, increases toward a maximum. The minimum left to the original essence of life is just self-preservation, which is analogous to the inertial laws ruling the conduct of a particle. The maximum transferred to the situation is the sum total of all those influences eliciting from mere self-preservation (by way of incidentally adaptive variability) that wealth of superstructure and superinduced behavior by which life as it were, entirely innocent of any foreshadowing disposition toward them, surprises itself—and its Creator if there is one. Mind was not foreseen in the amoeba, nor was the vertebrate structure, science no more than the opposable thumb:

one and the other were elicited in due—but unforeseeable—course in the enormous span of the changing vital situation. The variability is essentially instability, which itself testifies to the absence of a predetermined substantial form.

This reduction of the formal essence of life to the vanishing-point of a mere vital momentum without specific original content, and correspondingly the throwing open of the indefinite horizon of situation for the evoking of possibilities which were not pre-existing potentialities, have a familiar ring to those conversant with contemporary philosophies of Man. Indeed nineteenth-century evolutionism, which completed the Copernican revolution in ontology, is an apocryphal ancestor (along with the more official ones) of present-day existentialism. The latter's encounter with "nothingness" springs from the denial of "essence" which blocked the recourse to an ideal "nature" of man, once offered in his classical definition by reason (*homo animal rationale*), or in the Biblical one by creation in the image of God. The "image," in the absence of creation, had vanished with the original; and reason had been reduced to a means among means, to be judged by the efficiency of its instrumental role[4] in the survival issue: as a merely formal skill—the extension of animal cunning—it does not set but serve aims, is not itself standard but measured by standards outside its jurisdiction. If there is a "life of reason" for man (as distinct from the mere use of reason), it can be chosen only nonrationally, as all ends must be chosen nonrationally (if they can be chosen at all). Thus reason has no jurisdiction even over the choice of itself as more than a means.[5] But use of reason, as a means, is compatible with any end, no matter how irrational. This is the nihilistic implication in man's losing a "being" transcending the flux of becoming. Nietzsche's nihilism and his attempt to overcome it are demonstrably connected with the impact of Darwinism. The will to power seemed the only alternative left if the original essence of man had evaporated in the transitoriness and whimsicality of the evolutionary process. This is to say, not that Darwinism is *the* pro-

---

4. But to have an instrumental role, reason—i.e., mind—must have causative force, and this, as it challenges the self-sufficiency of materialism, also raises the whole issue of determinism connected with it: see Appendix to Fifth Essay.

5. Cf. Eighth Essay, especially sect. III.

genitor of existentialism, but that it conforms and contributes to all the other mental factors out of whose total setting existentialism logically grew. We mentioned the major role which evolutionism with the liquidation of immutable species played in the anti-Platonic trend of modern science: existentialism is the most radical conclusion drawn so far from the unreservedly accepted victory of nominalism over realism.

IV

In relating evolutionism to the Copernican revolution, we have especially in mind the fact that it extends to the realm of *life* that combination of natural necessity with radical contingency which the Newtonian-Laplacean cosmology resulting from that revolution had universally proclaimed. The combination of necessity and contingency seems paradoxical. The first obvious aspect of the universe in the modern scientific scheme was indeed the strict rule of causal law, in the function and consequently also in the genesis of things, and this seems rather to exclude any kind of contingency from nature. It certainly does exclude contingency in the sense of accidents outside the law. In another sense, however, the modern causal scheme is the very principle of an overall contingency of existence as such, insofar as the necessity here operating is external for any given entity within its pluralistic setting and does not proceed as an autonomous law of becoming from its intrinsic nature. Nor does it proceed from a transcendent plan, in the comprehensive design of which the particular things and their destinies are integrated. Rather is the necessity that of the sum total itself in the interaction of its parts, each of which contributes its quantity and is itself determined by the distribution of quantities around it. Though everything in this interaction is governed by causal law, the resulting formations are metaphysically contingent: none fulfills a particular end of reality, there being no intrinsic preference in reality for this rather than another outcome of the arithmetic of interrelated quantities. External necessity of the summative type is therefore the corollary to the most radical contingency of every particular existence. Some initial conditions being different, the solar system would not exist or would be otherwise than it is, and the completeness of nature as an equilibrium-system would be none the worse for it. "Necessity plus contingency" can be most simply expressed here by saying that there is the complete concourse of *causes* but no *reason* for the system as it happens to exist.

The same logic applies to life under the categories of evolutionism. The combination of necessity and contingency appears in all the features which we have discussed.

1. One such feature was the reversal of the older belief in the superior status of origins. Since perfection is not a standard intrinsic in nature itself, the so-called "higher" structure may well emerge from more primitive ones *accidentally,* i.e., by the agency of entirely primitive forces. If higher levels happen to emerge in the dynamics of the primitive, their quality as levels is wholly contingent, though their factuality is necessary. The importance of this idea of descent for the self-understanding of life is obvious.

2. Another feature was the reversal of the traditional relation assumed between pre-existing structure and function, and here too we meet the character of contingency. Organic structure, though in each given case the condition for specific function, is itself the function of a vital dynamic in the sequence of generations which is concerned not at all with the achievement of a particular structure but with the business of living and the continuance of life as such. (We shall presently see that "concerned" is a metaphorical expression only.) Species, a relatively stable, temporarily self-perpetuating structure, is an incidental result of life's history with no terminal status in creation and no indication where it may lead next. The flux of dynamism replaces essence and qualifies what appears as such with a radical contingency.

3. In the emphasis on environment we have a third feature pointing up the rule of "necessity and contingency." When we said before that in the evolutionary conception the patterns of organic structure appear as themselves products of life, the meaning was not that the emergent form is considered an autonomous achievement of the living substance which would unfold in this series of emergence its original potentialities. The explanatory accent lies rather, in accordance with the physical ontology we have been discussing, on the external conditions as the chief agency in evolution. Only when the term "life" comprises the interplay of organism and environment is it correct to say that "life produces species." Even the saying that the

emergent forms are "adaptations" to conditions, credits, by Darwinian standards, too much to the bearer of life if adaptation suggests a
performance on its part. The adaptations rather represent a dynamic
equilibrium, working itself out between the conditions of the environment and the haphazard possibilities offered by organic instability.
Thus we observe the same shift from substance and its intrinsic properties to the function of a plural system of relations which character-
izes the physical world-concept in general and leads to the combination of necessity and contingency here discussed.[6]

Regarding the distribution of causality between organism and environment as the factors of the evolutionary situation, we have to make
a final observation. According to Darwinism the distribution is:
chance-variation (or mutation) on the part of the organism, natural
selection on the part of the environment. The first of these rests
ultimately on the fact that nothing in nature is completely stable;
the second, on the fact that life is continually put to the test under
the alternative of being and not-being inherent in it. What, then, is the
respective share of either of these two causes? Theoretically, the
mechanics of selection, in which no purpose intervenes, is to take
the place of teleology in that it decides on the merits of the random
material offered it, and it does so by criteria which, mechanical as

---

6. It may be pertinent to point out the bearing of all this on the
classical idea of "perfection." As long as in the Aristotelian or even
Cartesian sense there was such a thing as the definitive pattern of a given
species, it was possible to speak of a more or less perfect realization of an
essence in the lives of individuals. One could argue that an individual is in
a greater or lesser degree what it is destined to be, viz., a representative of
its species. "Perfection" here means the completeness with which the
pattern of the tree or dog or of man comes to actualization in the individual development of a specimen of the species. Again, for the comparison of species with one another and for their ordering in a scale one could
postulate certain standards of perfection. But the picture is changed when
it is admitted that species is only relatively stable, and that this stability
represents only the temporary equilibrium among the forces which generally determine the structure as successful. In this view, each given
structure represents a trying-out in the drama of adaptation and is on
principle open to unforeseeable revisions which, if pushed far enough,
may result in something which can no longer be regarded as the more
perfect realization of an original pattern, but must be termed a new
species.

they are, favor "progress" in certain directions. It is to be noted, however, that they "favor" by elimination. This is essentially a negative substitute for teleology: it accounts for the disappearance only and not for the emergence of forms—it suppresses and does not create. Thus it replaces teleology as a directing principle only on condition that it is offered the suitable material to select from. This means that the positive role, the emergence of forms, falls wholly to the random play of aberrations from pattern, which as aberrations are by themselves indifferently "freaks," and on which the distinction between deformity and improvement is superimposed by entirely extraneous criteria. Strained through their sieve, the fortuitous is held to turn constructive—and with no "cunning of reason" there results the paradox of advance through mischance, of ascent by accident. It has still to be shown that the infinitely complex and wonderfully adjusted organic "machines" and their ascending series can really be accounted for on these terms.

It is not for us to decide on questions of fact, but we can make explicit what the hypothesis implies. Plasticity is here instability, and we are left with the riddle of the latter's feigning creativity. For if the gene system is the transmittor of heredity, stability—the condition of faithful transmission—is its essential virtue. A mutation, then, is a disturbance of this stability, resulting in failure to transmit faithfully. Presumably the disturbance is due to some external influence (e.g., radiation) which has managed to break through the stabilizing barriers of the system, and whose action, from the point of view of the system itself, is nothing but a mechanical mishap. Since it is a mishap to the steering-system of a future organism, it will result in something which from the point of view of the original pattern can only be termed a deformity. However "useful" it happens to be, as a deviation from the norm it is "pathological." As similar mishaps continue to befall the same gene system in succeeding generations, an accumulation of such deformities under the premium system of selection may result in a thoroughly novel and enriched pattern: but the "enrichment" would still be an excrescence on the original simplicity, a slipping of the discipline of form multiplied over and over again under the licensing of selection; and thus the high organization of any animal or of man would appear a gigantic monstrosity into which the original amoeba has grown through a long history of disease. Tendentious as it sounds, this must be the picture so long as mutation is conceived as nothing more than a freak accident whose deleterious or beneficial quality (and deleterious is overwhelmingly the rule) is decided only *post hoc* in the lottery of natural selection, i.e., by the external *fiat* of environment (except where intrinsic viability is affected by the change). On this model, which reflects the present conceptual state of genetics, any "higher" form is indeed nothing but a sport, by itself indistinguishable from degeneration, of a "lower" form, but a sport which has turned out to have a differential survival-value. This extreme consequence of Darwinism squarely poses the question whether a mechanistic biology can do justice to the phenomena of life.

Let us sharpen the question by the following consideration. In the combination of Darwinism with modern geneticism which constitutes the rational core of present theory, a *new dualism* of model-conception supersedes any previous one in the interpretation of life. It is not, as might appear at first glance, the dualism of organism and environment—this pair rather forms one interactive system—but the dualism *germ: soma,* in which the soma (the actual organism) is itself part of the "environment," namely, the immediate environment for the germ plasm and the mediator of the effects on the latter's existence of the wider environment. These effects, however, as far as conducted through the *life history* of the soma, are merely in the either-or terms of admission or nonadmission of the germ to reproduction (i.e., to its continuation *qua* germ) and in no way include any reflex of the organism's experience and achievements in its lifelong dealings with the environment. The nontransmission of acquired characters precludes the latter possibility. Thus there arises within the materialist realm itself a strange parody of the Cartesian model of two noncommunicating substances. Weismann's theory of the continuity of the germ plasm is the clearest expression of this new biological dualism. There is on the one hand the blind automatism of a germ history enacted in the subterranean darkness which no light from the upper world penetrates; and on the other hand the upper world of the soma meeting the world in terms of life, pursuing its destiny, fighting its battles, taking the impress of its victories and defeats—and all this being of no other consequence for the hidden charge than that of its being either continued or eliminated. The vicissitudes of the *germ's* history, as expressed in mutations, are entirely separate from the vicissitudes of the soma's history, uninfluenced by the whole drama of life enacted in the light, though determining the latter through the next embodiment. On these terms, the short-lived macroscopic individual appears as something like a repetitious offshoot of the enduring germ plasm, sent up in succession to provide its nourishing and protecting "environment": all complexity of the temporary carriers (with its attendant enjoyment and suffering) is the ever more expensive elaboration of this their subservient function. Thus the Platonic-Aristotelian immortality of the species is here replaced by the immortality of the germ plasm as a continuous existence in itself; and in a reversal of the classical formula, one would have to say that the developed is for the sake of the undeveloped, the tree for the sake of the seed.

V

In one respect, the triumph which materialism achieved in Darwinism contains the germ of its own overcoming. The metaphysical importance of Darwinism lay in the comparative success of its attempt —imposed by the scientific commitment as such—to credit the automatism of material nature with the generation of the branching and ascending life forms. But by thus dispensing with the dualistic necessity for a creative principle different from the created, the resulting monism also drew upon deserted matter the full weight of a burden from which dualism had kept it free: that of having to account for the origin of *mind,* in addition to the physical organizations themselves. For the mental attributes are among the "sports" thrown up in the mechanics of organic mutation, and this genetic doctrine implies a more fundamental view of the relation of mind and body. Of this relation the early philosophers of modern science (though with important exceptions such as Hobbes and Gassendi) had taken a conveniently dualistic view, and only after science had reaped to the full the advantages of this view did it exchange it for a materialistic monism in the doctrine of universal evolution.

Let us recall what made science fasten upon a certain form of dualism as the ontological setting most suitable for its purpose, entrench itself in its portion of the patrimony, and finally discard the other half as redundant. Again we make reference to Descartes. The scientific advantage of dualism was, at its briefest, that the new mathematical ideal of natural knowledge was best served by, and indeed required, the clear-cut division between two realms which left science to deal with a pure *res extensa,* untainted with the nonmathematical characters of being. That reality *in toto* was not of this one desirable kind had been realized by Galileo, whose doctrine of the mere subjectivity of the "secondary qualities" (the expression is Locke's) initiated the extrusion of the undesirable features from physical reality. But subjects themselves are objective entities within reality, and the extrusion of features remained incomplete so long as their dumping-ground itself was a part of the world to be described by natural science. Now Cartesian dualism seemed the perfect answer to this difficulty. Here was one substance whose one essential attribute is extension, whose knowledge therefore is essentially in the mode of measurement and mathematical description; and another substance entirely separate and independent, whose one essential attribute is awareness (*cogitatio*), and the appropriate mode of whose knowledge and description was indeed much less clearly stated, but also of much less concern:[7] what mattered was its *isolation* from the other. The isolation of the *res cogitans* was the most effective way of securing the complete ontological detachment of external reality from what was not extended and measurable. Thus, besides constituting this reality as a self-contained field for the universal application of mathematical analysis, the division provided the metaphysical justification for the all-out mechanical materialism of modern science.[8] It must be

---

7. In histories of philosophy Descartes figures mainly as the discoverer of the *ego cogito,* i.e., the founder of the philosophy of consciousness which terminated in idealism. When we take into account, however, his preoccupation with the metaphysical and methodological foundation of a science of nature, we may suspect that the isolation of the *res cogitans* was made perhaps more for the sake of the *res extensa* than for its own.

8. The fact that both idealism and materialism could issue from Cartesianism is significant for the two positions themselves. It signifies (as the First Essay has shown) that they both are by their nature, not only in time, postdualistic positions—in fact, disintegration products of the final stage of dualism, and with the shadow of their origin always beside them. Ancient, predualistic materialism is an imperfect parallel to modern materialism: it has the innocence before the fall, as it originated before

stressed that this justification lay in assigning the excluded, nonextended and therefore nonmechanical, characters a separate and fully acknowledged domain of their own, not in denying them reality; in other words, it lay in dualism, not in monism, and it automatically lapsed with the subsequent abandonment of the spiritual complement: alone with itself, materialism became an absurdity.

Yet this abandonment was inevitable because of the well-known theoretical difficulties inherent in Cartesian dualism. Its forte from the point of view of corporeal science, the mutual causal unrelatedness of the two orders of being, was also its mortal weakness (of which "occasionalism" was the clear confession). In consequence, Cartesian dualism broke up into two alternatives; and, while Berkeleyan idealism and Leibnizian monadology boldly tried the side of the *res cogitans*, natural science had no option in its choice of "matter." Much as science would like to have its choice understood in terms of method only and to be spared a *confessio fidei*, there are those among its own proper objects that force it to face the issue of materialism on the ontological level. These objects are living organisms, the mysterious meeting-place of Descartes' two substances, though he himself acknowledged such a "meeting" in only one case.

Here we must mention the most extreme aspect of Descartes' mechanistic theory of the animal body, an aspect he could afford precisely under the protection of his dualism. The animal automata, though entirely determined by the rules of matter, are yet so constructed that their functioning suggests to the human onlooker an inwardness analogous to his own *without their possessing any such inwardness*. All signs of pleasure and pain in animals are deceptive appearance, i.e., taken for such signs only by an unjustified inference from the habitual connection that in our case obtains between them and certain feelings. We impute the latter when we observe the former, but the imputation is gratuitous. Animals, in other words, are nothing but bodies.[9] The gain of this *tour de force* lay in its confining

---

the discovery of the distinct concept of mind, which was the feat of dualism, had left its indelible mark on the ontological landscape.

9. Cf. Descartes, *Discourse on Method*, Part V; also *Treatise on Man*, and numerous passages in his *Letters*. From the last, e.g.: "We are so accustomed to persuade ourselves that the brute beasts feel as we do [a habit of thought engendered by "the resemblance existing between most

the locus of inwardness in nature to the solitary case of man. Puzzling as it was there, it was an exception to an otherwise universal rule and left the rest of living nature free for purely mechanical analysis. Having rid "body" in general of any relation to mind, and the science of body of any obligation to deal with the phenomena of mind, Descartes and the Cartesians could feel safe in treating the organism as just another instance of the *res extensa*.

Thus, at the cost of just one unmanageable metaphysical problem, the expurgation of the world of matter from the admixtures of mind was made defensible, since the claims of mind or inwardness were still honored by their allocation to a separate substance, with its independent set of phenomena under their own laws, even if its domain had to be contracted to the sphere of *human* consciousness: resolute dualism in one instance provided the good conscience for materialism in all other instances, and the unsolved enigma of man protected the nonenigmatic, if metaphysically meaningless, nature of the entire extrahuman biological realm. (See Appendix to this Essay.)

Now it is easy to see that the very *success* of the monistic venture, which this compromise with dualism had started on its course, even-

---

of the actions of the beasts and our own": *Letter to?* of March 1638] that it is difficult for us to rid ourselves of this opinion. But if we were as accustomed to seeing automata which imitate perfectly all those of our actions which they can imitate, and to taking them for automata only, we should have no doubt at all that the irrational animals are automata too" (*Letter to Mersenne* of July 13, 1640.) Already in a previous letter, of June 11, 1640, Descartes had declared to the puzzled Father: "I do not explain the feeling of pain without recourse to the soul . . . but I do so explain all the external motions which in us accompany that feeling: these alone are found in the beasts, and not pain properly speaking." The brazenness of the last assertion has something disarming. One cannot help wondering whether Descartes himself believed in the decree of his reasoning outside the charmed circle of theory, e.g., when actually dealing with animals. But the doctrine certainly stayed with him to the end—witness *Passions of the Soul,* Part I, art. 50 (published in 1650, three months before his death; see also the detailed statement in the *Letter to the Marquis of Newcastle* of November 1646.) The material is beautifully marshalled in Leonora Cohen Rosenfield, *From Beast-Machine to Man-Machine: Animal Soul in French Letters from Descartes to LaMettrie* (New York: Oxford University Press, 1941.)

tually withdrew from it the saving grace which the latter for a time could extend to it. For that success was achieved through the theory of evolution, and evolution precisely abolished the special position of man which had warranted the Cartesian treatment of all the remainder. The *continuity* of descent now established between man and the animal world made it impossible any longer to regard his mind, and mental phenomena as such, as the abrupt ingression of an ontologically foreign principle at just this point of the total flow. With the last citadel of dualism there also fell the isolation of man, and his own evidence became available again for the interpretation of that to which he belongs. For if it was no longer possible to regard his mind as discontinuous with prehuman biological history, then by the same token no excuse was left for denying mind, in proportionate degrees, to the closer or remoter ancestral forms, and hence to any level of animality: common-sense evidence was reinstated through the sophistication of theory—against its own spirit, to be sure.

Thus evolutionism undid Descartes' work more effectively than any metaphysical critique had managed to do. In the hue and cry over the indignity done to man's metaphysical status in the doctrine of his animal descent, it was overlooked that by the same token some dignity had been restored to the realm of life as a whole. If man was the relative of animals, then animals were the relatives of man and in degrees bearers of that inwardness of which man, the most advanced of their kin, is conscious in himself. Thus after the contraction brought about by Christian transcendentalism and Cartesian dualism, the province of "soul," with feeling, striving, suffering, enjoyment, extended again, by the principle of continuous gradation, from man over the kingdom of life. What both Spinoza[10] and Leibniz had enunciated as an ontological postulate, the principle of qualitative continuity, allowing for infinite gradations in obscurity and clarity of "perception," has through evolutionism become a logical complement to the scientific genealogy of life.[11] The highest could have been reached from the lowest only through all intermediary stages, whether

---

10. See my article "Spinoza and the Theory of Organism," *Journal of the History of Philosophy* 3/1 (1965), 43-57.

11. Even the Aristotelian biological hierarchy of "souls" is in a way restored under the form of genealogical sequence: the evolutionary "later" largely coincides with the Aristotelian "higher."

these were merely transitional or left in being as permanent representatives. Where, then, throughout the enormous extent of this series can we draw with reason a line with the "nothing" of inwardness on its far side and the incipient "one" of it on the near side? Where else than at the beginning of life can the beginning of inwardness be placed? But if inwardness is coextensive with life, a purely mechanistic account of life, i.e., one in outward terms alone, cannot be sufficient. The subjective phenomena defy quantification and accordingly cannot even have outward "equivalents" substituted for them. Appetition, for instance, as actuating behavior, cannot be replaced by physical momentum, the drive for self-preservation by inertia, and measured in terms of amounts of these. The fear of death is an absolute which can be more or less acutely felt (according to the general level of feeling), but is in these different cases not present in greater or smaller amounts of a measurable quantity, even if the powers to act which it commands are measurably greater or smaller.

So it happened that in the hour of the final triumph of materialism, the very instrument of it, "evolution," implicitly transcended the terms of materialism and posed the ontological question anew—when it just seemed settled. And Darwinism, more than any other doctrine responsible for the now dominant evolutionary vision of all reality, turns out to have been a thoroughly dialectical event. This becomes increasingly visible as its teachings are philosophically assimilated. Whatever their success so far, all contemporary revisions of traditional ontology indeed start, almost axiomatically, from the conception of being as *becoming,* and in the phenomenon of cosmic evolution look for the key to a possible stand beyond the old alternatives.

APPENDIX (p. 56)
The Meaning of Cartesianism for the Theory of Life

Cartesian dualism landed speculation on the nature of life in an impasse: intelligible as, on principles of mechanics, the correlation of structure and function became within the *res extensa,* that of structure-plus-function with feeling or experience (modes of the *res cogitans*) was lost in the bifurcation, and thereby the fact of life itself became unintelligible at the same time that the explanation of its bodily performance seemed to be assured. The impasse became manifest in Occasionalism: its *tour de force* of an extraneous, divine "synchronization" of the outer and the inner world (the latter denied to animals) not only suffered from its extreme artificiality, the common failing of such *ad hoc* constructions, but even at so high a cost failed to accomplish its theoretical purpose by its own terms. For the animal machine, like any machine, raises beyond the question of the "how" that of the "what for" of its functioning—of the purpose for which it had thus been constructed by its maker.[1] Its performance, however devoid of immanent teleology, must serve an end, and that end must be someone's end. This end may (directly) be itself, as indeed Descartes had implied when declaring self-preservation to be the *effect* of the functioning of the organic automaton. In that case the existence as such of the machine would be its end—either terminally, or in turn to benefit something else. In the former case, the machine would have to be more than a machine, for a mere machine cannot enjoy its existence. But since, by the rigorous conception of the *res extensa*, it cannot be more than a machine, its function and-or existence must serve something other than itself. Automata in Descartes' time were mainly for entertainment (rather than work). But the *raison d'être* of the living kingdom could not well be seen in God's indulging his mechanical abilities or in the amusement of celestial spectators—especially since mere complexity of arrangement does not create new quality and thus add something to the unrelieved sameness of the simple substratum that might enrich the spectrum of being. For quality, beyond the primitive determinations of the extended *per se,* is the subjective creature of sensation, the confused representation of quantity in a mind; and thus organisms cannot harbor it because as mere machines they lack mentality, and pure spirits cannot because they lack sensuality, or the privilege of confusion and thereby of illusion with its possible enjoyment. And as to their intellectual enjoyment, even that, deprived of the thrill of discovery by the same token, would pale in the contemplation of what to sufficiently large intellects is nothing but the ever-repeated exemplification of the same few, elementary (and ultimately trivial) truths.

There remained, then, the time-honored—Stoic as well as Christian— idea that plants and animals are for the benefit of Man. Indeed, since the existence of a living world is the necessary condition for the existence of any of its members, the self-justifying nature of at least one such member

---

1. The concept of "machine," adopted for its strict confinement to efficient cause, is still a finalistic concept, even though the final cause is no longer internal to the entity, as a mode of its own operation, but external to it as antecedent design.

(=species) would justify the existence of the whole. In Stoicism, Man provided this end by his possession of reason, which makes him the culmination of a terrestrial scale of being that is also self-justifying throughout all its grades (the end as the best of many that are good in degrees); in Christianity, by his possession of an immortal soul, which makes him the sole *imago Dei* in creation (the end as the sole issue at stake); and Cartesian dualism radicalized this latter position by making man even the sole possessor of inwardness or "soul" of *any* kind, thus the only one of whom "end" can meaningfully be predicated as he alone can entertain ends. All other life then, the product of physical necessity, can be considered his means.

However, this traditional idea, in its anthropocentric vanity never a good one even where it made sense, no longer did make sense in the new dualistic and occasionalist setting. For man, the supposed beneficiary of living creation, i.e., of all the other organic mechanisms, was now himself an inexplicable, extraneous combination of mind and body—a combination with no intelligible relevance of the body for the existence and inner life of the mind (as also, of course, vice versa). Therefore, even if it was shown that the existence of the organic world was necessary for the existence of human bodies, as indeed it is, it could not be shown that the existence of this very body was necessary for the existence of "man" considered as the thinking ego.[2] Furthermore, the very distinction of man's body within the animal kingdom, viz., to be at least partially an organ of mind—that distinction for the sake of which Descartes had been willing to brave the contortions of the pineal gland doctrine—was also nullified by the occasionalist fiction, in which the human body became no less completely an automaton than all other organisms. Thus, the existence of the entire living kingdom became utterly unintelligible as to purpose and meaning as well as to origin and procreative cause. A vast scheme of delusory "as ifs" superseded all question of real issue in the working of things.[3]

---

2. Berkeley, in due course, drew the conclusion from this theoretical redundancy: bodies are nothing but mental representations ("perceptions").

3. It is worth to note the profound change which the concept of "soul" underwent: from a principle of life and thus of action it became a principle of pure subjectivity—a dimension rather than a principle—and as such essentially powerless. This must be borne in mind when considering the two connected Cartesian ideas that "life" is a fact of physics alone, and that "soul" is a fact of man alone: according to the first, life is a particular corporeal *behavior* following from a particular corporeal struc-

All this amounts to saying that the main fault, even absurdity, of the doctrine lay in denying organic reality its principal and most obvious characteristic, namely, that it exhibits in each individual instance a striving of its own for existence and fulfillment, or the fact of life's willing itself. In other words, the banishment of the old concept of appetition from the conceptual scheme of the new physics, joined to the rationalistic spiritualism of the new theory of consciousness, deprived the realm of life of its status in the scheme of things. It is a measure of the compelling motives behind this conception, farfetched as it was, that it could hold its ground against the irrepressible voice of our psychophysical experience, every one of whose acts eloquently contradicts the dualistic division. Cartesian dualism created the riddle of how an act of will can move a limb, since the limb as part of the extended world can only be moved by another body's imparting its antecedent motion to it.[4] Yet after learning

---

ture which distinguishes a class of objects in nature, viz., the natural automata; according to the second, "soul," equated with consciousness of any kind, be it feeling, desiring, perceiving, thought (*anima=mens= cogitatio*), as such not required for physical function of any kind *and thus not for life,* is absent in animals and present in man, but is neither in *his* case a principle of "life," which remains a purely structural-behavioral phenomenon in all cases. Cf. Descartes' letter of May, 1641, to Regius (Adam-Tannery III, 370 ff.), where he explicitly rejects the traditional idea of *species* of souls—vegetative, sensitive, rational—arguing that the first two, the powers to grow and to move, which man shares with the brutes, "are *toto genere* different from mind" and "nothing else than a certain disposition of the parts of his body."

4. The counterexperiential principle which became axiomatic for theory was most succinctly stated by Spinoza: "The body cannot determine the mind to thought, neither can the mind determine the body to motion nor rest, nor to anything else, if there be anything else" (Ethics III, prop. 2). With Spinoza this was, ostensibly, a proposition subject to demonstration (duly supplied) from first truths. But in reality it was postulative, and the "first truths" were conceived with a view to it—more particularly, with a view to the second half of the proposition which alone seriously mattered. The real argument should have read thus: If there were interaction of body and mind, there could be no science of nature; but there must be a science of nature: ergo, there cannot be interaction of body and mind.—The positive complement to the negative rule shows where its real application lies: "A body in motion or at rest must be determined to motion or rest by another body, which was also determined to motion or rest by another, and so on ad infinitum" (*ibid.,* lemma 3 after prop. 13). At least in this application to the *corporeal* realm, the ontological rigor of the rule admits no exception; and we may add that

from theory that it cannot be, we still go on feeling that we do move our arms "at will." Theory, while invalidating this primary certainty, had yet to explain it. The "violence" of metaphysical speculation after Descartes, which dared common sense more than any previous one and needed accordingly greater ingenuity to carry it off, is in part explained by the enormity of what it had to cope with.[5] The "psychophysical problem"— the cost for the scientific revolution—loomed behind all its exertions. Never had the rift between reason and immediate knowledge been so great.

Besides the riddle of our practical experience, there was the riddle of degrees of organization which the animal kingdom so manifestly displays, but which no longer could be related to degrees of self-rewarding awareness. The new doctrine denied the means for connecting the perfection of a physical organization with the *quality* of the life supported by it: all it provided for was the connection between organization and observable behavior, i.e., organic function. The wealth of gradation in the animal world from the most primitive (i.e., simple) to the most subtle (i.e., complex) structure could not be overlooked, but had to remain meaning-

---

none of the leading thinkers of the period down to, and including, Kant ever challenged the validity of it. The motives for thus ruling out of court the most insistent evidence of common experience—that fear or love or deliberation can determine action and thus be causes of bodily motion— have been discussed in the Essay: whatever their theoretical merit, they commanded overwhelming consensus and still express the creed of the scientist.

5. Indeed, there is little "ingenuity" or inventiveness in former speculation, and perhaps it should have no place in philosophy. It makes its appearance only where theory has to uphold prior commitments, as e.g. in the case of certain problems posed to the Schoolmen by the competing authorities of revelation and reason (or, Scripture and Aristotle), which *had* to be reconciled. But the doctrine of God, creation, and salvation, though outside experience, surely does not contradict experience. Cartesianism was the first to create a situation in which theory self-confidently *clashes* with experience: this situation, as it demanded of theory a new kind of ingenuity to effect a "reconcilation," also allowed it a new, despotic ruthlessness in dictating the terms of it (a combination characteristic of the thought of Spinoza and Leibniz): theory could indulge in a radicalism unknown to it before. That this ruthlessness went by the name of "rationalism" is a historical circumstance which veils the imperiously willful element in the situation. Philosophy has reason to distrust the masterful manner in theorizing, and for more than the Humean or Kantian reasons: the question is whether the intellect conforms or prescribes to reality.

less. Since no other kind of soul than the rational was recognized, all the mechanical perfection displayed in animal organisms amounted just to a gigantic hoax, as no higher type of experient life corresponded to greater excellence of mechanical performance. Thus the very perfection in terms of external construction and function mocks all justification in terms of lives.

Obviously, with regard to both riddles, theory could not rest with the verdict of sheer unrelatedness, nor with its desperate reprieve by the continuous miracle of divine coordination: Spinoza's and Leibniz' grand attempts to improve upon the Cartesian position offered ingenious solutions to both aspects of the psychophysical problem. Yet they were solutions to the problem *as set* by Descartes, sharing the motives and the broad terms of his bifurcation (to which indeed all thinkers till after Kant remained committed). Their very ingenuity, as remarked before—a typically inventive ingenuity called forth in response to a difficulty never faced before and itself an invention of theory—makes us admire the thinkers but suspect their problem. Our admiration is in part that for a feat accomplished with the performer's hands tied behind his back.

Is God a Mathematician?
The Meaning of Metabolism

I

"From the intrinsic evidence of his creation, the Great Architect of the Universe now begins to appear as a pure mathematician." Thus Sir James Jeans[1] summed up the insights of contemporary cosmology, unaware (as the "now" suggests) that he was echoing a call that has been sounded through the ages. A proposition of that magnitude and lineage, once the philosophers' bosom-child, demands philosophical comment when it is uttered anew by an astronomer-physicist on a new theoretical stage.[2] Two questions must be asked of it: what does it say? and is it true?

The first question, that of meaning, turns necessarily historical, since the tradition behind the saying belongs to the meaning itself. What did "mathematics," "creation," "universe" mean when it was first pronounced? What do they no longer mean? what do they (and thus the proposition as a whole) mean now? The "no longer" in the "now" becomes part of the interpretation of the now. Our first task, then, is to retrace the transformations of the reasoning on which the proposition has lived from its Greek origin to scientific modernity,

---

1. J. H. Jeans, *The Mysterious Universe* (Cambridge: University Press, 1933), p. 122.

2. In a direction different from that to be pursued here, incisive philosophical comment was made by the late Suzan Stebbing in her refreshing book, *Philosophy and the Physicists.*

and thereby spell out the meaning it must have when pronounced in the context of today.

The second question, that of truth, must resort to the evidence which the proposition itself invokes: that of "creation." Since the whole of this evidence is never before us, but what is true of the whole must be true of any part, I have chosen to test the proposition against one particular mode of existence within the universe, that of living organisms. Jeans's assertion raises the question whether the mathematician that is the great architect of the universe is also the architect, great or little, of the amoeba. He must be both, or he is neither. For the amoeba is part of the universe and must be accountable for by its creative principle. Its minuteness is no disability in ontological relevance. Its intrinsic evidence, as one creation, forms part of the general evidence and must be heard all the more as in this instance "intrinsic" has a fuller meaning than applies to any other class of cosmic beings: it includes the fact of its own, felt inwardness. This gives it a preferential status in ontological evidence that outweighs its quantitative limitations. In other words, if *life* is not within the competence of an alleged cosmic principle, though it is in every sense within the cosmos, then that principle is inadequate for the cosmos as well. The alternative would be a metaphysical transcendence of life which, though perhaps conceded to the conscious being of man, will hardly be accorded to the amoeba. That is to say, the remedy of dualism is inoperable in the explanation of organism. Thus material life (we are not yet speaking of mind and consciousness) can serve as a touchstone for interpretations of matter or world-stuff, and can rectify a conception of God built on such interpretations. In this sense, the metaphysical statement "God is a mathematician" can be reduced to a definite ontological view and checked against knowledge of plain facts: the whole proposition is brought down from the dizzy heights of stars and spaces to our immediate and most intimate experience; but it still retains its full application to cosmology, and hence to the speculative question of what God may be—if indeed the world has anything to say about him. Jeans's statement implies this by accepting the world's recognizable being as "evidence for." In taking him at his word, we do not necessarily share his confidence. But even if the evidence is not accorded a positive bearing on what God is (let alone on whether he is), a negative bearing—regarding what God is not, or is not exclusively—would be implicit in its mere excess over what would be attributable to a Creator of this or that hypothetical nature. Since that nature has been derived in the first place from a certain reading of the evidence of creation, it is actually this reading that is tested when we try out the inferred concept of God on the experiential basis to which it makes final appeal. The concept of a mathematical God, when applied to reality in earnest, elicits the utter possibilities—merits or faults—inherent in the underlying ontological or epistemological outlook. If this should result in a reductio ad absurdum, the impossible concept has still, through its self-defeat, served a useful purpose.

II

Jeans's dictum comes late in a long and venerable tradition that is almost coextensive with the history of Western speculation. From the demiurge of Plato's *Timaeus* there is a direct line of descent to Leibniz' God who creates the maximum of the mathematically compossible: "Thus it is wonderfully made known to us how in the very origination of things a certain Divine mathematics or metaphysical mechanics is employed and the determination of the greatest quantity takes place."[3] "When God calculates and employs thought, the world is made."[4] Kepler before him, deeply imbued with the Pythagorean faith in the mathematical essence of things and the consequent harmony of the world, said that God, "too kind to remain idle, began to play the game of signatures, signing his likeness into the world," with the result that "all nature and the graceful sky are symbolized in the art of geometry."[5] This divine geometry he saw displayed in the laws of planetary motion as he discovered them—its presupposition having inspired the search for them in the first place. In the same vein is Galileo's credo that the great book of the universe is written in math-

---

3. Leibniz, "On the Ultimate Origination of Things" (1697), *The Monadology and Other Philosophical Writings,* trans. Robert Latta (Oxford: Clarendon Press, 1898), p. 342.

4. *Ibid.,* p. 342, n. 18, citing *De connexione inter res et verba* (1677).

5. J. Kepler in *Tertium Interveniens,* quoted in A. Koestler, *The Sleepwalkers.* (Reference supplied by Prof. F. J. Dyson—cf. his article "Mathematics in the Physical Sciences," *The Scientific American,* Sept., 1964, p. 129).

ematical language, the symbols of which are triangles, circles, and other geometrical figures.[6]

In this grand projection, concept of being and ideal of knowledge support each other mutually. Kepler was probably the first of the moderns to declare quantity (or magnitude) to be the, at once, essential and truly knowable aspect of reality: cognition accordingly consists to him in measurement and comparison of measurements. But measurement of what? Is the "mathematical nature" aimed at still the same as the classical-Greek one? Is the mathematics still the same? The ostensible return to the Pythagorean-Platonic "geometrization" of the world at the beginnings of modern science somehow masked a novel approach, which only the "algebraization" of physical description increasingly revealed. Algebra applied to geometry, rather than classical geometry itself, became the mathematics of the new physics. This alone would suggest that it no longer dealt with the intuitive objects of Greek ontological speculation. (See Appendix 1 to this Essay.) We may use this observation as a lead to uncover the more profound differences separating the modern from the classical concept of a "mathematical nature," and thus to determine the precise meaning that must attach to Jeans's idea of a mathematical Deity within the context of modern science.

It was the paramount interest in *motion,* as against the satisfaction with pattern, which prompted the ascendance of algebraic method in physics: motion instead of fixed spatial proportions became the main object of measurement. This marks a radically novel attitude. In the early stages of modern science, analysis of becoming supplants contemplation of being. The role of "t" in physical formulae indicates the new attitude. The "forms" here envisaged are no longer those of the terminal products, but those of the continuous processes of nature. Process, as such, is defined solely by its own form, the law of the

---

6. "Philosophy is written in that great book which ever lies before our eyes—I mean the universe—but we cannot understand it if we do not first learn the language and grasp the symbols in which it is written. This book is written in the mathematical language, and the symbols are triangles, circles, and other geometrical figures, without whose help it is impossible to comprehend a single word of it, without which one wanders in vain through a dark labyrinth," *Il Saggiatore* (Rome, 1623). See "The Assayer" in *Discoveries and Opinions of Galileo,* trans. Stillman Drake (New York: Doubleday & Company, Inc., 1957), pp. 237-38.

series, and in no way by its end (of which there is none) or any temporary formations en route. Greek geometry had considered the relations of unchanging figures and bodies—intuitive ultimates: the abstract algebra of analytical geometry and of the infinitesimal calculus made it possible to represent the geometrical form itself as a function of variables, that is, as a phase in their continuous growth, and so to formulate the laws of its "generation." These generative, determining laws became the true objects of mathematical cognition, instead of the descriptive, determinate forms, which had lost their independent status for that of transitional limits.

This, by itself an intramathematical development, had physical applications. Indeed, a different "nature" could be interrogated by a different mathematics. For what in the purely mathematical field appeared as the functional consideration supplanting the static one of intuitive entities, amounts in the field of physical description to the dissolving of the "substantial forms" of classical ontology into the elementary motions and forces by which they can be thought (and in experiment shown) to be generated. In this application, the functional generation of a mathematical curve becomes the mechanical generation of the path of a body. Here the product, namely, the form of the path, is not a complete, simultaneously present entity, but a sequence, that is, a series of instants, each of them determined anew by the component factors operative at that very instant. It has no transcending reality of its own. Any rational properties which such a series (e.g., a planetary orbit) may exhibit when viewed as an ideal, geometrical whole, are then due no longer to intrinsic reason or an aspiration toward "harmony" in the moving principle, as Kepler reverently believed, but—as Newton later showed in his mechanics of those motions—to the mere uniformity or constancy of the elementary factors involved. Each of these (e.g., gravitation and inertia) would by itself produce rectilinear motion only, the simplest and least "formed" of all motions: yet their mere addition to each other cannot but result, on the sole condition of their staying constant,[7] and without any aspiration toward such a result, in the highly rational forms

---

7. Or, if they were variable, the condition would be that the variation in turn be subject to constants: the essential premise for the possibility of laws of nature is the prevailing of any constants whatsoever, provided that between them they "distribute" the whole range of natural phenomena.

of celestial geometry. This is the sole remaining sense of saying that the courses obey a rule (capable of mathematical expression): it is the sufficient reason of order and law in nature. Thus rationality of order does not testify to a rational cause, intelligible form no longer represents perfection of being, obtaining reality for that very reason in preference to lesser forms or to disorder, but must itself be explained by reference to the lowest, that is, most elementary types of event: and the latter, far from being transformed or even affected by their entrance into the more articulated order, constitute this by mere persistence in their own, unarticulated quantity. Their singleness alone is the basically real, and the "wholeness" of their conjoint result is an appearance with no genuine ontological status. This is the import of the modern analysis, which transformed the celestial mathematics of the ancients into the very different thing that is celestial mechanics, that is, a case of mechanics in general.[8] The Pythagorean harmony has become the balance of unconcerned forces, calculable from the conditions of their meeting. The "measure" and the "mean" no longer bind the opposites, but are their inevitable sum.

Thus the relation of higher and lower, of more or less rational (more or less form), is replaced by that of complex and simple, and the old order of intelligibility is reversed. With the whole now to be explained by the parts, intelligibility means reducibility to that which, as elemental, is in the older sense least intelligible, because it least involves intelligence for its own performance. In a word, then, for the modern idea of understanding nature, the least intelligent has become the most intelligible, the least reasonable the most rational. At the bottom of all rationality or "mathematics" in nature's order lies the mere fact of there being quantitative constants in the behavior of

---

8. Galileo still expressed himself "traditionally" when he said that the symbols of nature's mathematical language were triangles, circles, and the like. Though triangles may occur as auxiliary constructions in dynamic analysis, and conic sections do actually result from the dynamics of nature, it would have been more adequate to the whole scientific trend which Galileo himself inaugurated if he could already have said that the symbols were constants and variables, functions and equations: in brief, the language of algebra. In fact, only Descartes, Newton, and Leibniz eventually supplied the mathematics for the new science of nature. Its means of expression is the differential equation rather than Euclid's propositions.

matter, or the principle of uniformity as such, which found its first statement in the law of inertia—surely no mark of immanent reason.

III

It is obvious that the different sense in which nature can be spoken of as "mathematical" must necessarily affect the idea of a mathematical Creator. From what has been shown, Jeans's "Great Architect," for all his being a "pure mathematician," cannot but be profoundly different from Plato's Demiurge. It may be taken for granted that a metaphysical point of view is not only the effect but also the cause of a scientific development. An event like the suppression of teleology and of substantial forms cannot be simply ascribed to any particular discovery or set of discoveries made in the investigation of nature, nor even to the invention of a new method: rather has the revolution in method, which the sudden obsolescence of these venerable concepts signalizes, itself to be accounted for. Indeed, certain metaphysical conditions were required even to make possible the new approach of post-Renaissance science to nature; and since we are dealing with the subject of creation, we may elucidate those conditions from this particular angle.

The God of the *Timaeus* created the world as the perfect "animal" or visible god, ensouled and intelligent. Looking to the intelligible pattern he formed the changeable in its likeness, and thus as far as possible in his own. For the intelligible and the intelligent are the same. Passive "matter" alone could certainly not be entrusted with preserving throughout change the forms and proportions imprinted on it, nor with providing the force for that motion of change itself by which the fair copy must imitate eternity in time. Thus *soul* is required as the continually spontaneous cause of motion, and *intelligence* as the cause of *rational* motion, that is, one that exhibits law. It is this double aspect of "soul"—that it is the cause of motion and the cause of order—which makes it a universal physical principle. Soul pervades the cosmos in degrees of divinity, that is, of intelligence. The more consistently rational a motion, the higher must be the intelligence of the moving soul. Hence the superior intelligence of the celestial bodies, as compared to that of terrestrial beings, including man: hence the religious venerability of the Cosmos as a whole—not for its magnitude, but for the coincidence of intelligibility and intelligence that underlies its visible beauty.

Compare with this the Judaeo-Christian conception that took its place. The created world of Genesis is not a god and is not to be worshiped instead of God. Nor has it a soul of its own that would account for its activity and its orderliness. It is merely made and in no sense maker. Jewish monotheism had abolished the deities of nature and all intermediary powers, leaving God and world in clean-cut division. The Christian hierarchy of angels and saints did not bridge the gulf between God and the world, but that between God and the human soul which, not being of the natural order itself, shares their preternatural status. Indeed man's soul is the only entity in the world—but not of the world—which is created in the image of God, even out of God, and is thus in a sense divine, while heavens and earth and all their host are only God's handiwork and not his image.[9] The essential division between God and world is thus repeated or mirrored in the essential division between mind and nature. Nature, created out of nothing, has no mind of her own, but mutely performs God's will by which alone she exists. Thus the idea of a mindless or "blind" nature, which yet behaves lawfully—that is, which keeps an intelligible order without being intelligent—had become metaphysically possible.

The possibility just indicated depended on the condition that "soul" was banished from the context of nature, and this again was possible only insofar as in the explanation of nature in general soul was not needed as the *cause of motion*. In fact, in a nature without mind, "soul" as a dynamic principle would be a source of irrationality and promote disorder rather than law. Now transcendental monotheism, by abolishing nature-gods and divine powers within the world, entirely favored this elimination of soul from the system of natural principles; and the same monotheism, moreover, worked toward the leveling of any inner-cosmic hierarchy of being by reducing all nature to the equal status of "creation"—equal before God: stars and dust,

---

9. That this religious distinction was realized in a sense conducive to natural science of the modern kind is shown in the passage from Bacon quoted in note 3 to Eighth Essay.

celestial and terrestrial nature alike. Finally, once motion came to be conceived as an initial and self-conserving endowment of creation that requires no further spontaneity on its own part, there could arise the conception of a nature not only mindless but also inanimate, that is, of a nature not only intelligible without being intelligent, but also moving without being alive.

IV

The metaphysics of modern science seized on precisely this possibility, offered by Judaeo-Christian transcendentalism and held for so long in abeyance by the medieval alliance of church doctrine with Aristotelianism. It is true that the Renaissance philosophy of nature —the most "pagan" interlude in Western thought—attempted to combine the new vista of the universe with a pantheistic animism in the true classical style: but the seventeenth century, in its more sober and much more "Christian" mood—though certainly not from entirely Christian motives—reverted to the rigors of Judaeo-Christian transcendentalism, to extract from it the idea of a nature not spontaneous but strictly subject to law. In thus reaping the fruits of dualism, which throughout its long and varied career had tended to drain nature of her spiritual and vital attributes, the new metaphysic of science itself added the last chapter to this career by producing its own version of dualism. Its classical representative is Descartes' division of substance into *res cogitans* and *res extensa:* since "nature" is entirely and exclusively the latter, i.e. external, while the former is in no sense "nature," that division provided the metaphysical charter for a purely mechanistic and quantitative picture of the natural world, with its corollary of mathematical method in physics. Here the character of dualism, and with it the status of mathematics, had radically changed. For the classical polarity of form and matter, active soul and passive body, intelligible and sensible (where the second term of the unequally matched pairs, deficient in itself, requires the first for its share in "being"), a new type of polarity was substituted, indicated by such pairs as: subject-object, mind-nature, consciousness-spatiality, inwardness-outwardness, where the second term enjoys independent—and finally even anterior—reality. The leading term for the spiritual is no longer the transcendent and selective one of "mind," but that of "ego" or "self" simply, comprising whatever is conscious; its correlative then is no longer "form," but all "not-I" as such. In this sweeping repudiation of Platonism, overlaid as it was at first by the rationalist fervor of the Cartesian school, the fate of Western thought was decided: the Platonic union of intellect with the intelligible, and of the intelligible with the real, was dissolved, and "nature" could now be identified with "matter," that is, with a matter that quite self-sufficiently exists on its own. This repeats the position of ancient atomism, but against a dualistic background which is alien to the classical precedent. With Descartes, dualism entered its last and lethal metamorphosis, shortly to disintegrate into the equally barren alternatives of idealism and materialism: for the first time in its long history, every kind of awareness, however sensual or emotional—in short, irrational—is grouped *with* reason on one side and set over against every kind of spatial being, including its mathematical, that is, rational, form, on the other side. "Matter" in fact, in the sense of "body," becomes more rational than "spirit."

Thus we have reached from the metaphysical end the same result to which we were previously led by the analysis of method: namely, that the least intelligent has become the most, nay the only, intelligible. For though Descartes professes to have shown the mind to be "better [or "more easily"] known than the body,"[10] his own scientific method belies the claim where knowledge as a demonstrative system is concerned. The ease of knowledge in the case of the mind means merely immediacy of self-beholding which, at the same time, leaves the beheld entirely unrelated to the total field of that knowable in which alone the method works, namely, the *res extensa*.[11] Since mind has retained no standing at all in the system of those rational objects which constitute Descartes' Nature, the theme of his science, there ensues the paradox that reason itself has become an irrational entity, intelligence entirely unintelligible within the intellectual

---

10. See his *Second Meditation*.

11. "All things which, speaking generally, are comprehended in the object of pure mathematics are truly to be recognized as external objects" (Sixth Meditation). Observe the relation here stipulated between "mathematical" and "external"!

scheme of the scientifically knowable: in other words, the knower himself is among his objects, that is, the world, the unknowable par excellence.

But we have seen that not only mind but also soul and therefore life became redundant in the explanation of nature. Motion without soul involves force without appetition, from which forms result without being ends. The "force" is in every case inertial, that is, a quantitative constant carried over from instant to instant in an endless series. Now, since life means spontaneous and teleological motion, while understanding is in terms of inertial motion alone, there follows the further paradox that not only the mindless but also the lifeless has become the intelligible as such, and "dead matter" the standard of intelligibility. But inasmuch as "life" is encountered as a fact within the totality of physical facts, its understanding must mean precisely its reduction to this standard, that is, its explanation in terms of the lifeless. Descartes' mechanistic theory of the organism, the animal automaton (the exemption of man was a mere inconsistency), is therefore a logical and unavoidable consequence from his whole metaphysical and epistemological principle which set the stage for modern science beyond its own brief historical hour. La Mettrie's *L'homme machine* (no less than modern behaviorism) is still heir to Cartesian dualism stripped of its spiritual half. And since modern science, as quantitative and measuring, continues to be enacted on the stage on which it was ushered in, the stage of a nature essentially understood as *res extensa* or "external reality," no other cognition of the organic is available to it than one in terms of the mindless and the lifeless; and this must be represented as a system of minimum quantities in space and time, the resolution into which constitutes the understanding of any given entity.

V

I have tried to show what the idea of a mathematical nature means in the modern context, and what is therefore asserted, though probably not to his own knowledge, in Jeans's statement that the architect of the universe is a pure mathematician. We are now sufficiently prepared to ask: *Is* God a pure mathematician?—that is, in the only sense which the assertion can have in the given scientific situation. To answer this question we shall try to look at creation through the eyes of the mathematical God and find out what objects he would, and what he would not, apprehend: what objects, therefore (since his thought is said to be the cause of things), he could have, and what objects he could not have, created.[12]

What the object world of the divine mathematician might be like we may gather, if not from the older picture drawn by Laplace, from the writings of the mathematical physicist Sir Arthur Eddington. His vivid descriptions of the shadow world of mathematical values, into which the solid objects of our experience dissolve (or similar popularizations of the scientific abstract of basic reality), we assume as sufficiently known not to require elaboration. And for argument's sake let us grant the possibility that this object picture, replacing familiar things with systems of quantitative relations between widely spaced nodal points of reality, may with all its lack of color and concreteness be the "truer" one. But suppose it is a living body, an organism, on which the gaze of the divine mathematician happens to rest. It may be unicellular or multicellular. What would the God of the physicists "see"?

As a physical body the organism will exhibit the same general features as do other aggregates: a void mostly, crisscrossed by the geometry of forces that emanate from the insular foci of localized elementary being. But special goings-on will be discernible, both inside and outside its so-called boundary, which will render its phenomenal unity still more problematical than that of ordinary bodies, and will efface almost entirely its material identity through time. I refer to its *metabolism,* its exchange of matter with the surroundings. In this remarkable mode of being, the material parts of which the organism consists at a given instant are to the penetrating observer only tem-

---

12. In performing this test—it might be objected—we are bound to the contemporary state of science, whose limitations would not bind the cognitive powers of God. But the problem lies not where science falls short of its program, but rather in the anticipated fulfillment of that program. That is, not any "dated" incompleteness of its results but their ideally imagined completeness within the conceptual framework of science as such has to be confronted with the ontological facts of organic existence. And this can be done by extrapolation from the present state in the direction indicated by it.

porary, passing contents whose joint material identity does not coincide with the identity of the whole which they enter and leave, and which sustains its own identity by the very act of foreign matter passing through its spatial system, the living *form*. It is never the same materially and yet persists as its same self, *by* not remaining the same matter. Once it really becomes the same with the sameness of its material contents—if any two "time slices" of it become, as to their individual contents, identical with each other and with the slices between them—it ceases to live; it dies (or becomes dormant as do certain seeds and spores whose life process stops, to be resumed under appropriate conditions.) [13]

---

13. We have to realize the all-pervasiveness of metabolism within the living system. The exchange of matter with the environment is not a peripheral activity engaged in by a persistent core: it is the total mode of continuity (self-continuation) of the subject of life itself. The metaphor of "inflow and outflow" does not render the radical nature of the fact. In an engine we have inflow of fuel and outflow of waste products, but the machine parts themselves that give passage to this flow do not participate in it: their substance is not involved in the transformations which the fuel undergoes in its passage through them; their physical identity is clearly a matter apart, affected neither by those interchanges nor by their own ensuing action. Thus the machine persists as a self-identical inert system over against the changing identity of the matter with which it is "fed"; and, we may add, it exists as just the same when there is no feeding at all: it is then the same machine at a standstill. On the other hand, when we call a living body a "metabolizing system," we must include in the term that the system itself is wholly and continuously a result of its metabolizing activity, and further that none of the "result" ceases to be an object of metabolism while it is also an agent of it. For this reason alone, it is inappropriate to liken the organism to a machine. The first to do so was Descartes, and his model (designed from the outset for animals only and not for plants) already provided, besides the *structure* of movable parts, for a source of *power* to make them move: the heat generated by the "burning" of the food. Thus the combustion theory of metabolism complements the machine theory of anatomical structure. But metabolism is more than a method of power generation, or, food is more than fuel: in addition to, and more basic than, providing kinetic energy for the running of the machine (a case anyway not applying to plants), its role is to build up originally and replace continually the very parts of the machine. Metabolism thus is the constant becoming of the machine itself—and this becoming itself is a performance of the machine: but for such performance there is no analogue in the world of machines.

At first glance, this is suggestive of a type of object with which physics is familiar. Mathematical description does deal with dynamic *wholes* enjoying an "identity" of their own in time different from that of their changing constituents. I believe the wave (in a material medium like water or air) provided the first model for such descriptive entities of a mediate order. The oscillating units of which it successively consists in its progress perform their movements singly, each participating only momentarily in the constitution of the individual "wave"; yet this as the comprehensive form of the propagated disturbance has its own distinct unity, its own history, and its own laws, and these can become independent objects of mathematical analysis, in abstraction from the more immediate identities of the substratum. Modern physics deals largely with such whole-structures of happening, and special mathematical techniques are employed in their description. Here, then, form re-enters the physical scene with a cognitive significance of its own. And this transcending form, an event-structure, is of a different order from that of a crystal-structure, where the form is inseparably allied to the persistence of the material.

Yet it must be noted, with a view to the following discussion, that to these integrated event-structures no special reality is accorded that is not contained in, and deducible from, the conjoint reality of the participating, more elementary events: hypothetically the latter must completely account for every character of the former, or there must be strict equivalence expressible in an equation: which means that there is no novelty in the whole as such; and to an infinite intelligence the simultaneous, discrete notion of all the individual components would still be the perfect knowledge.

Now the same (though immensely more sophisticated) would seem to apply to the "formal" propagation through time of the manifold *we* know as "organism." There too, the complete analysis of the Great Mathematician, unclouded by the fusing summations of sense, will ultimately fasten on the single transient elements ("transient" in relation to the whole), which alone provide the immediate identities for the mechanical construction of the compound and alone remain as the residue of its analysis. The life process will then present itself as a series, or a web of many series, of consecutive events concerning these single, persisting units of general substance: they are the real performers, moving in and out of configurations, each for causal reasons of its own. The particular configuration under view, which we call organism, makes no difference to their single identity nor to their mode of function (defined in its potential repertoire) and is in principle like any other configuration which they may enter and temporarily help to constitute. No other type of causality obtains inside than outside it, and the transient particle continues in its proper concatenation of cause and effect when entering, when inside, and when leaving it. That its place is taken by a successor is a new fact whose repetition adds up to a continuity of aggregate form, but does not affect the singleness of each happening. Thus there is no reason to posit a special entity for that particular form of togetherness with its normal set of interactions. Against the flow of the momentary constituent parts, the configurative permanence by replacement—and thus the continuity of the "whole"—is an abstraction. To illustrate once more by the example of the wave: strictly speaking, not its progress as a moving form causes the successive entering of new units into the collective motion of which it consists, but the transmission of individual motion among adjoining elementary units adds up to the seeming whole-form which progresses on their account. In the same light the organism must appear as a function of metabolism rather than metabolism as a function of the organism. Every happening involved, and consequently their sum total at each instant, can and thus must be accurately accounted for on the lines of the general scheme underlying the mathematical-mechanical world-picture: on the lines of teleological indifference, efficient cause, inertial uniformity, smallest particle, quantitative extensity, and so on. In an ideal analysis of this kind, the apparent sameness and individuality of the organic whole will resolve itself—even more thoroughly than that of ordinary bodies—as an incidental result into the network of all physical lines which converge here and now from the universe, and in whose interweavings its pattern fleetingly appears; and all the features of a self-related autonomous entity would, in the end, appear as purely phenomenal, that is, fictitious.

V I

Here again we should say that the object-view of the divine mathematician is less concrete and colorful than ours—but would we also grant it, as before, the possibility of being truer? Emphatically not in this case, and here we move on firm ground, because here, being living bodies ourselves, we happen to have inside knowledge. On the strength of the immediate testimony of our bodies *we* are able to say what no disembodied onlooker would have a cause for saying: that the mathematical God in his homogeneous analytical view misses the decisive point—the point of life itself: its being self-centered individuality, being for itself and in contraposition to all the rest of the world, with an essential boundary dividing "inside" and "outside"— notwithstanding, nay, on the very basis of the actual exchange. It may be the case for every other form of aggregate that its distinct unity as a whole is nothing but the product of our sensuous perception, thus not ontological but merely phenomenal. Its identity, then, as "this" —this stone, this drop of water—rests on the relative perseverance of the aggregation and is in the last resort reducible to the immediate identities of the component parts: a borrowed and mediate identity, which vanishes with their segregation, while that of the ultimate parts is presumably inalienable. But then, in living things, nature springs an ontological surprise in which the world-accident of terrestrial conditions brings to light an entirely new possibility of being: systems of matter that are unities of a manifold, not in virtue of a synthesizing perception whose object they happen to be, nor by the mere concurrence of the forces that bind their parts together, but in virtue of themselves, for the sake of themselves, and continually sustained by themselves. Here wholeness is self-integrating in active performance, and form for once is the cause rather than the result of the material collections in which it successively subsists. Unity here is self-unifying, by means of changing multiplicity. Sameness, while it lasts (and it does not last inertially, in the manner of static identity or of onmoving continuity), is perpetual self-renewal through process, borne on the shift of otherness. This active self-integration of life alone gives substance to the term "individual": it alone yields the ontological concept of an individual as against a merely phenomenological one.

This ontological individual, its very existence at any moment, its duration and its identity in duration is, then, essentially its own function, its own concern, its own continuous achievement. In this process of self-sustained being, the relation of the organism to its material substance is of a double nature: the materials are essential to it specifically, accidental individually; it coincides with their actual collection at the instant, but is not bound to any one collection in the succession of instants, "riding" their change like the crest of a wave and bound only to their form of collection which endures as its own feat. Dependent on their availability as materials, it is independent of their sameness as these; its own, functional identity, passingly incorporating theirs, is of a different order. In a word, the organic form stands in a dialectical relation of *needful freedom* to matter.

VII

Let us consider further this new element of *freedom* that appears in organism, with special reference to *form*. Form, we have seen, is an essential and a real, that is, efficacious, characteristic of life. It is only with life that the difference of matter and form, in respect to lifeless things an abstract distinction, emerges as a concrete reality. And the ontological relationship is reversed: form becomes the essence, matter the accident. In the realm of the lifeless, form is no more than a changing composite state, an accident, of enduring matter. And viewed from the fixed identities of the changing material contents, as the inventory of each moment would record them, the living form too is only a region of local and temporal transit in their own movements, its apparent unity a passing, configurative state of their multiplicity. But viewed from the dynamic identity of the living form, the reverse holds: the changing material contents are states of its enduring identity, their multiplicity marking the range of its effective unity. In fact, instead of saying that the living form is a region of transit for matter, it would be truer to say that the material contents in their succession are phases of transit for the self-continuation of the form. Yet, it will be asked, what can it mean that one view is "truer" than the other if both are possible, that is, equivalent as descriptions of the fact from different aspects? And if they are, why should the physical world-picture, satisfied in the one view, be disturbed or questioned by the other? We shall take up this question later.

The basic freedom of organism was found to consist in a certain independence of form with respect to its own matter. According to a strictly material world-account such independence is either an absurdity or a deceptive appearance. Its emergence with emerging life indeed marks an ontological revolution in the history of "matter"; and the development and enhancement of that independence, or freedom, is the principle of progress in the evolution of life, which in its course produces new revolutions—each an additional step in the initial direction, that is, the opening of a new horizon of freedom. The first step was the emancipation of form, by means of metabolism, from the immediate identity with matter. This also means emancipation from the type of fixed self-identity that is matter's, to give scope to a different, viz., mediate and functional, kind of identity. What is the nature of this identity?

The material particle, identifiable in its space-time position, is simply what it is, immediately identical with itself without need to maintain that self-identity as an act of its existence. The identity of its Now is the empty logical one of $A = A$; its duration is mere remaining, not reaffirmation; and in remaining it is successively "identical" by no other principle than that of the continuity of the dimensions—space and time—in which "its" states take place. It is this one and not that one, because this is now here and that now there; it "remains" this, that is to say, is "the same" at a different (later) point of space-time, because from its present to its new position there leads the continuous sequence of all intermediate positions which as it were hand it on from one to the next, without ever letting it outside their bond. Such sequence constitutes the "path" of the unit, and if it were discontinuous—if there were gaps—we should have no way to identify succeeding presences, no warrant even for applying the concept of identity at all; and there would be none—unless we endow (as Whitehead did) the elemental with an inwardness which by a kind of memory would bridge the discontinuity of actual event. But this is a transference from life, and frankly speculative. In purely physical description, no more than continuous presence in the containing continuum is assumed (but no less can be assumed) for the "sameness" of an entity; and thus, on physical terms alone, there is only this external identity conferred on discrete units (particles or fields) by the *principia individuationis* (space and time), or, equivalently, by the totality of the physical universe defining their place: in either case a matter of *external reference*. Of an internal principle of identity in physical particles we do not know, even if there be one.[14] (See Appendix 2 to this Essay.)

Organic identity, however, must be of a different nature altogether. In the precarious metabolic continuity of organic form, with its perpetual turnover of constituents, no inert substratum, no single "path" and no "bundle" of parallel paths of cotemporaneous members, is available as referent for external identity. (See Appendix 3 to this Essay.) Internal identity of the whole, transcending the collective one of the present and vanishing substratum, must span the shifting succession. Such internal identity is implicit in the adventure of form and is spontaneously assumed on its external, morphological evidence which alone is open to inspection. But what kind of inference is this? And by whom? How can the unprepared observer infer what no mere analysis of the physical record will ever yield? The unprepared observer indeed cannot: indeed the observer must be prepared, as the hypothetical "pure Mathematician" is not. The observer of life must be prepared by life. In other words, organic existence with its own experience is required of himself for his being able to make that inference, which he does make all the time, and this is the advantage —perennially disowned or slandered in the history of epistemology— of our "having," that is, being, bodies. Thus we *are* prepared by what we are. It is by this interpolation of an internal identity alone that the mere morphological (and as such meaningless) *fact* of metabolic continuity is comprehended as an incessant *act;* that is, continuity is comprehended as self-continuation.

The introduction of the term "self," unavoidable in any description of the most elementary instance of life, indicates the emergence, with

---

14. Concerning the single particle, then, the traceable steady presence in the continuum is the sole operational meaning of "identity," and the traced "path" is its complete verification: no obvious claim to an internal principle of identity, such as retentive historicity or protentive urge for "self"-perpetuation, issues from its manner of inert permanence. And lacking any suggestion of a *threat* to its existing, the imputation of conative inwardness to its enduring seems gratuitous.

life as such, of internal identity—and so, as one with that emergence, its self-isolation too from all the rest of reality. Profound singleness and heterogeneousness within a universe of homogeneously interrelated existence mark the selfhood of organism. An identity which from moment to moment reasserts itself, achieves itself, and defies the equalizing forces of physical sameness all around, is truly pitted against the rest of things. In the hazardous polarization thus ventured upon by emerging life, that which is not itself and borders on the realm of internal identity from without assumes at once the character of absolute otherness. The challenge of selfhood qualifies all this beyond the boundaries of the organism as foreign and somehow opposite: as "world," in which, by which, and against which it is committed to maintain itself. Without this universal counterpart of otherness, there would be no "self." And in this polarity of self and world, of internal and external, complementing that of form and matter, the basic situation of freedom with all its daring and distress is potentially complete.

VIII

It is the task of a philosophical biology to follow the unfolding of this germinal freedom in the ascending levels of organic evolution. For our present purpose, a few remarks must suffice to indicate some of the attributes which already the primary level, defined by metabolism as such, displays and offers to evolution for further elaboration. These would be such that belong to the essence of life.

Our first remark concerns what we may call the thoroughly "dialectical" nature of organic freedom, namely, that it is balanced by a correlative necessity, which belongs to it as its own shadow and as such recurs intensified at each step to higher independence as the "shadow" peculiar to that level. On the basic level, that defined by metabolism, this double aspect shows in the terms of metabolism itself: denoting, on the side of freedom, a capacity of organic form, namely to change its matter, metabolism denotes equally the irremissible necessity for it to do so. Its "can" is a "must," since its execution is identical with its being. It can, but it cannot cease to do what it can without ceasing to be. Thus the sovereignty of form with respect to its matter is also its subjection to the need of it, by the impossibility of its resting with any concretion attained, that is, with any simultaneous sum of stuff with which it happens to coincide in an instant of time. This indigence, so foreign to the self-sufficiency of mere matter, is no less unique a distinction of life than is its power, of which it is but the other side: its liberty itself is its peculiar necessity. This is the antinomy of freedom at the roots of life and in its most elementary form, that of metabolism.

A second observation immediately follows: in order to change matter, the living form must have matter at its disposal, and it finds it outside itself, in the foreign "world." Thereby life is turned outward and toward the world in a peculiar relatedness of dependence and possibility. Its want goes out to where its means of satisfaction lie: its self-concern, active in the acquisition of new matter, is essential openness for the encounter of outer being. Thus "world" is there from the earliest beginning, the basic setting for experience—a horizon of co-reality thrown open by the mere transcendence of want which widens the seclusion of internal identity into a correlative circumference of vital relationship. It is important to see that this "spatial" self-transcendence, opening into an environment, is grounded in the fundamental transcendence of organic form relative to its matter, for it is this which constitutionally refers it beyond its given material composition to foreign matter as needed and potentially its own. In other words, the self-transcendence of life in having a world, with all its promise of higher and more comprehensive stages, springs from the primary antinomy of freedom and necessity inherent in organism as such.

Third, there is inwardness or subjectivity involved in this transcendence, imbuing all the encounters occasioned in its horizon with the quality of felt selfhood, however faint its voice. It must be there for satisfaction or frustration to make a difference. Whether we call this inwardness feeling, sensitivity and response to stimulus, appetition or nisus—in some (even if infinitesimal) degree of "awareness" it harbors the supreme concern of organism with its own being and continuation in being—that is, it is self-centered—and at the same time bridges the qualitative gulf to the rest of things by selective modes of *relation* which, with their specificness and urgency, replace for the organism the general integration of material objects in their physical context. This restates in part what was said before about the self-transcendence of life. But the open horizon means affectivity as well as spontaneity, outward exposure as well as outward reach: only by being sensitive can life be active. In affection by a foreign agent, the affected feels itself, its selfhood excited, or illuminated as it were, against the otherness without and thus set off in its isolation. At the same time, beyond and "through" this inner state of excitation, the affecting presence is felt, its message of otherness, however obscurely, incorporated within. As felt, the affecting agent obtains a presence of sorts "within" the affected subject. With the first dawn of subjective reflex, the most germinal "experience" of touching, a crack as it were opens in the opacity of divided being, unlocking a dimension where things may exist once more in the mode of object: it is the dimension of inwardness. As the need-inspired interest seeks the other, so the uninvited presence of the other summons the interest. But even if uninvited, the readiness for presence as such is in the organism; and even rejection by act presupposes appropriation (i.e., interiorization) by sense. The primary solicitation of transcendence indeed issues from the organic want and is thus one with the commitment to activity: it is outgoing; but receptivity of sense for the incoming, this passive side of the same transcendence, enables life to be selective and "informed" instead of a blind dynamism. Thus, in facing outward, internal identity becomes the subject-pole of a communication with things more intimate than that between mere physical units, and so the very opposite of isolation emerges from the isolation of the organic self. Here again we meet the dialectical structure pervading all ontological characters of life, which can be grasped only as a paradox of material existence.

One last remark. By the "transcendence" of life we mean its entertaining a horizon, or horizons, beyond its point-identity. So far we have considered the horizon of environment with the presence of things, or, the extension of relatedness into simultaneous space. But self-concern, actuated by want, throws open as well a horizon of time that embraces, not outer presence, but inner imminence: the imminence of that future into which organic continuity is each moment about to extend by the satisfaction of that moment's want. Thus life is facing forward as well as outward and extends "beyond" its own immediacy in both directions at once. In fact, it faces outward only because, by the necessity of its freedom, it faces forward: so that spatial presence is lighted up as it were by temporal imminence and both merge into past fulfillment (or its negative, disappointment.)

Thus the element of transcendence we discerned in the very nature of metabolizing existence has found its fuller articulation: both horizons into which life continually transcends itself can be traced to the transitory relation of organic form to its own matter. The internal direction toward the next impending phase of a being that has to continue *itself* constitutes biological time; the external direction toward the co-present not-itself which holds the stuff relevant to its continuation constitutes biological space. As the here expands into the there, so the now expands into the future.

It follows that, in the internal horizon extended by the self-transcendence of the organic "now" into the process of its continuity, the anticipation if imminent future in appetition is more fundamental than the retention of past in memory. Some measure of the latter must indeed be assumed in all life as the subjective form of its identity in duration. For absorption of the past into each emerging present, that is, "historicity" as such, even of the briefest span, is the prerequisite of duration. But future is the dominant time-horizon opening before the thrust of life, if *concern* is its primary principle of inwardness.

It then also follows that with respect to the organic sphere, the external linear time-pattern of antecedent and sequent, involving the causal dominance of the past, is inadequate: while mere externality is, at least can be presented as, wholly determined by what it was, life is essentially also what it is going to be and just becoming: in its case, the extensive order of past and future is intensively reversed. This is the root of the teleological or finalistic nature of life: finalism is in the first place a dynamic character of a certain mode of existence, coincident with the freedom and identity of form in relation to matter, and only in the second place a fact of structure or physical organization, as exemplified in the relation of organic parts to the whole and in the functional fitness of organism generally. With this Aristotelian reminder we may return from analysis to discussion.

I X

None of the features just sketched has a place in mathematical description of physical entities; and the organism undeniably is a physical entity and as such subject to the uniform description in extensive, spatiotemporal terms. Externally its organization presents itself as a pattern *in extenso,* and its functioning as the exceedingly subtle mechanics of this pattern: the physicochemical analysis of life aims at the complete unraveling of both, which must amount to their complete subsumption as a special case under the general laws of physical patterns. This is because "unraveling" means reduction to the elementary, which is "inorganic," that is, lifeless, and general, that is identical throughout nature—so that the scientific understanding of life comes to mean its conceptual assimilation to that which is not life. In the fullness of success this would result in the disappearance of life as such, coincident with the explanation of all its outward phenomena—except for the fact that the scientific undertaking itself is an act of life, and the scientist is a living being and thus by original experience of life saved from forgetting that there is "something else" to it. But if we credit the mathematical God with the fullness of that which human science aims at by reductionist terms—the ultimate "analysis"—while denying him as a pure incorporeal intellect the benefit of organic experience, then to him, with the extensive pattern furnishing all the data for its own explanation, life itself would not even become visible, nor yet a blank in its place. Eye would not be recognized as eye, feeler not as feeler, organism not as organism. For, taken by themselves (as pointed out before), the material elements satisfy, in this precisely as in any other configuration, all the requirements of the mechanistic scheme and of its modes of explanation or description: particles are drawn into and pass through certain configurations, enter certain combinations, are engaged in certain energy transactions—pass out again into other fields of relation. To the outside, or extensive, view there is nothing else to it. The greater complexity of such a system is no essentially new feature. True, it is a physically improbable system, but the improbable, when it happens, is just as necessary as the most probable case. And with the divine mathematician, for whom the whole difference of probability and improbability is resolved into the one universal necessity, the unitary description in terms of that necessity would be ideally complete, and to the same degree exclusive: not only would it cover all the facts, as facts go for this object-pattern, it would also in its closeness leave no room for slipping in an additional, heterogeneous principle. In other words: the divine mathematician, being the ideal physicist in complete possession of the data and with perfect power of analysis, would account on his lines as exhaustively for this phenomenon as for any other in the physical universe; he would be neither in need nor in command of any other aspect: there would be nothing lacking within that context and he would miss nothing.

Yet, we know that this is not the whole truth because of what science likes to call "subjective" evidence. This can be dismissed as irrelevant for the exposition of physical objectivity on either of the following two counts: either that the phenomena of "subjectivity" constitute an entirely separate field which, whatever its metaphysical standing, does not reach beyond itself (not, for instance, by interaction) and is thus as if it were nonexistent in the system of natural causes and effects; or that they stand in a relation of unilateral dependence to this system and can therefore at best lay claim to a derivative and secondary reality, to be explained by the primary one, but itself redundant in any immanent account of the latter. The first of these alternatives represents dualism of the Cartesian kind, the second "epiphenomenalism," that is, the materialist assertion that mind, or awareness generally, is only a powerless "epiphenomenon" or byplay of physical happenings which follow their own rules entirely. Of these two, the materialistic alternative is easily disposed of since, denying the autonomy of thinking, it invalidates thought and thus disqualifies itself as a rational context of thought, that is, an argument claiming truth on the merits of its reasons and not on the merit of its factual happening. (See Appendix to Fifth Essay.) The dualistic alternative, however, being logically consistent in itself, must be judged by recourse to the facts, of which "organism" is a crucial one. We therefore recast Jeans's God now into a version of Descartes' God who created bodies *and* minds: his being a mathematician then relates to the first department, while his knowledge, of course, must comprise both. We endow him thus with a knowledge, on the one hand, of the complete space-time data of the extensive manifold, and *another* knowledge of all the instances of "inwardness" scattered through it without being part of it.[15] What, then, would such a God

---

15. We must, of course, adopt a strictly noninteractive version of dualism, such as was designed, in the diverse forms of psychophysical parallelism, with the specific purpose of safeguarding for science the homo-

behold when sometimes surveying his creation?

God in his creative knowledge would behold, besides the dead world of extended objectivity, a multiple host of individualized subjectivity, of many shades of obscurity and clarity—each with a correspondingly shaded phenomenal (perceived, sensed, felt) "objectivity," which varies but always coincides with some segment or other of real extensity, presenting it in a particular, occasionally shifting "perspective" from within the extended manifold; and each with one preferred, unvarying region at the center of the variable perspective, distinguished as "belonging" to itself as its "body": and behold, this phenomenal region happens in each case to coincide with some actual material system of *peculiar arrangement* within real extensity! These systems are what we call organisms and living (but they are part of the dead), and we may call them that either by reason of their peculiar physical arrangement and behavior, or (the choice is ours) by reason of their coincidence with the phenomenal "mine"-region of a subjectivity which thus, though itself nonspatial, seems localized in them. Either-or, coincidence, and happening are all that the premises warrant to say, and this leaves open, in these particular cases, two parallel and complementary ways of describing what is locally the same event: either in terms of outwardness or in terms of inwardness, neither description interfering with the other and neither requisite for the internal completeness of the other; that is, more specifically for our case, no terms of the inward description are requisite for the completeness of the outward description.

Now if this construction, however artificial, proves tenable in the face of the facts, we will grant Jeans's contention with the sole qualification, mentioned above, that it is the "architect of the *material* universe" that appears as a pure mathematician. But it is just in the face of organism that the dualistic construction does break down. Far from there being just a coincidence of inwardness with some indifferent parts of extensity that simply happen to serve as the center-regions of a phenomenal outwardness, these particular parts—

---

geneity and closure of the material realm. On the other hand, we take the "mental" realm to comprise *all* forms and grades of subjective being, down to the dimmest "feeling" of the amoeba, which is thus included in the psychophysical dichotomy.

organisms—are obviously *organized for* inwardness, for internal
identity, for individuality—and less obviously perhaps from them as
well. True, this is obvious only to a mind enjoying organic existence
himself, or to a corporeal subject, and is entirely outside the grasp of
bodyless intellect when confronted with a *res extensa* which (on the
dualistic premise) is nothing else. But if, on the premises of the
experiment, the external facts of organism indeed are absorbed with
no remainder in the total account of divine mathematics, at the cost
of their not being recognizable *as* facts pertaining to organism, this
perfect solution of the computing task would not betoken the self-
sufficiency of the spatial considered as this and nothing else, but the
deficiency of a merely extensive description of that which exhibits this
aspect. For (with apologies for the truism) eyes do have in their
physical make-up a reference to seeing, and ears to hearing, and
organs generally to their performance—and, more generally still,
organisms to living. This is not just an additional aspect of them, or
an optional mode of interpretation: it is their own teleological nature.
However complete the physicochemical analysis of the composition
of the eye and of the processes attending its stimulation may be, no
account of its construction and functioning is meaningful without
relating it to seeing. And what is plain in so highly specialized a case
is true in principle for the whole class of material things we call
organisms, though it becomes easier to disregard, for purposes of
physical description, the more we descend to the lower rungs of the
ladder of life-forms, that is, with decrease in complexity of organization and in differentiation of function (and, presumably, corresponding decrease of awareness). But there is always the purposiveness of
organism as such and its concern in living: effective already in all
vegetative tendency, awakening to primordial awareness in the dim
reflexes, the responding irritability of lowly organisms; more so in
urge and effort and anguish of animal life endowed with motility and
sense-organs; reaching self-transparency in consciousness, will and
thought of man: all these being inward aspects of the teleological side
in the nature of "matter." How this finalism tallies, in the same
world, with mechanical causality whose reality cannot be denied
either is a problem not to be "solved" by sacrificing an evidence
(purposiveness) to a theorem (exclusiveness of *causa efficiens*)
which was derived by generalization from another evidence; but, if
solvable at all, only by treating it as the profoundly challenging and

as yet completely unsettled problem it is. At all events, the teleological structure and behavior of organism is not just an alternative choice of description: it is, on the evidence of each one's own organic awareness, the external manifestation of the inwardness of substance. To add the implications: there is no organism without teleology; there is no teleology without inwardness; and: life can be known only by life.

X

This is the advantage we poor mortals have over Jeans's mathematical God: happening to be living material things ourselves, we have in our self-experience, as it were, peepholes into the inwardness of substance, thereby having an idea (or the possibility of having an idea) not only of how reality is spread and interacts in extensity, but of how it *is* to *be* real and to act and to be acted upon. And we can still contrive, by certain acts of abstraction, to be *also* mathematicians and mathematical physicists: "also"—to be "nothing but" a mathematical physicist is plain absurdity.

The evidence we find in ourselves is an integral part of the evidence concerning life which experience puts at our disposal. That it must be used critically to avoid the pitfalls of anthropomorphism goes without saying. But used it must be—and as a matter of fact, most of the time it is, however much biologists and behaviorists may assure us and themselves of the contrary. Else they would altogether miss the existence of life around them and thus have no object for inquiry—the concrete *from* which to make their abstractions—to begin with. They would then share in the divine poverty of the "nothing but" (I take this to be the meaning of "pure") mathematician-creator: not the most complete analytical record, down to the minutest detail, of the space-time data of an eye+optic nerve+visual cortex, etc., if such data be his *only* terms, would enable *him* to infer that in a given case an act of vision occurs—not knowing in the first place what "seeing" could possibly mean. But where his disembodied geometrical intelligence fails, we "of the earth, earthy," and having eyes ourselves, do know (and not merely infer) that the organic individual endowed with those structures sees with them, whatever the physics involved.

We begin to suspect that the "material" which the Great Mathematician had to use for embodying his ideas had an intrinsic nature of its own, unknown to him and unprovided for in his scheme—properties which found their opportunity along the course of mechanical evolution to realize, in the seeming automatism of causal sequence, some of the hidden potentialities of original substance: of which realization we are instances. Thus betrayed into constructing a manifold with a tendency of its own, what the mathematician creates he knoweth not. For him eyes do not see, and ears do not hear. He resembles much more the Demiurge of the Gnostics, who creates the world in ignorance of what he lets himself in for, than the Demiurge of Plato who creates the world out of knowledge.

The end of our inquiry is only the threshold of much larger tasks, which, I believe, are more than ever imposed on philosophy. They are: a philosophical biology without which there cannot be a philosophy of man on the one hand and a philosophy of nature on the other; and a new examination of *causa* without which these three cannot be brought into line. But with regard to the immediate issue of this essay I trust that the foregoing suffices to show why I conclude "from the intrinsic evidence of his creation" that its Creator must be different from what the metaphysician Jeans thinks him to be—to the same extent that creation, that is, being, is different from what the mathematical physicist Jeans conceives it to be. Therefore, our final answer to the question, "Is God a Mathematician?"—meaning essentially and purely a mathematician, even with respect to the *material* universe alone—is a distinct "No."

APPENDIX 1 (p. 67)

Note on the Greek Use of Mathematics in the Interpretation of Nature

To apply mathematics to natural phenomena, or to claim a mathematical character for such phenomena, can mean different things depending on whether it refers to the structures or to the dynamics of nature, to its forms of order or to the changes in the course of which they emerge. The Greek approach represents the first alternative. For the Pythagoreans, the mathematical interpretation of reality consisted in defining a structural whole by the numerical proportions, primarily of spatial dimensions, that hold among its principal parts or between itself and related structures. This matrix of proportions in which a manifold was found to be interrelated provided the distinctive, ordering feature of it and was therefore regarded as the rationale of its wholeness. The "ratio" is the *"logos"* of a thing, that which constitutes it the thing it is. For example, the octave has the ratio two to one: this then is its *logos,* the principle of its being, which antecedes and outlasts any particular occurrence of it. Since one and the same abstract ratio would recur in different entities and on vastly different scales in the order of things, analogies or equations could be established throughout the universe; and the discovery of this possibility in a few striking instances prompted the sweeping conception of one all-comprehensive *Logos* as the principle of "proportion in itself," pervading the whole universe, which by this fact assumes the character of one cosmos. It follows that *logos* as applied to reality is a selective standard which some phenomena come up to and others do not. For only that is a true "ratio" which can be expressed in "rational" numbers, while incommensurate proportions are "irrational": the infinity involved in them is a deficiency to the Greek mind, which cherished finiteness as the mark of true being and the prerequisite for its being known. The latter is really the reason for the former—the first instance in history of this recurrent *quid pro quo.* The intellectual satisfaction in these determinate relations, geometrical and numerical, and in their intrinsic rationality, transposed itself directly into the belief that here is true being and perfection. The tones of a harmony come and go, and it may be impure: the *logos* which makes them a harmony is imperishable, and the same each time the imperfect material harmony occurs. As its eternal truth, the *logos* is the measure of, and at the same time the reason for, each instance of temporal harmony. Thus measures and proportions, ultimately expressible in numbers, are the essence of things.

If we ignore the metaphysical aspect and look only at the way in which mathematics is here applied to phenomena, we find that this application is morphological, and descriptive not of the interplay of component factors but of the form of selected compound wholes. Its objects are such enduring structures of form as may be extracted from the flux of things but are not of the flux, and can be described in terms of stable numerical relations. Their expression forms a statement of "that" and not an explanation of "how" and "why." The theory of the heavens, being "theory" in the original sense of contemplation, gives not the mechanics of the heavens, but a synthesis of its "resultant" (as *we* should say) physiognomy of geometrical and arithmetical features. As descriptive morphology, this *characteristica mathematica* of reality is essentially static, gathering its data into the "present" of the quiescent form. Even where motion is involved among the unchanging traits in the picture, as with the stars in their courses, the successive phases are registered as it were in ideal juxtaposition, as mere moments in the self-completion of the total form. The relative durations are themselves enduring morphological features in the exhibited whole, together with the geometrical properties of the spatial courses described through their sequence. In fact there is the encompassing present of eternally recurring self-performance, where all phases are on an equal footing as integral parts of the one and identical whole. In evidence of this, the heavenly bodies were conceived not as points within a void, which would have no reference to a path in past and future, but as fixed each in a complete sphere, the "orb," which contains its successive path, the "orbit," in the simultaneity of an ever-present form.

The Pythagoreans believed these heavenly orbs to be arranged in numerical ratios of distances equaling those of the concordant intervals in the musical scale and so conceived the magnificent idea of the harmony of the spheres. This may seem to be an aesthetic rather than a scientific or rational conception, but it must be remembered that the correlation of the cosmic with the musical harmony was based on strictly mathematical (though astronomically erroneous) grounds, and the inaudible cosmic music was inferred from them.

Ideas of beauty or perfection are as alien to modern physics as they were inherent in Greek cosmology of the dominant type (the Atomists always excepted). Aristotelian cosmology provides another example. The perfection of the celestial motion, then conceived as spherical, resides in the mathematical virtues of the circle, the most perfect of figures; and this excellence, entailing as it did permanent completeness and immutability, made the stellar world the purest embodiment of the divine (i.e., rational) nature of the universe, the closest temporal approximation to the timeless self-containedness of the Unmoved Mover who keeps the universe going as its final cause. Once again the combination of a geometrical ideal with a teleological pattern of causality is an idea for which modern science has no room. By the time of the great Alexandrian astronomers, to be sure, scientific rigor had suppressed much of the speculative fancy of earlier times. Yet the morphological approach remained; even a Ptolemaeus did not dream of violating the integrity of the celestial motions by any reduction to vulgar, sublunar mechanics; and the perfection of the circle still haunted Copernicus as an axiom of astronomy.

Thus the application of mathematics to nature conformed to the whole spirit of Greek natural philosophy which dwelt on complete structures of form, with an autonomous status to their wholeness, and patterned cosmology accordingly. The system of the world was one of wholes within wholes of ever-widening comprehensiveness, culminating in the Cosmos himself, the ultimate all-embracing whole, the supreme "One in Many" of his own end, in the likeness of a living body. To the same pattern corresponds every entity in nature, if in lesser degrees of completeness and self-sufficiency. Each is part of a greater whole, an end in itself and a whole for its parts. Thus the integral whole, represented by form as such and realized in the universe as the total form, was the ultimate term in this ontology, just as conversely the smallest part—of matter or energy—is the ultimate term in the modern ontology. In both cases what is here called "ultimate term" serves as the last resort of intelligibility and therefore of explanation. To the one's deduction of the parts, and of their function, from the independent nature of the whole, as envisaged in original synthesis, corresponds the other's construction of the complex whole out of the interaction of independent parts, as isolated in antecedent analysis.

APPENDIX 2 (p. 82)
Note on Whitehead's Philosophy of Organism

Whitehead, who significantly called his general theory of being a "philosophy of organism," in effect turned the difference between life and nonlife from one of essence into one of degree. In this as in some other respects he followed Leibniz, and like him he has no real place for death in the conceptual account of life. Concerning the subject of "identity" with which the Essay has been dealing (see above, pp. 81 f.), Whitehead's ontology solves the problem of *physical* identity (in our example: that of particles) by extending to it a principle of *organic* (biological) identity—thereby incidentally depriving the latter of the specific challenge it poses by normal physical standards: it has been converted into a case of what universally holds. This end, the overcoming of an annoying dualism, is achieved by an ingenious conceptual scheme straddling both sides of the fence.

Simple location is replaced by graded omnipresence, permanent substance by actual occasions of feeling, endurance of existence by the transmission of characters from occasion to succeeding occasion: the latter inherits a past by appropriating the yield of the antecedent into its inwardness, and initiates a future by becoming inheritable itself when its own actualization is completed. In between lies what is its own contribution to the heritage: the laying hold of, and incorporating of, some "eternal objects." Thus, what on the outside looks like continuity of existence is in fact a sequence of atomic events, forming a nexus in virtue of the cumulative inclusion of the past in each new present. Herewith "identity," in the only sense conformable to the system, is brought about.

This is a doctrine of permanent creation, of which the conservation laws are the mere phenomenal summing-up. But it is an immanent creation (self-creation of nature); and one with an infinite number of concurrent individual strands; and in each of these proceeding by atomic steps: in all three respects different from the permanent creation postulated by Descartes, who held matter each moment to be renewed in existence by its transcendent creator; and his *fiat* to be summarily one for all matter each time; and to go on continuously throughout time: an act of reconfirmation rather than creation. It is the difference between the theistic view which denies creativity to the created—indeed the mechanistic nature conceived on this basis is emphatically noncreative—and the modern, immanentist view which transfers the attribute of creativity to nature itself. This is the only rational alternative open to naturalism after the loss of the transcendental counterpole provided by dualistic metaphysics, in whose shelter alone an unadulterated "materialism" in physics was rationally possible.

I cannot here discuss this bold proposition of basic ontology, whose intellectual force and philosophical importance are unequaled in our time. Its bearing on our particular problem is that, as "inheritance," nay, historicity, is made the universal principle of identity, biological identity ceases to be the puzzle which by normal physical terms it is. I wonder whether this is a gain. The blurring of the difference between inanimate and animate nature, which the spread of inwardness down to the physical foundations entails, seems a high price to pay for the claimed atomicity of "actual occasions" which requires this universal inwardness to obviate their otherwise inevitable monadic isolation: the result is a submersion of discontinuity where it matters—between life and nonlife—against its injection where it is hypothetical—between phases of physical duration.

One further comment: while the polarity of self and world, as also that of freedom and necessity, is taken care of in Whitehead's system, that of being and not-being is definitely not—and therefore not the phenomenon of death (nor, incidentally, that of evil): but what understanding of life can there be without an understanding of death? The deep anxiety of biological existence has no place in the magnificent scheme. Whitehead, in this respect like Hegel, has written in his metaphysics a story of intrinsically secured success: all becoming is self-realization, each event is in itself complete (or it would not be actual), each perishing is a seal on the fact of completion achieved. "Death, where is thy sting?"

APPENDIX 3 (p. 82)

Note on the Nonparticipation of DNA in Metabolism

The statement on page 82 that in the metabolizing organism, "with its perpetual turnover of constituents, no inert substratum, no single 'path' and no 'bundle' of parallel paths of cotemporaneous members is available as referent for external identity" in its space-time career, must be qualified in one respect: one such "bundle" does seem to escape the general metabolic shift. Recent findings of microbiology indicate that the set of chromosomal DNA molecules which in each cell represents the genetic code, while controlling the metabolism of the rest of the cell, is itself exempt from metabolism, i.e., not subject to exchange. It thus stays physically the same, not merely in number, kind and order of components, but with these selfsame component-individuals throughout the lifetime of the cell: the molecules concerned are there once for all, not sharing in the general flux of the living substance which they on their part control. The persistence here, then, is not that of pattern only but of the substratum itself. While all the rest of the cell material—its overwhelming bulk—is involved in the metabolic turnover and in its course is gradually replaced, this steering core would be found at the end still to consist of the same material units present there at the beginning if they could have been "labeled" at that time for later identification.[1]

In the case of the metazoic (multicellular) organism the situation is somewhat more complicated. For there, replacement takes place not only on the molecular level as in the cell, but on the cellular level as well: cells in turn are being replaced. Thus, while each cell for itself may be said to possess in the fixed system of nuclear DNA molecules a material core of "identity" as long as it lives, an analogous core for the metazoic complex would in turn require a fixed system of *cells* which are nonregenerative, never replaced, coeval with the organism (once formed) from beginning to end; and which, moreover, in their entirety (as a "system") exercise controlling functions relative to the whole analogous to those which the nucleus exercises relative to the single cell. Now there are indeed such cells and such a system of them: the neural cells, and the

---

1. Accession of new material to this chromosomal system (leaving aside the abnormal incident of mutation) takes place only at its replication in cell division, i.e., in the original building up of such a system from an existing one. Apart from this reproductive event, which marks respectively its beginning and end as this one, it is "closed," and its interaction with the rest of the organism is merely "catalytic," leaving itself unaffected.

nervous system they form. This accordingly would be the stable carrier of "identity" in material as well as functional terms. But since the constancy of neural cells is again reducible to that of their nuclear cores, while the bulk of their material is (presumably) as subject to metabolism as that of cells in general, it is finally the *repetitious network of neural chromosomes* strung throughout the body which represents the true "physical" invariant in the general molecular shift of the organic whole. Thus the hypothetical "total resolution" of the divine spectator which I tried to reconstruct, would exhibit (e.g.) the human body somewhat like this: a permanent, fine tracery of molecular groupings reiterating one pattern over and over again (=the DNA nuclei of the nervous system), surrounded by an immensely larger, impermanent multitude of variously grouped elements in constant coming and going (but among which the same molecular grouping also recurs over and over again, viz., in each nonneural cell): that stable tracery provides as it were a "skeleton" of abiding identity for the otherwise ever changing composition of the whole. According to this refined picture there would be after all a strictly physical, external, if very residual, evidence in terms of pure space-time readings for the enduring sameness of the organism in the face of its continual metabolic turnover: the latter would not be strictly *all*-engulfing.

I do not think that this seriously changes the overall picture I have drawn so as to affect the argument based on it, viz., that vital identity is different from physical identity. For one, considering the dynamic control exercised by this "skeleton" (unlike the inert skeleton of support which an organism may lay down from products of its living activity), it is still the functional aspect and not that of mere material persistence that matters in organic identity. Furthermore, it is the replicable pattern and not the individuality of its building blocks that matters: each of these *could* be replaced by a like atom or molecule without consequence to the function and thus to the total identity. Here, too, the principle is continuity of form and not of matter, even where material continuity happens to obtain. Finally, the "identity" of the organism is that of the whole living individual and not that of the physical device by which it is operationally secured: and *that* identity is the paradoxical one of constant renewal through metabolic exchange.

To Move and to Feel:
On the Animal Soul

I

Three characteristics distinguish animal from plant life: motility, perception, emotion. The necessary connection of locomotion with perception is obvious and has been noted already by Aristotle; that with emotion calls for closer scrutiny, which will show that all three manifest a common principle.

The emergence of perception and motility opens a major chapter in the history of freedom that began with organic being as such and was adumbrated in the primeval restlessness of metabolizing substance. Their progressive elaboration in evolution means increasing disclosure of world and increasing individuation of self. Openness toward the world is basic to life. Its elementary evidence is the mere irritability, the sensitiveness to stimuli, which the simple cell displays as an integral aspect of its aliveness. Irritability is the germ, and as it were the atom, of having a world, just as the cell itself is the germ and the atom of the larger organism. That germ of sensing unfolds to distinct world-relationship, just as the cells grow into the differentiated, composite organism. In both cases, the more complex is also the more individualized: in both cases, the elementary starting-form (cell in itself, irritability in itself) continues to be what it is, but acts as an atomic constituent in the synthesis of the higher order.

A real world-relation emerges only with the development of specific senses, defined motor structures, and a central nervous system. The differentiation of sentience, with the central integration of its diversified data, furnishes the beginnings of a true world of objects; the active commerce with this world through the exercise of motility (in turn implying centralization, viz., of control) subjects it to the self-assertion of freedom, which thus answers on a higher plane to the basic necessity of the organism.

The faculties here manifested must be understood as developments of the element of "transcendence" which (as the preceding Essay has shown) is inherent in metabolizing existence. The transitory relation of organic form to its matter distends from the beginning two "horizons" "into" which life continually transcends itself: internally that of time as the next impending phase of its own being toward which it moves; externally that of space, as the locus of the co-present "other" on which it depends for this very continuation. Life by its nature faces forward and outward at once. Now it is the main characteristic of *animal* evolution as distinct from plant life that *space,* as the dimension of dependence, is progressively transformed into a dimension of freedom by the parallel evolution of these two powers: to move about, and to perceive at a distance. In fact, only by these powers is space really disclosed to life, while the initial situation of irritability and irritant confines the experience of the inside-outside differential to that of mere contiguity which allows the outward no true dimension but lets it diffusely coincide with the sensitive surface of the organism itself.

What is less obvious and shall be argued on the following pages, is that the other dimension of "transcendence," *time,* comes in a like manner to be disclosed by the simultaneous evolution of yet another power, that of emotion, and on the same principle, that of "distance" between the self and its object—in this case temporal distance. This is less obvious, *inter alia,* because unlike sentience and motility, emotion has no external organs by which to be identified and to force its way into a physical account, and this invisibility or complete inwardness (any outward expressions being feats of motility) seems to make it dispensable in a scientific description of organic behavior, as long ago Descartes and most recently Cybernetics have illustrated. We shall try to show the insoluble interconnection of the three animal powers, in particular the linkage between motility and emotion, and to interpret its meaning in the greater framework of a general theory of life.

II

Locomotion is toward or away from an object, i.e., pursuit or flight. A protracted pursuit, in which the animal matches its powers of movement against those of the intended prey, bespeaks not only developed motor and sensor faculties but also distinct powers of emotion. It is safe to assume that the number of intermediate steps over which the purpose can extend itself is a measure of the stage of emotional development. The very span between start and attainment which such a series represents must be bridged by continuous emotional intent. The appearance of directed long-range motility (as exhibited by the vertebrates) thus signifies the emergence of emotional life. Greed is at the bottom of the chase, fear at the bottom of flight. If appetition is the basic condition of motility, pursuit is the primary motion. Appetition also stands nearest to the preanimal urge of living things in general, i.e., to the basic concern of life in continuing itself by the ceaseless carrying on of its metabolic process. However, though distinct appetite is the translation of this basic life-thrust into animal terms, these terms are really different from the vegetative ones, and it is motility which makes the difference visible: it consists in the interposition of *distance* between urge and attainment, i.e., in the possibility of a distant goal. Its apprehension requires distant perception: thus development of sentience is involved. Its attainment requires controlled locomotion: thus development of motility is involved. But to experience the distantly perceived *as* a goal and to keep its goal quality alive, so as to carry the motion over the necessary span of effort and time, desire is required. Fulfillment not yet at hand is the essential condition of desire, and deferred fulfillment is what desire in turn makes possible. Thus desire represents the time-aspect of the same situation of which perception represents the space-aspect. Distance in both respects is disclosed and bridged: perception presents the object "not here but over there"; desire presents the goal "not yet but to come": motility guided by perception and driven by desire turns *there* into *here* and *not yet* into *now*. Without the tension of distance and the deferment necessitated by it there would be no occasion for desire or emotion generally. The great secret of animal life lies precisely in the gap which it is able to maintain between immediate concern and mediate satisfaction, i.e., in the loss of immediacy corresponding to the gain in scope.

Of this *principle of mediacy,* sentience, emotion, and motility are different manifestations. If emotion implies distance between need and satisfaction, then it is grounded in the basic separation between subject and object and thereby coincident with the situation of sentience and motility, which equally include the element of distance. "Distance" in all these respects involves the subject-object split. This is at the bottom of the whole phenomenon of animality and of its departure from the vegetative mode of life. Our concern is to understand the nature of this departure.

I I I

Among the fundamentals which constitute the existence of such a thing as an organism is the inside-outside relation, commonly expressed by the concept-pair "organism-environment." From this original fact of life's having commerce with an environment we should exclude all premature suggestion of the duality of subject and object. The original condition is an environment contiguous with the organism: in this stage environment is nothing but the immediate surroundings with which the chemical interchanges of metabolism take place. This situation of material contiguity means also continuity in the process of exchange and thus immediacy of satisfaction concurrent with the permanent organic need. In this condition of continuous feeding there is no room for desire. Need passes of itself over into satisfaction by the steady operation of the metabolic dynamics. It still remains true that this dynamism itself, the very condition for there being a need, manifests the basic concern of life with its own continuation, which can be secured only by constant self-renewal. But the continuous availability of the matter needed for the renewal of form gives no occasion for the concern in such renewal to turn into appetite. Environment and self still form one context functioning of itself, and not until some sort of separation between the two takes place can appetite and fear come into play. It is life itself which brings about this separation: a particular branch of it evolves the capacity and the necessity of relating itself to an environment no longer contiguous with itself and immediately available to its metabolic needs.

The division between immediate and mediate environment-relation coincides with that between plants and animals and must thus be related to the basic difference in their modes of metabolism. By its ability to synthesize inorganic matter directly into organic compounds the plant is enabled to draw its sustenance from the ever-ready mineral supply of the soil, while the animal has to depend on the unassured presence of highly specific and nonpermanent organic bodies. Furthermore, the intake of solid food which the animal mode of nutrition requires as against the mere osmotic absorption of dissolved nutriment by plants, involves the interposition of an auxiliary, "mechanical" stage (of conveying, shredding, etc.) before the direct, chemical stage of metabolic appropriation. On these counts the plant shows a superiority rather than a deficiency in comparison with animals. But the possession of this one power of direct synthesis, and the sufficiency which it affords, are the very reason for the absence of all those other features which the animals were constrained to evolve on the basis of their more precarious mode of metabolism. We note here that independence as such cannot be the ultimate good of life, since life is just that mode of material existence in which being has exposed itself to dependence (of which metabolism itself is the prime form) in exchange for a freedom closed to the independence of stable matter. The attainment of a highly satisfactory independence within the sphere of metabolism may thus close avenues of evolution into which that freedom would otherwise, at the price of increased dependence, move.

In roots, plants "invented" the most efficient means of exploiting the inherent advantages of a photosynthesizing organism. Possessing them, the plant is relieved of the necessity (as it is also deprived of the possibility) of movement. Through their continuous contact with the source of supply, the organism-environment relation functions automatically and no further apparatus for adaptation to short-term changes is necessary. Here we have immediacy guaranteed by constant contiguity between the organs of intake and the external supply. In the uninterrupted exchange the current need, though ever renewed, cannot take on the keen edge of want. As satisfaction is contemporaneous with the vital activity, there is no gap across which need could become felt by itself and activity would have to be performed by itself, under the spur of appetition.

I V

If we consider the situation we discover three aspects of what a "gap" or its absence here means. There is first the material contiguity between the plant and the environment nourishing it: for the animal the relevant items of its environment are always at a distance. Environment therefore means in the case of the plant something fundamentally different from what it means in the case of the animal. With its adjacent surroundings the plant forms one permanent context into which it is fully integrated, as the animal can never be in its environment. Second, there is the temporal continuity or discontinuity between need and satisfaction. Here again the animal has to span a gap which represents in time what the gap between itself and the relevant objects represents in space. As the latter gap is provisionally spanned by perception, so the former is by emotion. Both modes express the mediacy of animal existence or the split between self and world: the immediacy of plant life knows of no such split and therefore offers no room for those modes. The "room," in the case of animal life, is provided by the gap with which it has surrounded itself in place of the continuous surroundings of the plant.

Last, there is, in consequence of these gaps in space and time, the separateness of action from its purpose, or the phenomenon of intermediate activity, in animals. The typical plant activity is part of the metabolic process. In the motions of animals, on the other hand, we have activity made possible by the surplus from previous metabolism and directed toward safeguarding its future, but itself a free expenditure dissociated from the continuing vegetative activity, and thus action in a radically new sense. It is external action superimposed on the internal action of the vegetative system and parasitic on it: only its results are destined to benefit those functions. This mediacy of vital action by external motion is the distinguishing mark of animality. The arc of its detour is the locus of the freedom and risk of animal life. The outward motion is an expenditure to be redeemed only by the eventual success. But this success is not assured. The external action, in order to be a possibly successful one, must be such that it also can go wrong. It must, in other words, be an activity which disposes freely of the resources of the nutritive system—freely, i.e., for better or for worse. The possibility of error or failure is correlative to that of success under the conditions of mediate action. The resources for the latter are made available by the nature of animal metabolism, which, by breaking down the results of vegetable synthesis, is as a whole parasitic on plant life. Only by this exploitation is the energy-surplus obtained which can then be expended in nonvegetative acitivity. Thus animal metabolism makes mediate action possible; but it also makes it necessary. The animal, feeding on existing life, continually destroys its mortal supply and has to seek elsewhere for more. In the case of flesh-eaters, whose food is itself motile, this need is increased in proportion and forces the mutual development of that agility in which so many other faculties of the animal must participate.

The mediacy of animal existence is at the root of motility, perception, and emotion. It creates the isolated individual pitted against the world. This world is at once inviting and threatening. It holds the things needed by the solitary animal, which has to go out and seek them. It also holds the objects of fear, and since the animal can flee, it must flee them. Of this world the animal is no stable part. Survival becomes a matter of conduct in single actions, instead of being assured by well-adapted organic functioning in itself. This precarious and exposed mode of living commits to wakefulness and effort, whereas plant life can be dormant. Responding to the lure of the prey, of which perception has given notice, alertness turns into the strain of pursuit and into the gratification of fulfillment: but it also knows the pang of hunger, the agony of fear, the anguished strain of flight. Pursuit itself may end in the disappointment of failure. In short, the indirectness of animal existence holds in its wakefulness the twin possibilities of enjoyment and suffering, both wedded to effort. The two evolve together, and the liability to suffering is not a shortcoming which detracts from the faculty of enjoyment, but its necessary complement. The suffering intrinsic in animal existence is thus primarily not that of pain (which is occasional and a concomitant) but that of want and fear, i.e., an aspect of appetitive nature as such. Appetition is the form which the basic self-concern of all life assumes under the conditions of animal mediacy, where it emancipates itself from its immersion in blind organic function and takes over an office of its own: its functions are the emotions. Animal being is thus essentially passionate being.

V

In terms of mere biological safety, the advantages of animal over plant life are highly questionable, and in any case they are bought at a heavy price. The ability to go out in search of food merely answers to the necessity which its mode of metabolism imposes upon the animal and from which the plant is free. Motile existence is fitful and anxious: plant life is nothing of the kind. But doubtful as are the gains of motility in a balance of mere survival values, the survival standard itself is inadequate for the evaluation of life. If mere assurance of permanence were the point that mattered, life should not have started out in the first place. It is essentially precarious and corruptible being, an adventure in mortality, and in no possible form as assured of enduring as an inorganic body can be. Not duration as such, but "duration of what?" is the question. This is to say that such "means" of survival as perception and emotion are never to be judged as means merely, but also as qualities of the life to be preserved and therefore as aspects of the end. It is one of the paradoxes of life that it employs means which modify the end and themselves become part of it. The feeling animal strives to preserve itself as a feeling, not just a metabolizing entity, i.e., it strives to continue the very activity of feeling: the perceiving animal strives to preserve itself as a perceiving entity—and so on. Without these faculties there would be much less to preserve, and this *less* of what is to be preserved is the same as the *less* wherewith it is preserved.

Ultimately it is the fact of individuation which decides the issue between animal and plant. The original condition of organism, even on the unicellular level, exhibits individuality as the venture of freedom by which a form maintains its identity through the change of its matter. The freedom is dialectically balanced by necessity, the autonomy by dependence. The selfhood here adumbrated has from the beginning its counterpart in the otherness of the world. The further accentuation of this dualism with all its inherent burden is nothing but the accentuation of life itself. Its dialectic cannot but make each more developed state of it more double-edged. From this point of view we see wherein the real advance of developed animality lies. Its mediacy of world-relation is an increase of the mediacy which is already peculiar to organic existence on the first (metabolizing) level, as compared to the immediate self-identity of inorganic matter. This increased mediacy buys greater scope, internal and external, at the price of greater hazard, internal and external. A more pronounced self is set over against a more pronounced world. The progressive nervous centralization of the animal organism emphasizes the former, while correspondingly the environment becomes open space in which the free-moving sentient has to fend for itself. In its greater exposure and the pitch of awareness that goes with it, its own possible annihilations becomes an object of dread just as its possible satisfactions become objects of desire. Its enjoyment has suffering as its shadow side, its loneliness the compensation of communication: the gain lies not on either side of the balance sheet but in the togetherness of both, i.e., in the enhancement of that selfhood with which "organism" originally dared indifferent nature. Its price from the beginning was mortality, and each further stage of separation pays in its own coin—the same in which it also acquires its fulfillment. The kind of coin determines the value of the enterprise. The rift between subject and object, which long-range perception and motility opened and which the keenness of appetite and fear, of satisfaction and disappointment, of pleasure and pain, reflect, was never to be closed again. But in its widening expanse the freedom of life found room for all those modes of relation—perceptive, active, and emotional—which in spanning the rift justify it and by indirection redeem the lost unity.

Cybernetics and Purpose: A Critique

I

In 1782 James Watt patented the flyball governor for his steam engine. It consists of two balls linked to a vertical spindle which is rotated by the engine; their weight, tending to keep them down and close to the spindle, is counteracted by the centrifugal force of the rotation. With an increase in speed this force causes the balls to fly out and up, while a decrease makes them fall. In thus moving, they operate a lever so connected with the throttle-valve between the boiler and the engine as to close it when the speed exceeds a normal value and to open it when the speed falls short of that value. The beauty of this self-regulation is in the fact that the machine performs it as part of the output to be controlled, and through the very acts of excess or deficiency which are the objects of the corrective action.

Note here the two important aspects of this control mechanism. First, a part of the output energy, though of insignificant magnitude, is redirected to the controlling apparatus farther back in the causal order of the system; this feature is called "feedback." Second, this feedback is such as to counteract the action of the machine, that is, it is corrective, not reinforcing; this is called "negative feedback." When properly functioning it will keep the performance around a mean value by reacting alternately to the "plus" or "minus" departures from it.

More than eighty years later, in 1868, Clark Maxwell, in a paper

"On Governors," read before the Royal Society, gave the first theoretical account of this type of mechanism. And again eighty years later, in 1948, Norbert Wiener of the Massachusetts Institute of Technology lifted from the font a new science which he christened cybernetics, taking the name from the Greek word *kybernetes*—helmsman, pilot—of which our "governor" is a derivative.

Little did Watt dream of these consequences. His governor was an auxiliary device for his steam engine, the purpose of which was the production of mechanical power for industry. From the plentiful availability of such power stemmed the industrial revolution, or what Wiener prefers to call the first industrial revolution. Its dominant technological aspect was power engineering. The pilot function of the governor was confined to assuring the steady running of the power engine, and anything that Watt and his contemporaries may have been able to foresee of his invention's effects was surely in terms of the moving force generated by the new machines and of its impact on economy—that is, in terms of the first industrial revolution.

Lately, however, automatic pilot devices have come into their own with a difference. Modern technology, going beyond the mere production and application of power, tends increasingly to couple the power engine with robot mechanisms—mechanisms that replace man's perception and judgment in the serving of the machine, just as the power engines replaced man's arms in supplying the moving force. The difference lies not only in the function but also in the technology; automatic control is a branch of communication engineering, as distinct from power engineering. It is the rise of these servomechanisms, and the fact that they supersede human functions very different from those superseded by the mere power engine—generally speaking, "higher" functions—which causes Wiener and others to speak of a second industrial revolution. Familiar examples of servomechanisms are the thermostat, self-correcting steering engines in ships, automatic fire control in antiaircraft artillery, target-seeking torpedos, electronic computers, automatic telephone exchanges. In all of them, feedback plays an important part.

That the common principles involved in these different devices and the problems posed by them require a unified theory, and that this theory is of sufficient autonomy and range to deserve the name of a new science, was a matter for the workers in the field to decide, and no quarrel can arise with their practical decision. If this were all the status claimed by cybernetics, the philosopher would not have to engage in a critique of it.

But cybernetics is not as innocent as that. There is a strong and, it seems, almost irresistible tendency in the human mind to interpret human functions in terms of the artifacts that take their place, and artifacts in terms of the replaced human functions. The power engine, with its levers and joints and its voracious fuel consumption, was a slaving giant, and, correspondingly, the human or animal body was a fuel-burning power machine. The modern servomechanism is described as perceptive, responsive, adaptive, purposive, retentive, learning, decision-making, intelligent, and sometimes even emotional (but this last only if something goes wrong), and, correspondingly, men and human societies are being conceived of and explained as feedback mechanisms, communication systems, and computing machines. The use of an intentionally ambiguous and metaphorical terminology facilitates this transfer back and forth between the artifact and its maker. In former days, dealing in such analogies was left mainly to the imaginative writer, and certainly had no part in the terms of reference of the scientist as such; but this sort of transference is precisely what cybernetics is concerned with, and on this account it is subject to philosophical criticism. The literature, which has been growing rapidly since the publication of *Cybernetics* by Norbert Wiener in 1948, abounds with cybernetical explanations of human behavior, processes of thought, and sociocultural organisms.

This is something new. The classical mechanist, dealing with matter and motion, was content to speak of the "machine of the body" and, in method if not in metaphysics, to follow Descartes, originator of the notion of the "animal automaton," who had removed mind from the very terms of physical science. Later materialists repudiated the Cartesian dualism in name only. That mind is an epiphenomenon of material processes in the brain, as they held, remained a summary assertion not leading to such actual correlations and transformations as would invade the field of mind itself with the symbolism of physical science. Now is offered, for the first time, a mechanistic model which, it is claimed, applies to material and mental phenomena at once, not only equivalently but identically—that is, without involving passage from field to field.

This would indeed mean an overcoming of the dualism which classical materialism had left in possession by default: for the first time since Aristotelianism we would have a unified doctrine, or at least a unified conceptual scheme, for the representation of reality. Needless to say, this would be of the utmost philosophical importance—and the spokesmen of cybernetics are not restrained by any timidity from pointing out these implications in very explicit statements. It is with this aspect of the new discipline, not with the mathematics and technology of communication engineering and automatic control, that this essay proposes to deal.

There are three major topics facing such a scrutiny, indicated by the terms "teleology," "information," and "mind." I have chosen for analysis here the first of them: the cybernetical concept of purpose and teleology. This is basic to the whole scheme, and I grant at the outset that if cybernetics makes good its claim with regard to these terms—that they can be evolved from mechanical premises alone—it has carried its main point and resolved an age-old dualism. I propose to show that the resolution claimed is spurious and mainly verbal.

II

Before entering into detailed discussion, let me show by a stock example from cybernetical literature what kind of analogies we are about to deal with in this field.[1] The analogy in question is between a servomechanical and a neurological disturbance. This is the mechanical side: a feedback may be inadequately "damped" and result in overcorrections, thereby in effect becoming positive instead of negative; in such a case a machine, say one that is designed to hit a moving target, will "overshoot" in alternate directions in a series of ever-larger oscillations, and thus "miss the goal." And now the neurological analogue: if a cerebellar patient "is asked to carry a glass of water from a table to his mouth . . . the hand carrying the glass will execute a series of oscillatory motions of increasing amplitude as the glass approaches his mouth, so that the water will spill

---

1. The example, and the quotations in this section, are taken from a joint paper by A. Rosenblueth, N. Wiener, and J. Bigelow, "Behavior, Purpose and Teleology," in *Philosophy of Science*, Vol. 10/1 (January, 1943), pp. 18-24.

and the purpose will not be fulfilled." The condition described is called "purpose tremor."

It is contended that the two cases are "strikingly similar." However that may be, one point at least should be clear from the outset: the patient himself *wills* to bring the glass to his mouth, that is, he wants it there. This *end,* motivating the action from the start, is intrinsic in all the part-motions, providing the reference by which they are in themselves failures and make the whole undertaking a failure. Presumably the patient finds his inability to perform distressing. But the machine, for all we know, may just as well be said, instead of being distressed, to abandon itself with relish to its wild oscillations, and instead of suffering the frustration of failure, to enjoy the unchecked fulfillment of its impulses.

"Just as well" amounts of course to "neither." Manifestly neither "distress" nor "enjoyment" fits the *modus operandi* of a machine—not even as an operational analogy, since the machine is equally "satisfied" in each and any single step of behavior as it occurs, the occurrence as such being its own sole and sufficient vindication. In the case of the machine "missing the goal" means, of course, missing *our* goal, the goal for which it has been designed, namely by us, it "having" none itself; whereas the unfortunate patient truly misses his goal, which is his not because he has been designed for it but because he has formed and entertained the design. These elementary distinctions, for whose probably exasperating obviousness I apologize, have to be kept firmly in mind during the following deliberations. The example itself, however, belongs to a later stage in the logical development, to which I now turn.

In the cybernetical study referred to, the concept of purpose emerges in a process of dichotomy to which the basic concept of "behavior" is subjected. Since "by behavior is meant any change of an entity *with respect to its surroundings,*" the whole sequence remains within the terms of external relationships. Purposeful behavior appears as a subdivision of active behavior, and "the term purposeful is meant to denote that the act or behavior may be interpreted as directed to the attainment of a goal—i.e., to a *final condition* in which the behaving object reaches a *definite correlation* in time or in space with respect to another object or event" (italics mine).

Obviously the whole definition turns on the meaning and relevance of the term "final condition." Now what condition is to be regarded as final? We are not permitted to answer "the one in which the goal is reached," since it is the finality of the condition which alone gives meaning to the term "goal"; this meaning is not derived, for example, from the anticipatory presence of such a condition in the initiation and throughout the successive stages of the motion. Nothing remains but to understand as "final" the condition in which the action ends, that is, a condition of rest, in the broad relativistic sense indicated by the phrase "in which the behaving object reaches a definite correlation . . . with respect to another object." This sounds almost Aristotelian, except that to Aristotle a body comes to rest in its natural place because this *is* the aim of its motion, while to our authors the motion "may be interpreted" as having had that aim because it ends where it does.

The difference is not a minor one. Aristotle could distinguish between the mere ending and the intrinsic "end" of a motion, a distinction without which, as he points out, death would have to be considered the aim of human life. But to our authors, if they stick to their definition, death—the most definite correlation to the environment reachable, and inevitably reached, by an organism—indeed *is* the goal of the total motion of life as one sequence of "active behavior," and I see no way for them to escape this conclusion. To generalize this, we may say that "running down," that is, increase of entropy, defines the direction of all natural processes, and therefore maximum entropy is the goal to whose attainment all behavior may be interpreted as being directed. In this sense all behavior is purposeful—by the terms of the definition.

This criticism may seem unfair, since it does not consider the kind of mechanism to which the authors intend their definition to apply, and which, by its statable difference from other, "nonpurposeful" kinds, exemplifies the true meaning of the definition. Indeed, we are not concerned with verbal shortcomings. Let us therefore look at some of the examples given to illustrate the meaning—first at a nonpurposeful mechanism.

"First may be mentioned mechanical devices such as a roulette, designed precisely for purposelessness." What a mechanism is designed for, by its maker, is of course entirely irrelevant, because extraneous, to the description of its working. The mention of the purpose of the human designer in this context arouses our suspicion that also in the general theory the human—that is, the familiar, the noncybernetical—meaning of "purpose" is insinuated into a description which purports to deal in terms of external behavior alone. We shall find this suspicion amply confirmed as we go on. As regards the roulette itself, it attains in each run one final condition, though one that is unpredictable by its designer or user, and is thus by itself "purposeful." It may be argued that it does not come under a definition by which "purposeful" is a subdivision of "active" behavior, since the whole action of the roulette can be traced to the immediate input of energy, the push by a hand. But instead of losing time with showing that the distinction between active and passive behavior is irrelevant to the issue, let us go on to the next example, which is not open to this objection.

"Then may be considered devices such as a clock, designed, it is true, with a purpose, but having a performance which, although orderly, is not purposeful—i.e., there is no specific final condition toward which the movement of the clock strives." This is a glaring example of illicit mixing of points of view. The statement that there is no specific final condition toward which the movement of the clock strives is true only as an expression of desirability from the point of view of the human user, who intervenes—by periodical rewinding, for example—to secure this desirable state. Left to itself, to its own "striving," the clock will run down: the spring will extend to its maximum, the zero point of tension, or the weight will come to rest, at the latest on reaching the center of gravitation, and the final condition of the clock itself will be that standstill which marks the attainment of complete equilibrium or maximum entropy. I cannot see any other striving in the clock as a piece of physical mechanism, though I can see a striving of a very different nature in the *user* of the clock to counteract the clock's own "purpose."

On the other hand, it seems arbitrary to exclude the regular performance as a whole from the conditions "in which the behaving object reaches a definite correlation in time or in space with respect to another object or event," and thus to disqualify it from representing the goal of the process. The "definite correlation" may well be a series, which it is in the case of a continuously energized clock (and, on the human level, in the case of all those activities that have their end in themselves); and thus in this respect too the example fails to illustrate nonpurposive as opposed to purposive behavior in a mechanism. It seems that once we have abandoned the original meaning of "purpose" as the *propositum,* that which someone sets *before* himself as the whereto of his action, we are reduced to the necessity of granting purpose to *all* action—thereby depriving the definition of all defining force.

Let us now look at our author's counterexamples. "Some machines, on the other hand, are intrinsically purposeful. A torpedo with a target-seeking mechanism is an example. The term servomechanisms has been coined precisely to designate machines with intrinsic purposeful behavior." Why is a target-seeking or self-steering torpedo intrinsically purposeful? We must of course beware of succumbing to the suggestiveness of such words as "seeking" and "self." In observing the behavior of the torpedo, its "change with respect to its surroundings," we notice that it does not simply follow its initial course, but alters it occasionally, with the general effect of keeping on the target, which may be a moving one. We see these changes occur in response to changes in the relative positions of the two entities, and may then speak of "compensatory action" on the part of the torpedo. We do this provided the changes of behavior are due not directly, in terms of force, but only indirectly, in a sense to be specified, to the influence of the other entity. Otherwise any magnetic particle changing its path with the displacement of a magnetic pole, or a gravitating body changing it with the relative displacement of the source of gravitation, would have to be regarded as coming under the same category.

The latter example is instructive. A planet may be said to respond continuously to the relatively changing position of the sun, and the curvature of its actual path may be said to be a compromise between two conflicting "strivings," one to continue in a straight line by its momentum, the other to fall toward the sun by its gravity. Each factor embodies its own "purpose," and if the first should grow steadily smaller the revolution of the planet will become a decreasing spiral in which the margin of "error" with regard to the second "purpose" will be progressively diminished. Yet we would not say that the planet "corrects" or "adjusts" its course. The reason is that here the changes are a direct function of the forces involved; especially, the energy that provides the "stimulus" (the "pull" of the sun) is the same as that which effects the "response." In other words, we cannot here even make the distinction, since action and reaction are one and the same event.

An analogous situation would obtain if the torpedo altered its course by direct magnetic attraction between itself and the target. This would certainly be "purposive" behavior according to any reasonable interpretation of the previous definition, which has been shown to be worthless in any case, but it would not be "teleological" behavior according to the definition we are soon to deal with. What constitutes the difference in the two cases, assuming that magnetic principles operate in both, is that in the self-steering torpedo the magnetic factor does not itself provide the *power* for the acceleration of the entity whose steering arrangement it affects, and the effect on the latter is not a function of the *quantity* of the magnetic force acting on it. Given sufficient sensitivity, this force may be as small as you please, and given efficient coupling and sufficient motor resources, the effect in terms of power may be as large as you please. The torpedo is not attracted but is steered toward the target—in response, to be sure, to an influence emanating from it, but this influence is of the order of "message" and not of acceleration. Thus it is the difference between receptor and effector elements, and the steering of the latter's output by the former's input, which characterize this type of adaptive behavior. On the human level this is tantamount to saying that purposive behavior involves perception.

Obviously the division, and at the same time connection, between receptor and effector organs is one of the essential conditions of the freedom of animal action: it makes *possible* action governed by purposes (for the goal-object must be perceived, and movement guided by such perception be performed)—provided the entity in question is one that can have purposes. This instrumental *condition* for goal-directed action, viz. (in the animal analogy), "motility and sentience," which is no other than the "feedback" of the control engineers, provides the cybernetician with his definition of "teleological behavior" itself: behavior controlled by negative feedback. Thus it is a subdivision of "purposive behavior," and it escapes the meaninglessness of the generic term through being thus specified by a definite technical pattern.

With negative feedback an entity's function is controlled by the amount of discrepancy which it shows from moment to moment with reference to some defined state, the amount being continually compensated. The process thus appears to be goal-directed. Can it therefore be called "teleological" in any more relevant sense than that of a verbal definition—in a sense that would justify the choice of the name from the connotations it has prior to the definition? The question is tantamount to asking whether the differentia of "feedback" can supply the concept of *purpose* which the logical genus failed to yield; this again amounts to the question whether the technical *condition* for purposive action can itself constitute purpose; and this, finally, involves the question whether effector and receptor equipment—that is, motility and perception alone—is sufficient to make up motivated animal behavior.

III

With these questions in mind let us look again at the target-seeking torpedo. Its *telos* would be said to be the hitting of the target, because this will be the result of its behavior if successful, and the behavior is said to be purposeful and teleological because it is self-adaptive with regard to this result. Note that in the term "successful" we have introduced an element of human evaluation into the description, and that in saying "adaptive with regard to the result" we have allowed ourselves another anthropomorphic latitude, since there is nothing in the single operations of adaptation that relates directly to the outcome of the action as a whole, even though retrospectively we can adjudge the single adaptations to have contributed to it. Each of the adaptations in itself only restores the equilibrium of the moment, which on its own terms is a self-sufficient situation. I will not press these points here, but rather ask what *part* of the mechanism embodies the purposiveness.

It cannot be the propulsion engine, because this—whether it is a battery-fed electromotor, a jet or internal-combustion engine, or whatever—simply works toward the equalization of energy levels, that is, it is governed by the law of entropy. But so too is the sensitive receptor, whose action from moment to moment consists in the leveling-out of a magnetic or electric potential or some other internal disequilibrium; and the same is true for the transmission of its "message" through whatever channel, and for its amplification, and for the relay actions involved, and so on, back to the operation of the steering device as such. Each of these actions runs its course entirely in the tracks of its own mechanical necessity—"blindly," as the expression is—and is as unrelated to the previous and following steps in its own series as to the actions of the other elements in the system. None of them is as such engaged in the attainment of the "goal," the sole "concern" of each being the attainment of its own "purpose" in terms of entropy.

Thus the overall purpose, since it does not reside in any part, must reside in the whole, in the receptor plus the effector plus the coupling, and in the form of organization of the multiple system. This indeed is the cybernetical contention, and therefore the question becomes that of whether the mechanism *is* a "whole," having an identity or selfness that can be said to be the bearer of purpose, the subject of action, and the maker of decisions.

That it is not can be shown by a simple mental experiment. Imagine the torpedo, not fully mechanized, to be manned by a human pilot—and of course you may immediately substitute for this image the everyday example of the driver in his car. One would no more regard the torpedo plus the sailor, or the car plus the driver, as a single purposive entity than one would declare the ax to participate in the purposiveness and the teleological behavior of the lumberjack who swings it. Any sane person would say that the sailor, the driver, the lumberjack, is the bearer and agent of purpose in the combination, and uses its other elements to his purpose. And this situation is not altered at all if the pilot, for example, has no firsthand perception of the goal but does his steering by the data of mechanical receptor devices such as radar. In this case we should have mechanical feedback input and mechanical energy output coupled by a human link at the control point, but this still would not bring the machine a jot nearer to merging with the human agent into one purposive whole. The man can step out of the contrivance and walk away and take the "purpose" with him, complete and unabridged.

In certain cases, therefore, we *can*, within an overwhelmingly mechanical system of interlocking functions, including even servomechanisms, *localize purpose* in one single controlling part—provided this part or link is such an entity as for itself *has* purpose and *acts on* purpose. All the rest of the machinery is then simply his tool. Why, then, if we now replace this one agent by a mechanical link, which taken by itself has no purpose, should the quality of purposiveness shift from this locus in the configuration and suddenly expand over the whole of the system, and the former tools assume, together with the replacing element, the characteristics of intrinsic purposeful behavior? The idea is absurd. We may say, of course, that the whole contrivance, judged from without, behaves "as if" it were purposeful; only we must immediately add "but we know better."

Why do we know better? To answer this question let us concentrate for a moment on the hypothetical human pilot of the target-seeking torpedo. He carries out certain actions, i.e., his limbs perform certain motions—those that would be carried out in the alternative case by the interpolated mechanical device. Why does he perform those motions as and when he does? The cybernetical answer would be that he does so in response to certain information from his receptors, or, he acts as determined by the latter—in other words, he functions as a feedback mechanism himself.

But this is patently untrue. Everyone in his right senses will say that the pilot operates a certain switch not because he has received a certain sense-message but because he wishes to keep the torpedo on the target, and *in the light of this purpose* he takes the occurrence of certain perceptions as the occasion for performing certain actions conducive to the end in view. It is the prior and coextensive purpose which qualifies the incoming data as messages if they are relevant to the purpose. It is I who let certain "messages" count as "information," and as such make them influence my action. The mere feedback from sense-organs does not motivate behavior; in other words, sentience and motility alone are not enough for purposive action—not even for the original conditioning of reflexes which, once set up, may then substitute for purposive action. The reflex arc embodies in its mechanized pattern the vital purposiveness or concern that went into the making of it. The feedback combination of a receptor-effector system (which an organism indeed is among other things) lends itself to purposive action precisely if and when it is *not* a mere feedback *mechanism*—that is, if the two elements are not coupled directly, but if interposed between them there is will or interest or concern.

This amounts precisely to saying that purposive behavior requires the presence of purpose. That statement is no mere tautology, for cybernetics is an attempt to account for purposive behavior without purpose, just as behaviorism is an attempt at a psychology without the "psyche," and mechanistic biology a description of organic processes without "life."

If then everything turns on purpose itself, let us eye more closely the purpose of our torpedo pilot. We said he acts so and so because he wishes to keep the torpedo on a certain course. But the matter does not end here. This being only the most proximate purpose, we immediately have to ask why he wishes the torpedo to follow this course.

One answer might be that he wishes the torpedo finally to hit and sink the enemy cruiser. And why should he wish that? This is all the more relevant to ask as the desired success may entail his own destruction, and we may credit the agent with a concurrent desire to live. The answer may be that he wishes it out of patriotic fervor, or for honor and glory, or out of hate or revenge, or to win a bet, or to commit a spectacular suicide. But in each of these cases, or in a combination of them, we again have to ask why, and thus launch into a consideration of what the welfare of his nation, or honor or glory or revenge or whatever, means in the total teleological economy of his person. This investigation will lead to his ultimate concerns, the ends by which he lives, at least at the present juncture.

But the first answer might have been not "because he wishes to sink the cruiser," but "because he has been ordered to steer the torpedo to that effect," and then the next question would be "why does he make obedience to orders his purpose in this sequence of action?" Here the answers might be that he does so out of a sense of duty, or out of fear of his superiors, or to win their approval, or because he wants to earn his pay, or to conform to a social pattern. Each of these answers leads again into an ascending and expanding series of mediate purposes or concerns, and when followed through will end up in a picture of the total purposiveness of the man.

The point is that, however limited and possibly heteronomous the immediate motivation may be, it can become a motivation only on the basis of the concernedness of all life with itself, its performance, its content. Only on this basis can the "feedback" operate in the control of purposive action. Even the appeal to obedience and the widest use of habit must ultimately draw on this fund of spontaneity and interest.

But our second set of hypothetical answers is instructive in a further respect. We assumed that the purpose once removed from the immediate purpose of "keeping on the target" was "carrying out orders." Although this, as we have seen, will itself fall into the pattern of the agent's own overall purposiveness, it points also to somebody else's purpose, which the agent can be said to be carrying out with his action. This need not mean that he has made the commander's purpose his own, but he certainly has made its execution, as far as entrusted to him, his present purpose, and this for purposes of his own, as we observed before.

From the point of view of the commander, however, these purposes of the pilot do not matter at all. All he is interested in is that he can reasonably rely on the agent to execute his orders, for whatever reasons, so that in his own pragmatic account he can substitute for those reasons his own orders as the sole effective determination of the other's behavior. He can do so, of course, only if he knows that the agent's own purposiveness includes the accepting of orders from him —and of such orders as the one given. But once this condition is observed, as it will be by any intelligent commander, he may indeed forget about the other's motives. He then can with some right consider his subordinate for the duration of the action to have abdicated his "person", with the spontaneity of its own purposiveness—and to that extent to have, in effect, *become mechanized* (one of the aims of military training, after all). In other words, the commander can regard the pilot during his mission as his robot, his tool.

Seen in this way the pilot indeed merges with the torpedo into one instrumental entity, and the whole represents a servomechanism. But this means just that the combination so considered is *devoid*—in fact, *has been voided*—of *intrinsic* purposefulness and merely carries the purpose of its user of which even the human co-agent has become a mere executive. And this is the very case of the pilotless, "self-steering" torpedo. The human pilot *can* be replaced by a mechanical device precisely because his own intrinsic purposiveness has been voided anyway and does practically not count in this context; what counts is only the purpose of the commander who, by the "remote control" of his orders, or by the instructions "fed in" at the outset, operates the "machine"—propulsion engine, pilot, and all.

Thus there is indeed a sense in which we can say that a purposive action is being performed by the whole complex, whether with or without a human pilot in its combination. We still remain in agreement with the stated axiom that purposive behavior requires the presence of purpose, if the purpose here present is understood to be that of the commander, that is, a purpose *extrinsic* to the system. In the absence of that, the mechanism, even with identical action, becomes purposeless on this level of consideration—though by being active it inevitably performs the "purpose" intrinsic to all mechanical action, the attainment of entropy; or, if it includes a human element, this will assert its own purposiveness and (perhaps) steer the machine and itself to safety.

IV

The irony that scientists, for so long the very abjurors of anthropomorphism as the sin of sins, are now the most liberal in endowing machines with manlike features, is only dimmed by the fact that the real intent of the liberality is to appropriate the donor, man, all the more securely to the realm of the machine. The mirroring-back takes place under the cover of names. In terms of mere semantics we may say that the whole cybernetical doctrine of teleological behavior is reducible to a confusion of "serving a purpose" with "having purpose"; and more specifically to the confusion of "carrying out a purpose" with having purpose. One naturally tends to say that to carry out a purpose one must have it; and then, that one must have it *while* carrying it out; and then, that one must keep it before himself in the carrying-out. This can be but need not be the case, even when I am my own executive agent. Having once formed my purpose and adopted a standard course of action appropriate to it, I can turn myself into a kind of automaton and go through the required steps routinely and insofar "blindly"—not with respect to their immediate objects but with respect to their overall goal; or I may leave the execution, whole or parceled out, to others who may be entirely ignorant of the purpose though each knowing his assigned object (and perhaps, but not necessarily while doing it, his own purpose in doing "as told"): they are even more "goal-blind," and surely their goals are irrelevant to mine as mine is to theirs; or I can even reduce the steps to such primitive elements that I can dispense with human agents altogether. It is precisely this dissociability of purpose and execution which permits us to delegate the latter so extensively and distributively to others, to whole chains of subagents, and even to machines. The manifest organization of such an action context for a purpose, and its actually realizing it in its outcome, have nothing to say about the presence or absence of purpose among its members or in the system as a whole, however persuasive the behavioral analogy may be for mixing terms and making the imputation. And so an indubitable context of "goal-directed" action need not in the least mean that the agency itself or any part of it has those goals or any goals at all. The evidence for *this* is not the mere performance, and even less the formal applicability of names.—Similar considerations would apply, *mutatis mutandis,* to the cybernetic concepts of "information" and "reasoning," where similar imputations occur under the spell of formalized terms. But semantic confusion does not explain the phenomenon; it serves only to diagnose it.

We come nearer to an understanding if we realize that the cybernetician looks at his objects in a theoretical situation somewhat like the practical situation in which our commander looks at his subordinate—that is, a situation in which indeed the distinction between man and machine is irrelevant and the two become interchangeable. But the commander, although in his handling of the situation he takes the subordinate as a robot, does not take himself to be one—and this in spite of his being well aware that in the action context of his superiors he in turn is to them a robot, instrumental to their purposes —and so on. His knowledge that he is thus viewed from without, and that he is always capable of being thus viewed, does not cast doubt on the knowledge he has of himself from within. Reflecting on this, if he has the time, he will apply the same consideration to his subordinate and grant him that he is, of course, not really a robot.

It is this reflection which the cybernetician fails to perform. He himself does not come under the terms of his doctrine. He considers behavior, except his own; purposiveness, except his own; thinking, except his own. He views from without, withholding from his objects the privileges of his own reflective position. If asked why he embraces cybernetics, he would for once answer not in cybernetical terms of feedback, circular loops, and automatic control, but in terms like these: "because I think it to be true, and I am interested in truth"; or "because I think it to be useful for such and such ends, and I am interested in those ends"; or "because it is the rising fashion, and I like to keep up with the times"; or whatever else may be truthfully or untruthfully answered in such cases.

But if asked why a group of persons other than himself organize a conference on cybernetics, he might answer that there are "many regenerative loops" in the single nervous systems which, in their circular paths, perpetuate signals as "universals," and that "by joining these loops universals can be related" and "thereby the postulates of any . . . theory . . . constructed"; and that if such a "related system of impulses in reverberating circuits . . . gets into a nervous system so as to define the form of its activity [it may] determine the pattern of firing of motor neurons, and so literally, causally and neurologically determine an overt, objective, social and institutional fact."[2] Nothing could be more devastating for this account of theory-forming than to be found self-illustrative. Professor Northrop would be justly indignant were I to suggest that this theory of his has no other logical status than that derivable from the kind of genesis it describes; and were I, in his own case, to substitute the process there propounded for his seeking after and conforming to truth.

We are here, as in so many other cases, in the presence of what I would call split-personality theorizing—a phenomenon unavoidable, and to that extent excusable, in some of the special sciences, but inadmissible and fatal in philosophy, and hardly less so in those sciences that include man among their objects. *In abstracto* the behaviorist must count himself among the objects of his method. But *in*

---

2. To quote F. S. C. Northrop, "The Neurological and Behavioristic Psychological Basis of the Ordering of Society by Means of Ideas," in *Science,* Vol. 107 (April 23, 1948), pp. 411 ff. It is against philosophical transferences of this kind (of which this is merely one example), much more than against the specialistic work of the cyberneticians proper, that the present criticism is directed.

concreto he must make the implicit reservation of self-exemption, at least with regard to his reasoning in support of the behavioristic thesis, for the sake of its claim to validity. Furthermore, expecting his argument to be evaluated on its merits, he must also exempt those to whose judgment it is addressed in scientific discourse, while at the same time considering them as instances of those "other than myself" to whom the method should apply. And he himself is being considered by them with the same duplicity—inside and outside the discourse. If he reflects sufficiently he may even be aware of all this. The same necessary duplicity obtains in the case of the materialistic biologist, the same in the case of the cybernetician. (See Appendix to this Essay.)

These cases need not too much disturb us, since the special sciences, after all, are concerned not with the whole but with isolated aspects which they tackle in their terms at the declared cost of unity. But what are we to say of philosophers who, taking their cue from one or another of the special sciences, cast themselves with the abandon of self-abnegation into the disavowal of the *ego cogitans?*

This is a subject too wide to broach here, sadly as it needs broaching. But in the present case cybernetics cannot be entirely absolved from guilt. It is not the innocent special science which seduces susceptible philosophy by its passive beauty: from its inception it has been out to capture her. From its inception it has pretended to the status of a unified theory of mechanism, organism, the nervous system, society, culture, and mind; and by its suggestive employment of the terms behavior, purpose, goal, information, memory, decision, learning, initiative, value, and thought it has so inflated its initially modest definitions that their resulting use amounts to hardly more than verbal trickery.

V

In conclusion, and for an observation transcending the mere negative criticism with which this essay has had to be filled, let me single out one level—the biological—from all the levels of reality to which cybernetics applies itself. Until corrected on this point by more competent experts, this layman is ready to concede that the sensor-effector combination in animals does in certain respects represent a feedback pattern and, to the extent that it does, conforms to the model evolved by cybernetics. Where, then, does that model fall short?

The answer can be compressed into one statement: living things are creatures of need. Only living things have needs and act on needs. Need is based both on the necessity for the continuous self-renewal of the organism by the metabolic process, and on the organism's elemental urge thus precariously to continue itself. This basic self-concern of all life, in which necessity and will are bound together, manifests itself on the level of animality as appetite, fear, and all the rest of the emotions. The pang of hunger, the passion of the chase, the fury of combat, the anguish of flight, the lure of love—these, and not the data transmitted by the receptors, imbue objects with the character of goals, negative or positive, and make behavior purposive. The mere element of effort lifts bodily activity out of the class of mechanical performance, and the fact that movement requires effort means that an animal will move only under the incentive of an interest.

The cybernetical model reduces animal nature to the two terms of sentience and motility, while in fact it is constituted by the triad of perception, motility, and emotion. Emotion, more basic than the two it binds together, is the animal translation of the fundamental drive which, even on the undifferentiated preanimal level, operates in the ceaseless carrying-on of the metabolism. A feedback mechanism may be going, or may be at rest: in either state the machine exists. The organism has to keep going, because to be going is its very existence —which is revocable—and, threatened with extinction, it is concerned in existing. There is no analogue in the machine to the instinct of self-preservation—only to the latter's antithesis, the final entropy of death.

According to cybernetics, society is a communication network for the transmitting, exchanging, and pooling of information, and it is this that holds it together. No emptier notion of society has ever been propounded. Nothing is said on what the information is about, and why it should be relevant to have it. The scheme allows no room for such a question even to be raised. Any theory of man's sociability, however crude or distorted, that takes into account his being a creature of need and desire, and that looks for the vital concerns which bring men together, is more to the point. Grim old Hobbes showed himself infinitely better informed than the information specialists when he contended that fear of violent death and the need for peace brought men into the covenant of commonwealth and continue to hold the body politic together. One-sided as his doctrine may be, it is valid in that it ascribes man's action to a striving after some good, even if this be the mere preservation of life—nay, even if it be the mere avoidance of supreme evil. Without the concept of good, one cannot even begin to approach the subject of behavior. Whether individual or social, intentional action is directed toward a good. According to some, the scale of lesser and greater goods that can become the objects of desire, and thus motivate behavior, culminates in a highest good, the *summum bonum*. In the case of man this may well be, in a sense very different from that of cybernetics, *in-formation*.

APPENDIX (p. 125)
Materialism, Determinism, and the Mind

Darwinists, behaviorists, cyberneticians, adopt in effect the Cartesian position without its metaphycial cargo. Mental attributes are not denied in themselves, merely kept out of the physical record. In the Darwinian view, e.g., such attributes may be among the "sports" thrown up in the mechanics of organic mutation, but only their behavioral aspect counts in the mechanics of selection, viz., by its differential survival value, and this aspect alone in its given outwardness is treated by science. To state the view more generally: certain animal actions may be, and probably are, accompanied by states of awareness, but these are scientifically irrelevant under the axiom that external actions can be explained on external, i.e., physical terms alone. If the chain of sensory excitation, afferent nerve-conduction, central synapses, efferent conduction, muscular excitation, can be constructed in its unbroken sequence, there is neither need nor room for the interpolation of the mental anywhere as a *link* in the chain, although its secondary occurrence somewhere "along" the chain is granted. Redundant in the dynamic account and not even an observational datum, it does not enter the universe of scientific description. By this economy behaviorism contrives to enjoy the advantages of the Cartesian position without incurring the disadvantages of its dualism. Yet the implied doctrine of the causal redundancy of mind is itself a *metaphysical position* which behaviorism cannot disown.

The metaphysical position is that of materialism, which as a general doctrine of being has to face the metaphysical issue involved in conscious life. It does so with the general formula that what appears as "mind" is a function of body, and wholly unilaterally so, i.e., with no reciprocity. Evidently the formula is not a causal one by the standards of materialism itself—in fact it does not fit at all into the general scheme of quantitative correlation of cause and effect. It is *ad hoc* designed to suit the interests of science, namely, to retain for science the methodological benefits which the preceding dualistic division had secured with the causal closure of the material realm, and at the same time to make the mind-generating role now assigned to matter so peripheral for matter itself that its former concept is left practically unimpaired. This technical purpose is served by the theory of mind as an "epiphenomenon," i.e., its being a byplay of particular material processes in particular material systems (brains), which systems behave in those processes entirely in accordance with the deterministic laws of matter.

The relevant aspect of "epiphenomenalism" lies in its implied negative statements. Its overt, affirmative thesis, that matter is responsible for mind, is proffered without any attempt to show how such a performance can be related to the known properties of matter.[1] It is nothing more than an assertion of the occult. But negatively the concept of the epiphenomenon does say something more. It is meant to denote an effect which, unlike all other effects in nature, does not consume the energy of its cause; it is not a transformation and continuation of such energy, and therefore, again unlike all other effects, it cannot become a cause itself. It is powerless in the absolute sense, a dead-end alley off the highway of causality, past which the traffic of cause and effect rolls as if it were not there at all. Even to call mind an "iridescence" on the material substratum would be too much, since in exchange for the appearance of an iridescence in the physical sense some quantity present in the preceding physical transaction will have disappeared, and again another will replace it on its disappearing in turn (and these successive replacements will be found to be quantitatively equivalent), whereas no equivalent is deemed missing from the material account with the appearance of the epiphenomenon. Thus the closed system of material causality is safeguarded as effectively as in Cartesian dualism, and yet mind has been made, by the stratagem of unilateral dependence, a part of that nature which cannot tolerate its interference. But epiphenomenalism itself, apart from the grandiose point-

---

1. E. Du Bois-Reymond included this problem among those on which he pronounced his famous *"ignorabimus"* (*Über die Grenzen der Naturerkenntnis*, 1872). Although at the time it provoked violent protests, most thoughtful scientists today will probably share his view.

lessness in which nature would have indulged with the luxury of consciousness, involves difficulties and even absurdities which seem too heavy
a price for the scientific convenience for whose sake it was devised.

One point easily overlooked is that a "matter" called upon to account
for spirit is no longer the same matter that science took over in the
dualistic expurgation. Materialism inherited the estate of dualism without
being fully aware that the left-over to which it succeeded carried an
obligation which it could never hope to discharge from its own resources:
the obligation to support theoretically those phenomena too that had
formerly been taken care of by the vanished half of dualism's estate. This
task had inescapably devolved upon materialism once it established itself,
on its part-domain, as a self-sufficient monism. Its bequest was the secret
revenge for one of the greatest usurpations in the history of thought.
Actually, materialism cannot, by the law of its birth, ever attain to the
legitimate status of monism. For it represents but one side, taken in
isolation, of a dualism which had first torn asunder an earlier unity.
Materialism continues *logically* to presuppose transcendental dualism, for
only by having unavowedly in the background the "other world" of dualism can materialism *in its own field* afford to disregard the spiritual
evidence and to interpret reality, as far as it deals with it, in terms of pure
matter. Plain materialism, therefore, lived by this implied carry-over from
dualism, and its lease on life expired with the renouncing of the spiritual
complement: deprived of the dualistic shelter, lonesome "matter" must
now account for mind and thereby loses the unambigous nature of "mere
matter" as once conceived. In other words, its concept is, by this very
demand upon it, already reabsorbed into a concept of substance that
transcends the aspect which materialism isolated under the name of matter; and this in effect reopens the issue of ontology which materialism
claims to have settled. The glib formula of epiphenomenalism betrays this
very fact by trying to hide it.

Apart from the ontological difficulty, there is a logical absurdity involved in epiphenomenalism in that it denies itself the status of an argument by depriving any argument of that status. The present argument, no
less than that against which it argues, is by this view the epiphenomenon
of physical occurrences determined by necessities of sequence entirely
foreign to "meaning" and "truth." The only possible reference which the
epiphenomenon may have to truth is the accidental agreement of its
symbols with facts other than the cerebral facts carrying it, but there is no
way on the part of those engaged in the argument, marionettes as they are
to those necessities, to evaluate the issue on its merits, and thereby to
decide between two alternatives, equal as they are in the factuality of their

physical occurrence. Thus materialist monism, while ensuring to the *res extensa* the methodological fitness for science it had acquired in Cartesian dualism, avoids the latter's psychophysical impasse only at the price of destroying any possible understanding of mind, even by destroying the very idea of mind; and at the same time, as we have seen, it adulterates the clean concept of matter by charging it with an occult faculty, that of generating the "epiphenomenon."

But let us concede at least one virtue of "epiphenomenalism": it does away with the preposterous concept of intra-mental determinism and puts determinism back where it belongs, i.e., where alone it makes sense—in the realm of matter. For the causal principle underlying scientific determinism is by no means satisfied with the trite proposition that every event has its cause and in turn causes something else (which simply means that the existence or happening of anything makes a difference to what comes next, or: that presence and absence of entities are consequential for the progress of event), but in addition to the principle of "sufficient reason" it requires the principle of "quantitative equivalence" between cause and effect, which in turn requires assignability of quantity to defined items, which in turn requires measurability—and this requires a whole set of further conditions: that the items are severally identifiable, with a separate identity to each through time; which requires that they are isolable and each distinguishable from its contemporaries; which requires that they are external to each other—and this they can be only if distributed in an extended continuum with simultaneous dimensions that provide for discrete location (multiple co-presence) as well as for magnitude to be measured; and the extension must be homogeneous for measurement to be uniform, and transfer of location must permit traceable intersections of paths. In short: *space,* which alone fulfills these requirements, is the indispensable condition for verifiable, i.e., computational, causal law (whose test is prediction); and apart from this condition, the principle of "sufficient reason" has a different meaning altogether which offers no hold for the construction of a deterministic scheme and no evidential data for its verification. (A noncommittal blank form of determinism can, of course, always be held by way of metaphysical conviction, or religious faith, or general mood, or plain superstition.)

Yet the will-o'-the-wisp of a *science* of intramental determinism has been chased ever since the scientific idea of causal rule began to bestride the stage of knowledge. From the beginning it was natural for the *mathematical* ideal of knowledge, once Descartes had promoted it to a universal norm, to urge its own application to every field of objects, therefore also to objects of the internal sense—though by rights the dualistic division would exempt the mathematician himself, as a mind and thus not a *res extensa*, from the claim of his method. But Cartesian dualism, unlike any previous dualism, intrinsically tended to fit and to serve the cause of the *res extensa* more than that of the *res cogitans*, and there was no particular resistance against the former's invading the latter with its standards of knowledge if the success of mathematical method promised to repeat itself there. Descartes had held out that promise, but some instinct or prudence restrained him from putting it to the test. (His *Passions de l'âme* is anything but a mathematics of the soul.) Spinoza's was the only radical attempt in that direction, and here the obvious incongruity of the *more geometrico* method was enough to refer mathematics back to its cognate field of objects: the attempt was not repeated.

But if not mathematics, at least the *causal* principle seemed to apply to psychological no less than to physical sequences, for the cause-effect relation (going by the mere definition of the concepts) seems prima facie only to describe a time sequence and not by itself to involve space. Why, then, should not the time sequences of the inner world, provided they have their *own* dynamics and do not simply reflect those of another field, also conform to the universal rule? And determination in fact, of course, renders its subject determinable in knowledge. Thus there should be possible an "analytics" (factor analysis) of inner phenomena analogous to that of bodies, and eventually a general dynamics of the mental field yielding a predictive calculus—in its pattern of antecedent and consequent no less exclusive of "final causes" than that obtaining in the time dimension of external intuition.

It is a testimony to the irrational force of rational faith that no amount of failure to execute this program has ever discouraged its devotees. What is their claim? Something like this. Given (e.g.) a number of "motives" A, B, C . . . at time t_1, the "strongest" will decide what the person will decide at t_2. (It is a question of detail whether "the strongest" *one,* by an either-or rule, emerges as the sole determinant, or whether *all* of them contribute as "components" to the ensuing "resultant" according to their relative strengths, or whether—somewhere in-between—a preponderant and fusible combination carries the day.) "Motive" comprises whatever is a factor in the situation: immediate emotional drives, short and long term expectations, rational evaluations, beliefs, social indoctrination, dispositions, habits, memories, moods . . . Now how do I measure, item by item, the absolute and relative "force" of these? Answer: by the outcome. *Since* such and such is the mental state now, motive A (or combination A+B . . .) *must have been* the strongest, for *why else* should situation t_1 have resolved itself as found at t_2? This circular argument, which affords triumphant *vaticinia ex eventu,* is in the last analysis the whole logical arsenal of psychological determinism, which assigns quantitative values in retrospect. A motive is "overwhelming," not because it predictably *will* overwhelm its rivals by a measurable excess of force, but because it can be depicted, in the light of a subsequent state, as *having* overwhelmed them: I really speak of this later state when I endow what prevails there with a magnitude in "its" past that would account for its prevailing now—a pseudo-explanation if ever there was one. For there is no reversal of the way, viz., independent and separate measurement first, confirmation of the predictive calculus later. Thus the model of forces and relative magnitudes is here not a working tool but a pious or prestigious ornament.

In all these efforts, undertaken under the hypnotism of natural science, it was strangely overlooked that (as indicated before) the scientific concept of causality is inseparably bound up with spatiality: in space, entities are isolable; by reference to its coordinates they can be measured and positionally identified; by means of this reference, velocity and acceleration can be determined, and in this way "effect" can be *quantitatively* correlated with "cause." A geometrical illustration is the parallelogram of forces, whose construction requires a minimum number of dimensions— no less than two, besides time. Thus when the causal scheme is transferred to the "inner world," the simple fact is overlooked that the idea of efficient causation in its quantitative aspect (which is the decisive one) refers to conditions of representation and verification that obtain in the *res extensa* only, and is therefore not really dissociable from the possibility of mathematical analysis. It makes sense only where motion in space is involved.[2] "Time" alone, the form of order of the internal mani-

---

2. A characteristic fact is the wavering of Kant in this matter. On the one hand, he was aware, indeed emphasized, that to apply the categories (among them "cause-effect") to objects "we need *outer* intuitions" (*äussere Anschauungen*), i.e., space: *Critique of Pure Reason,* 2nd ed., pp. 291 ff. Yet in the Third Antinomy and its solution, the rule of causality clearly extends to the events of inwardness *as phenomena,* i.e. to psychology: *ibid.,* pp. 560 ff. The wavering is due to an ambiguity in Kant's argument: as "conditions of possible experience," the categories must fit *every* object *qua* phenomenon, for to be this is to be so constituted by the transcendental unity of apperception as to be fit *for* the categories. But in the concrete development of the argument it becomes clear that it holds good only where the "form of external intuition," i.e., space, is involved and not for objects of the internal sense. And so Kant must assert psychological determinism and then again, by implication, deny it. The reason for the ambiguity can be traced to Kant's insistence on treating the

fold, is not a dimension in which to construct causal sequences: there is more than one coordinate required for such construction. Consequently, the naïve transfer of "cause" from its native to a foreign field resulted in a ludicrous concept of psychological determinism in which "motives" were treated, not as elements of meaning in a context of meaning, but like causes of ascertainable size and vector magnitude in an extended continuum, and the age-old problem of free will degenerated into a sorry ontological misunderstanding.

But finally, with the rise of materialist monism, the whole problem of psychological determinism could safely be dropped into the lap of omnipotent matter, where it ceased to be psychological. It is the one merit of "epiphenomenalism" to defer to the truth that determinism in its scientific sense can only mean a description of matter and has no possible application outside it. Thus *if* there is to be total determination (but nobody, of course, has ever shown that there is), then let there be total materialism (which indeed somehow looms behind Spinoza's deterministic "parallelism"): then "mind" *can* be only an epiphenomenon of matter, with no causality of its own—neither external nor even internal. At its own heavy price, therefore, the "epiphenomenalist" explanation relieves its proponents from the impossible task set by intramental determinism, viz., to fashion the flow of consciousness into a causal system—because it no longer matters: as a specious byplay of what is certainly determined by mechanical cause alone, purpose becomes in any case a mere illusion. Yet its utter redundancy for the chain of events renders its gratuitous presence a puzzle more vexing than any posed by dualism, and incidentally affords a rather Mephistophelian commentary on the adage that nature does nothing in vain. In fact, the concession of this redundancy, which is nothing less than a charge of fraud, serenely casts nature in the role of that "deceiving demon" from whose unsettling idea Descartes sought sanctuary in the veracity of a benevolent God.

Mechanistic matter raised to monistic omnipotence *is* the deceiving demon whom Descartes (the early champion of that matter) strove to avoid.[3] The science of life pays homage to his rule. As part of the history

---

inner world as one of sensuous "phenomena" (appearances) on a par with those of the outer world, denying self-consciousness a privileged status: this again can be traced to his treating *time* as a mere "form of intuition" on a par with space, instead of as an ultimate reality.

3. Descartes himself says so in the *First Meditation:* "There may be those who would deny the existence of any such powerful god rather than believe all other things to be uncertain. We need not quarrel with them and may grant that all this about a god [with the power to deceive] is a

of life's quest to know itself, materialistic biology, its arsenal newly strengthened by cybernetics, is an attempt to apprehend life by eliminating that which affords the possibility of the attempt itself—the authentic nature of awareness and purpose. The attempt, therefore, in disowning itself as evidence of its subject matter, contradicts itself with the kind of understanding it achieves of its subject matter. In eliminating itself from the account, it makes the account incomplete, yet does not tolerate a completion that would transcend the self-sufficiency of its principle, in virtue of which the account is closed in itself. Thus the attempt not only leaves itself unaccounted for, and unintelligible by its own terms: even more, with the epiphenomenalist depreciation of inwardness, it invalidates its own finding by denying to thinking a basis of possible validity in an entity already completely determined in terms of the thoughtless. It is the Cretan declaring all Cretans to be liars.

---

fiction: if, instead, it is by fate, or chance, or the continuous series of antecedents, or in whatever other way, that they suppose me to have become what I am—it would hold that, since to err and deceive oneself is a defect, the probability of my being so imperfect as to deceive myself always will be the greater, the less powerful the cause of my being is assumed to be." In other words: blind nature can perfectly fill the place of the divine arch deceiver.

The Nobility of Sight:
A Study in the Phenomenology
of the Senses

Since the days of Greek philosophy sight has been hailed as the most excellent of the senses. The noblest activity of the mind, *theoria,* is described in metaphors mostly taken from the visual sphere. Plato, and Western philosophy after him, speaks of the "eye of the soul" and of the "light of reason." Aristotle, in the first lines of the *Metaphysics,* relates the desire for knowledge inherent in the nature of all men to the common delight in perception, most of all in vision. Yet neither he nor any other of the Greek thinkers, in the brief treatments of sight itself which we have, seems to have really explained by what properties sight qualifies for these supreme philosophical honors.[1] Nor have the different virtues of the several senses been properly compared and assessed. Sight, in addition to furnishing the analogues for the intellectual upperstructure, has tended to serve as the model of perception in general and thus as the measure of the other senses. But it is in fact a very special sense. It is incomplete by itself; it requires the complement of other senses and functions for its cogni-

---

1. Aristotle in the same passage sums up the virtues of vision by stating that it is the sense yielding the most knowledge and excelling in differentiation (*Met.A,* 980 a 25); and he emphasizes that we enjoy vision for its own sake, apart from its utility. This evaluation merely hints at the qualities which elevate sight over the other senses.

tive office; its highest virtues are also its essential insufficiencies. Its very nobility calls for the support of more vulgar modes of commerce with the importunity of things. In this sense, in which all eminence pays for itself the price of increased dependence, the "nobility of sight" will be considered in the following discussion. As one of its results, we shall find the ancient claims for sight substantiated and at the same time qualified.

The unique distinction of sight consists in what we may provisionally call the *image*-performance, where "image" implies these three characteristics: (1) *simultaneity* in the presentation of a manifold, (2) *neutralization* of the causality of sense-affection, (3) *distance* in the spatial and mental senses. In considering these three characteristics we may hope to contribute not only to the phenomenology of the senses by themselves but also to the evaluation of their role in the higher mental performances based upon them in the case of man.

1. THE SIMULTANEITY OF IMAGE OR THE TIME-ASPECT OF SEEING

Sight is *par excellence* the sense of the simultaneous or the coordinated, and thereby of the extensive. A view comprehends many things juxtaposed, as co-existent parts of one field of vision. It does so in an instant: as in a flash one glance, an opening of the eyes, discloses a world of co-present qualities spread out in space, ranged in depth, continuing into indefinite distance, suggesting, if any direction in their static order, then by their perspective a direction away from the subject rather than toward it. The theme of depth will engage us later under the head of "distance." Sight is unique already in beholding a co-temporaneous manifold as such, which may be at rest. All other senses construct their perceptual "unities of a manifold" out of a temporal sequence of sensations which are in themselves time-bound and nonspatial. Their synthesis therefore, ever unfinished and depending on memory, must move along with the actual progress of the sensations, each of which fills the now of the sense from moment to moment with its own fugitive quality. Any present quality is just a point of passage in the transition from the preceding to the subsequent one, none is closed in itself, and only one is there at a time. Thus the content is never simultaneously present as a whole, but always in the making, always partial and incomplete. These more

temporal senses therefore never achieve for their object that detachment of its *modus essendi* from their own, e.g., of persistent existence
from the transitory event of sense-affection, which sight at any
moment offers in the presentation of a complete visual field. We may
illustrate the difference by the cases of hearing and touch, the two
senses which in certain respects deserve particular comparison with
sight.

a. Hearing

The case of hearing is obvious: according to the nature of sound as
such it can "give" only dynamic and never static reality. The wholes
which it achieves by the synthesis of its manifold are strictly temporal
ones, and their objective time-measure is identical with the time of
the sense-activation itself: the duration of the sound heard is just the
duration of hearing it. Extension of object and extension of its perception thus coincide. What the sound immediately discloses is not an
object but a dynamical event at the locus of the object, and thereby
mediately the state the object is in at the moment of that occurrence.
The rustling of an animal in the leaves, the footsteps of men, the
noise of a passing car, betray the presence of those things by something they do. The immediate object of hearing is the sounds themselves, and then these indicate something else, viz., the actions producing those sounds; and only in the third place does the experience
of hearing reveal the agent as an entity whose existence is independent of the noise it makes. I can say that I hear a dog, but what I hear
is his bark, a sound recognized as the bark of a dog, and thereby I
hear the dog barking, and thereby I perceive the dog himself in a
certain way. But this way of perceiving him arises and ceases with his
act of barking. By itself it does not reveal anything beyond it, and
that there is an agent preceding and outlasting the acoustic act I know
from information other than the acoustic one. The object-reference of
sounds is not provided by the sounds as such, and it transcends the
performance of mere hearing. All indications of existents, of enduring
things beyond the sound-events themselves, are extraneous to their
own nature.

On the other hand, precisely because of this looseness of external
object reference and thus of representative function, sound is eminently suited to constitute its own, immanent "objectivity" of acoustic

values as such—and thus, free from other-representative duty, to represent just itself. In hearing music, our synthesis of a manifold to a unity of perception refers not to an object other than the sensory contents but to their own order and interconnection. Since this synthesis deals with succeeding data and is spread over the length of their procession, so that at the presence of any one element of the series all the others are either no more or not yet, and the present one must disappear for the next one to appear, the synthesis itself is a temporal process achieved with the help of memory. Through it and certain anticipations, the whole sequence, though at each moment only atomically realized in one of its elements, is bound together into one comprehensive unity of experience. The acoustic "object" thus created is a time-object that lasts just as long as the act of its synthesis lasts, that is, as the sequence of hearing itself does (or its recreation in fantasy), with whose progress the "object" part for part coincides. It has no other dimension than that of time.

It is true that hearing, though wholly governed by succession, knows also juxtaposition of simultaneous acoustic content—witness polyphony in music, or the separable voice strands in the vocal babel of a cocktail party. One may even speak of a kind of inner-acoustic "space" in which a manifold can coexist. But this is a metaphor. The "coexistence" is always one of common procession in time, i.e., of strands of movement and change; and their distinction requires qualitative difference (in pitch, timbre, etc.) whose continuation in the sequence lets "strands" be identified: two notes of identical quality sounded together simply reinforce each other and make one (except for the "stereo" effect from the spacing of their sources), whereas real space is a principle of co-temporaneous, discrete plurality irrespective of qualitative difference. Also the "identity" of the single strands in a polyphony, and thus the conservation of discrete simultaneity through time, is a function of certain figural coherences (such, e.g., as make a tune) which come under the "Gestalt" principle and thus make the juxtaposition of plurality not a primary datum of the *now* but a feat of ongoing organization—i.e., a product itself of process. Even so the limits for a simultaneous manifold allowing integrity to its members are narrow in the world of sounds: a strong sound drowns its weaker contemporaries; to relate more than a few at a time to different source-loci in space becomes difficult, and beyond a limited number any multiplicity of sounds merges into a compound noise. There is no "keeping to one's place" in the community of acoustic individuals. The simple fact is that sounds are dynamic events, not just static qualities, and thus trespassers by nature.

This brings us to what is perhaps the most important feature to be considered in our comparison of hearing with seeing: sound, itself a dynamic fact, intrudes upon a passive subject. For the sensation of hearing to come about the percipient is entirely dependent on something happening outside his control, and in hearing he is exposed to its happening. All he can contribute to the situation is a state of attentive readiness for sounds to occur (except where he produces them himself). He cannot let his ears wander, as his eyes do, over a field of possible percepts, already present as a material for his attention, and focus them on the object chosen, but he has simply to wait for a sound to strike them: he has no choice in the matter. In hearing, the percipient is at the mercy of environmental action, which intrudes upon his sensibility without his asking and by mere intensity decides for him which of several qualities distinguishable at the moment is to be the dominant impression. The strongest sound may not be the vitally most important one in a situation, but it simply seizes the attention from among the competing ones. Against this the freedom of selective attention is extremely limited.

In view of these characteristics we understand why for our ears we have nothing corresponding to the lids of our eyes. One does not know when a sound may occur: when it occurs it gives notice of an event in the environment and not merely of its permanent existence: and since an event, i.e., a change in the environment, may always be of vital import, ears have to be open always for this contingency. To have them closed could be fatal, just as it would be useless to open them at arbitrarily chosen moments. With all the initiative left to the outer world, the contingency aspect of hearing is entirely one-sided and requires therefore continual readiness for perception. The deepest reason for this basic contingency in the sense of hearing is the fact that it is related to event and not to existence, to becoming and not to being. Thus hearing, bound to succession and not presenting a simultaneous coordinated manifold of objects, falls short of sight in respect of the freedom which it confers upon its possessor.

b. Touch

The case is different with touch, though it shares with hearing the successiveness of apprehension, while it shares with vision the synthesis of its data into a static presence of objects. A proper analysis of touch is probably the most difficult in the phenomenology of sense-perception, because it is the least specialized and in its physiology and achievements the most compound of the senses. In fact, "touch" serves as a blanket label for a very complex set of functions. The most elementary level in this complexity is the contact-sensation in which the presence of a contiguous body is felt at the point of incidence. I leave for later consideration the important fact that the contact-situation always involves pressure and therefore a modicum of force as part of the experience. Here we deal as far as possible with the mere qualities sensed. The first observation to be made then is that *shape* is not an original datum of touch, but a construct which emerges additively from a serial multiplicity of single or continuously blending touch sensations, and this in conjunction only with proprioceptive motor sensations. The single touch-sensation confined to the point of contact and without correlation to more of its own kind is rather barren of information. Already the simple tactile qualities, such as soft and hard, and even more so rough and smooth, are not really an instantaneous experience but require a series of changing sensations obtained by pressure and by friction, i.e., generally speaking by movement. Thus in their very constitution, a synthesis on the part of the percipient is involved, extending over the time-span of the series and, by a short-term retention, unifying its elements into one impression. Touch and hearing agree in this respect: that their primary objects, the qualities sensed, have process character and are thus essentially time-entities. (This observation, incidentally, disposes of the rather sterile question whether all sentient life is endowed with memory. In the form of immediate short-term retention, memory enters into the very consitution of sensibility, and is thus coeval with it.) But in hearing, the process is purely passive, while in touching it involves bodily activity.

For the tactile situation moves to a higher level when the sentient body itself becomes the voluntary agent of that movement which is required for the acquisition of this serial sequence of impressions.

Then touch passes over from suffering to acting: its progress comes under the control of the percipient, and it may be continued and varied with a view to fuller information. Thus mere touch-impression changes into the act of feeling. There is a basic difference between simply having a tactile encounter and *feeling* another *body*. The former may be said to be the atomic element in the more complex totality of the latter, but this totality is more than the mere additive result of such atomic touch-sensations. The *motor* element introduces an essentially new quality into the picture: its active employment discloses spatial characteristics in the touch-object which were no inherent part of the elementary tactile qualities. Through the kinesthetic accompaniment of voluntary motion the whole perception is raised to a higher order: the touch-qualities become arranged in a spatial scheme, they fall into the pattern of *surface,* and become elements of *form.* This is a synthesis of a higher order, superimposed on that already operative in the constitution of the simple sense-qualities, which integrate their own time-series of atomic contact-sensations but now enter as material into the larger unit of spatial order. In this order the manifold concresces into a shape. The higher order of synthesis means also a larger time-span for its performance, and thus involves more of the memory inherent in all perception. But what in hearing results in a time-object, in touch results in the copresence of a space-object: the data successively registered are entered into a matrix of static simultaneity.

An organ for real shape-feeling exists probably only in the human hand, and there is more than mere coincidence in the fact that in his hand man possesses a tactile organ which can take over some of the distinctive achievements of his eye. There is a mental side to the highest performance of the tactile sense, or rather to the use which is made of its information, that transcends all mere sentience, and it is this mental use which brings touch within the dimension of the achievements of sight. Briefly, it is the image-faculty, in classical terms: *imaginatio, phantasia,* which makes that use of the data of touch. Only a creature that has the visual faculty characteristic of man can also vicariously "see" by touch. The level of form-perception at the command of a creature will be essentially the same for both senses, incommensurable as they are in terms of their proper sensible qualities. Blind men can "see" by means of their hands, not because they are devoid of eyes but because they are beings endowed with the general faculty of "vision" and only happen to be deprived of the primary organ of sight.

c. Comparison with sight

We are engaged in showing the unique position of sight with respect to simultaneity of presentation, the thesis being that all the other senses operate on the basis of time-series in the presentation of their qualities. Hearing, so we found, stays entirely within this dimension in that the results of its synthesis, the extensive acoustic objects (such as a tune), retain the successiveness of elements which the succession of experience itself originally possessed. Melody not only is generated by sequence, it *is* a sequence. The time-measure is an essential aspect in the content of the sound-experience. A visual value, the presence of a color, may have a long or short duration: this may make a difference to the percipient for reasons of his own, but it does not make any difference to the experience-content itself. This color-quality has no intrinsic reference to time. With touch we found that already the single "atomic" sensation includes a time-element as part of the sense-content itself, the time without which such a quality as rough cannot be "generated" for experience and in which alone it presents itself; and moreover we found the composite tactile objectivity to emerge from a successive synthesis of such sensations. But the result of the synthesis itself, in the case of surface- and shape-perception, represents a spatial and not a temporal entity, and we have here presentation of simultaneity through successiveness.

In this presentation the original time-order of the atomic sensations becomes irrelevant and has no voice in the synthesized content now "present." It was merely the accidental order of the acquisition of data, which could be *ad libitum* changed and still procure the same result, whereas in hearing the order of the acquisition of data is the order of the object itself.

Thus it would seem that the three cases can be distinguished in this formula: Hearing—presentation of sequence through sequence; touch —presentation of simultaneity through sequence; sight—presentation of simultaneity through simultaneity.

According to this formula sight retains its unique position even in relation to the most developed case of tactile performance. We may take it that the achievement is at its best in the case of blind people who have learned to glean full information about shape and spatial situation of objects from the tactile data which they collect through their own activity. Yet even the densest distribution of the point-determinants collected and correlated in the course of extensive scanning by touch still leaves areas to be supplied by imagination. Knowledge of the complete form emerges progressively in this series of partial delimitations, and from a certain stage onward it is for all practical purposes "complete." How complete it can be is testified by the work of blind portrait sculptors. But this completeness is the product of an elaborate synthesis of many single perceptions, integrated into the one simultaneous form in whose presentness to the imagination the time sequence of its building-up is forgotten.[2] Thus we have here to distinguish what in the case of sight is identical, namely, the feat of the sense itself and the feat of the image-presentation *on the basis* of this sense-performance. The second is strictly speaking no longer a matter of touch but a kind of seeing by means of the heterogeneous material of touch. But however many data may be registered in succession and entered into the plane of simultaneous presentation, they can never fill a horizon such as is disclosed to one glance of the eyes. There are bound to remain blank spaces in between and an unrealized horizon in depth beyond the proximity of the actually contacted resistant objects.

d. Seeing and time

With sight, all I have to do is open my eyes, and the world is there, as it was all the time. We have shown that the case is different with hearing; and touch has to go out and seek the objects in bodily motion and through bodily contact, and this narrows down the actual object-relation to one particular instance: the realized relation is committed by the previous choice in which it originated, whereas in sight selection by focusing proceeds noncommittally within the field which the total vision presents and in which all the elements are simultaneously available. The particular focus impairs nothing of this simultaneous presentness. It has not committed freedom to this one choice at

---

2. Cf. the excellent analysis, by Pierre Villey, a blind author, in *The World of the Blind: A Psychological Study,* trans. by Alys Hallard (London: Duckworth, 1930), pp. 187 f.

the expense of all the other possible ones, which remain at its instantaneous disposal without involving the kind of action that would change the situation obtaining between the subject and its vis-à-vis, the environment. Only the simultaneity of image allows the beholder to compare and interrelate: it not only offers many things at once, but offers them in their mutual proportion, and thus objectivity emerges preeminently from sight.

As regards the time-aspect as such, the simultaneity of sight is not only of practical advantage, in that it saves the time needed to collect the manifold data successively, but it introduces the beholder to a whole time-dimension otherwise not disclosed to him, namely, the *present* as something more than the point-experience of the passing *now*. In the case of every other sense, no instant is closed in itself, and no instantaneous datum tells its story. Sensation has to go on, to follow up the beginnings made in the evanescing antecedent, datum has to follow upon datum to let the larger units of experience in process emerge. Sound exists in sequence, every *now* of it vanishing into the past while it goes on: to arrest this flow and "view" a momentary "slice" of it would mean to have not a snapshot but an atomic fragment of it, and strictly speaking nothing at all. Transience is thus of the very essence of the *now* of hearing, and "present" is here a mere following in the stream of onmoving process. The situation is similar with touch, only that here the sequence is one more of active performance than of mere incoming data. In neither case is there a static present; to put it in Platonic terms, they are senses not of being but of becoming. Only the simultaneous representation of the visual field gives us co-existence as such, i.e., the co-presence of things in one being which embraces them all as their common present. The present, instead of being a pointlike experience, becomes a *dimension* within which things can be beheld at once and can be related to each other by the wandering glance of attention. This scanning, though proceeding *in* time, articulates only what was present to the first glance and what stays unchanged while being scanned. The time thus taken in taking-in the view is not experienced as the passing away of contents before new ones in the flux of event, but as a lasting of the same, an identity which is the extension of the instantaneous *now* and therefore unmoved, continued present—so long as no change occurs in the objects themselves. When it does, then time starts rolling visually. Indeed only the simultaneity of sight, with its extended "present" of enduring objects, allows the distinction between change and the unchanging and therefore between becoming and being. All the other senses operate by registering change and cannot make that distinction. Only sight therefore provides the sensual basis on which the mind may conceive the idea of the eternal, that which never changes and is always present. The very contrast between eternity and temporality rests upon an idealization of "present" experienced visually as the holder of stable contents as against the fleeting succession of nonvisual sensation. In the visual presence of objects the beholder may come to rest and possess an extended *now*.

Over these wider issues we must not forget the immense advantage which an instantaneous survey of the whole field of possible encounters represents in the biological situation. In the simultaneous field of vision a coordinated manifold, as yet outside active communication with me, offers itself to my selection for *possible* action. In this connection simultaneity means selectivity, and is thus a major factor in the higher freedom of the self-moving animal.

2. DYNAMIC NEUTRALIZATION

The freedom of choice just mentioned is dependent not only on the simultaneity of presence but at the same time on the fact that in seeing I am not yet engaged by the seen object. I may choose to enter into intercourse with it, but it can appear without the fact of its appearance already involving intercourse. By my seeing it, no issue of my possible relations with it is prejudged. Neither I nor the object has so far done anything to determine the mutual situation. It lets me be as I let it be. In this respect sight differs decisively from touch and hearing. The obtaining of the touch-experience itself is nothing but the entering into actual intercourse with the object: i.e., the very coming into play of this sense already changes the situation obtaining between me and the object. A fuller information then involves further such changes, each of which affects the object and my body at once and so is itself already a phase in my practical commerce with the object, for which on the other hand my sense-information is meant to prepare me. We therefore do not have in touch that clear separation between the theoretical function of information and the practical conduct, freely based on it, that we have in vision. Here again we have in the very constitution of a sense and its physical conditions the organic root of a highly spiritual distinction on the human level: that between theory and practice. While in touch subject and object are already doing something to each other in the very act in which the object becomes a phenomenal presence, the presence of the visual manifold leaves me still entirely free as to actual commerce, as I see without doing and without the object's doing anything.

In hearing, it is true, there is also no doing on my part, but all the more on the part of the object. Things are not by their own nature audible as they are visible; it does not belong to their mere being to emit sound as it belongs to them to reflect light. I can therefore not choose to hear something, but have to wait till something happens to a part of my environment to make it sound, and this sound will strike me whether I choose or not. And since it is an event of which sound informs me and not merely the existence of things in their total configuration, my choice of action is determined for me by the acoustic information. Something is going on in my surroundings, so hearing informs me, and I have to respond to that change, which affects me as an interested party not free to contemplate: I have to strain myself toward what may come next from that quarter, to which I am now bound in a dynamical situation.[3]

Now, it is the complete absence of such a dynamical situation, of any intrusion of causality into the relation, which distinguishes sight. I have to do nothing but to look, and the object is not affected by that: and once there is light, the object has only to be there to be visible, and I am not affected by that: and yet it is apprehended in its self-containment from out of my own self-containment, it is present to me without drawing me into its presence. Whatever dynamic commerce there is in physical fact between source of light, illuminated object, and perceiving eye, this context forms no part of the phenomenal result. This complete neutralization of dynamic content in the visual object, the expurgation of all traces of causal activity from its presentation, is one of the major accomplishments of what we call the

---

3. This is not even considering the fact that sound may be specifically *addressed* to me—that its uttering, in outcry, growl, or speech, is meant for my heeding: in this case, communicative intent reinforces the dynamical claim peculiar to the acoustic situation as such. (Visual signs have not this intrinsic, or natural, power to enforce attention, but only acquire some of it through symbolic convention.)

image-function of sight, and it results in a subtle balance of gain and loss in the cognitive economy of man, the pre-eminently seeing creature.

The gain is the concept of objectivity, of the thing as it is in itself as distinct from the thing as it affects me, and from this distinction arises the whole idea of *theoria* and theoretical truth. Furthermore, the image is handed over to imagination, which can deal with it in complete detachment from the actual presence of the original object: this detachability of the image, i.e., of "form" from its "matter," of "essence" from "existence," is at the bottom of abstraction and therefore of all free thought. In imagination the image can be varied at will. This is also the case with sound, it is true, of which "imagination" can compose a freely created world of its own: but this has no reference to the world of things and therefore no cognitive function, whereas even the freest exercise of visual imagination retains this reference and may reveal properties or possibilities of the external world, as the case of geometry shows. Only the peculiar causal "indifference" of visual presence provides the material and engenders the attitude for these mental feats.

The loss, on the other hand, consists in the very feature which makes these higher developments possible, namely, the elimination of the causal connection from the visual account. The pure form-presentation which vision affords does not betray its own causal genesis, and it suppresses with it every causal aspect in its objects, since their self-containedness vis-à-vis the observer becomes at the same time a mutual self-containedness among themselves. No force-experience, no character of impulse and transitive causality, enters into the nature of image, and thus any edifice of concepts built on that evidence alone must show the gap in the interconnection of objects which Hume has noted. This means only that we have to integrate the evidence of sight with evidence of another kind which in the exclusiveness of *"theoria"* is all too often forgotten.

Let us consider more closely this causal detachment by which sight is the freest and at the same time the least "realistic" of the senses. Reality is primarily evidenced in resistance which is an ingredient in touch-experience. For physical contact is more than geometrical contiguity: it involves impact. In other words, touch is the sense, and the only sense, in which the perception of quality is normally blended with the experience of force, which being reciprocal does not let the

subject be passive; thus touch is the sense in which the original encounter with reality as reality takes place. Touch brings the reality of
its object within the experience of sense in virtue of that by which it
exceeds mere sense, viz., the force-component in its original make-up.
The percipient on his part can magnify this component by his voluntary counteraction against the affecting object. For this reason touch
is the true test of reality: I can dispel every suspicion of illusion by
grasping the doubtful object and trying its reality in terms of the
resistance it offers to my efforts to displace it. Differently expressed,
external reality is disclosed in the same act and as one with the
disclosure of my own reality—which occurs in self-action: in feeling
my own reality by some sort of *effort* I make, I feel the reality of the
world. And I make an effort in the encounter with something other
than myself.

The effortlessness of sight is a privilege which, with the toil, fore-
goes also the reward of the lower sense. Seeing requires no perceptible activity either on the part of the object or on that of the subject.
Neither invades the sphere of the other: they let each other be what
they are and as they are, and thus emerge the self-contained object
and the self-contained subject. The nonactivity of the seen object in
relation to the seeing subject is not impaired by the fact that, physically speaking, action on its part (emission of light) is involved as a
condition of its being seen. The singular properties of light[4] permit
the whole dynamic genesis to disappear in the perceptual result, so
that in seeing, the percipient remains entirely free from causal involvement in the things to be perceived. Thus vision secures that
standing back from the aggressiveness of the world which frees for
observation and opens a horizon for elective attention. But it does so
at the price of offering a becalmed abstract of reality denuded of its
raw power. To quote from our own earlier account (see above p.
31): The object, staying in its bounds, faces the subject across the
gap which the evanescence of the force context has created. Distance

---

4. The smallness of the disturbances in which light consists affords all
the major advantages of sight over the other senses: the distance of reach,
the detachment from the cause-effect situation, its replacement by a
quiescent image, the simultaneous representation of a manifold, and the
extreme minuteness and precision of point-to-point "mapping" in this
representation.

of appearance yields neutral "image" which, unlike "effect," can be looked at and compared, in memory retained and recalled, in imagination varied and freely composed. Thus becomes essence separable from existence and therewith theory possible. It is but the basic freedom of vision, and the element of abstraction inherent in it, which are carried further in conceptual thought; and from visual perception, concept and idea inherit that ontological pattern of objectivity which vision has first created.

Thus in speaking of the advantage of the causal detachment of sight, it must be borne in mind that this results also in the causal muteness of its objects. Sight, more than any other sense, indeed withholds the experience of causality: causality is not a visual datum. And as long as percepts ("impressions" and "ideas") are taken as just more or less perfect instances of the model case of visual images, Hume's denial of causal information to them must stand. Vision, however, is not the primary but the most sublime case of sense perception and rests on the understructure of more elementary functions in which the commerce with the world is maintained on far more elementary terms. A king with no subjects to rule over ceases to be a king. The evidence of sight does not falsify reality when supplemented by that of the underlying strata of experience, notably of motility and touch: when arrogantly rejecting it sight becomes barren of truth. (For a more detailed discussion, compare the whole Appendix "Causality and Perception" to the First Essay.)

3. SPATIAL DISTANCE

Neither simultaneity of presentation nor dynamic neutrality would be possible without the element of distance. A manifold can be presented simultaneously only if it does not crowd my immediate proximity where each item observed would block out the rest. And causality could not be neutralized if the object invaded my private bodysphere or its closest vicinity. Now sight is the ideal distance-sense. Light travels farther than sound and smell and does not suffer distortion on its way over any distance. Indeed, sight is the only sense in which the advantage lies not in proximity but in distance: the best view is by no means the closest view; to get the proper view we take the proper distance, which may vary for different objects and different purposes, but which is always realized as a positive and not a defective feature in the phenomenal presence of the object. By distance up to a point sight gains in distinctness of detail, and beyond that point in comprehensiveness of survey, in accuracy of proportions—generally speaking, in integration. We consciously stand back and create distance in order to look at the world, i.e., at objects as parts of the world: and also in order to be unembarrassed by the closeness of that which we wish *only* to see; to have the full liberty of our scanning attention. It is different with the other two distance senses, hearing and smell. Smell never gains, always loses by distance. And as to hearing, though within a narrow range of local vicinity it also may have optimal distance and suffer by overcloseness (e.g., with large volumes of sound sources such as an orchestra), further withdrawal will not disclose new "vistas" to it, as to sight, which would compensate it for the loss of distinctness. Its case then becomes similar to that of smell. Both may bridge distance effectively, i.e., overcome what is in itself a disadvantage, but can only lose from its increase and will always tend to gain better information by closing the range.

Besides this quantitative aspect, the most telling characteristic is the *manner* in which distance is experienced in vision. Sound or smell may report an object as merely distant, without reporting the state of the intervening space: in sight the object *faces* me *across* the intervening distance, which in all its potential "steps" is included in the perception. In viewing an object there is the situation of a "vis-à-vis," which discloses the object as the terminal of a dimension leading from me toward it, and this dimension lies open before me. The facing across a distance thus discloses the distance itself as something I am free to traverse; it is an invitation to forward motion, putting the intervening space at my disposal. The dynamics of perspective depth connects me with the projected terminus.

This terminus itself is arbitrary in each given case, and my glance even if focused on it includes as a background the open field of other presences behind it, just as it includes, as a corona fading toward the edges, the manifold co-present in the plane. This indefinite "and so on" with which the visual perception is imbued, an ever-ready potential for realization, and especially the "and so on" in depth, is the birthplace of the idea of *infinity,* to which no other sense could supply the experiential basis. Touch conjoined with locomotion certainly also includes awareness of the potentiality of going on to the next point, and thence to the next, and so on. But touch does not already adumbrate these imminent realizations in its perceptual content, as a marginal part into which the core continuously blends. In the visual field it is this continuous blending of the focused area into more and more distant background-planes, and its shading off toward the fringes, which make the "and so on" more than an empty potentiality: there is the co-represented readiness of the field to be penetrated, a positive pull which draws the glance on as the given content passes as it were of itself over into further contents. No such blending of actual and potential content is given in touch; there is merely the abstract possibility of replacing the present by a subsequent content, and the whole results only from the progressive addition of discrete parts. Sight includes at any given instant an *infinite* manifold at once, and its own qualitative conditions open the way into what lies beyond. The unfolding of space before the eye, under the magic of light, bears in itself the germ of infinity—as a perceptual aspect. Its conceptual framing in the idea of infinity is a step beyond perception, but one that was taken from this base. The fact that we can look into the unbounded depth of the universe has surely been of immense importance in the formation of our ideas.

To revert to the straight phenomenon of distance, it goes without saying that sight by this mere widening of the horizon of information confers a tremendous biological advantage. Knowledge at a distance is tantamount to foreknowledge. The uncommitted reach into space is gain of time for adaptive behavior: I know in good time what I have to reckon with. The apprehension of distant objects therefore means an immediate increase in freedom by the mere increase which remoteness allows in the time-margin for action; just as we found simultaneity of presentation to mean an increase in freedom by the opportunity of choice it offers in the presented manifold. It has been said before that these two aspects of the freedom of sight are closely interrelated. Their union in one performance is the crowning achievement of freedom in the sphere of sentience.

It would not be correct to say that in sight the distant is brought near. Rather it is left in its distance, and if this is great enough it can put the observed object outside the sphere of possible intercourse and of environmental relevance. In that case, perceptual distance may

turn into mental distance, and the phenomenon of disinterested beholding may emerge, this essential ingredient in what we call "objectivity," of which we have found another condition in causal neutrality.

We turn back to the beginning, the partiality of classical philosophy for one of the bodily senses. Our investigation has shown some
grounds for this partiality in the virtues inherent in sight. We even
found, in each of the three aspects under which we treated vision, the
ground for some basic concept of philosophy. *Simultaneity of presentation* furnishes the idea of enduring present, the contrast between
change and the unchanging, between time and eternity. *Dynamic
neutralization* furnishes form as distinct from matter, essence as distinct from existence, and the difference of theory and practice. *Distance* furnishes the idea of infinity.

Thus the mind has gone where vision pointed.

APPENDIX
Sight and Movement

The "Nobility of Sight" has dwelt on the nondynamic quality of the visual
world and the "quietive" transmutation by which this distillate of reality is
obtained; and reference was made to its need for cognitive complementation from other senses and from the sphere of action. We must add that
the latter, or the *motility of our body* generally, is not called in *post hoc*
only but is already a factor in the very constitution of seeing and the seen
world themselves, much as this genesis is forgotten in the conscious result.
Lest our preoccupation with the finished product in its contemplative
"nobility" be taken as a similar forgetting on our part, some remarks on
the role of *movement* in the production of it are in order. They naturally
involve the more general question of the share of *praxis* in the bringing
about of so seemingly "theoretical" a thing as the perceived world, or
more generally still, the question of our active part in the organization of
our sensa. Our particular concern here is with the visual province; but
though we do *not* regard vision as a *model* of the other senses, its extreme
of aloofness challenges the thesis of a practical dependence of perception
more than any other sense, and so what is found of such dependence to
inhere even there should hold *a fortiori* for the less privileged rest.

Kant posed the question of the cognitive organization of our percepts
as the question of the relative shares of "receptivity" and "spontaneity,"
of the passive and active components of our being. But by "activity" in
this context he understood mental activity alone (the formal articulation
of the sense material through the categories of the understanding), not

bodily action of the psychophysical person in his practical dealings with the world. It is strange how little the command of our limbs entered into the long history of the problem. To Kant, the "theoretical" subject is self-sufficient for the cognitive task of constructing from primitive data a meaningful perceptual whole called "world;" and the "practical" subject—becoming this under the spur of need or the moral will—acts in and on a world already constituted by the theoretical faculties of sense and reason. Kant only exemplifies a long-dominant trend: the idea of the theoretical subject separable from *praxis,* and more particularly of the passive or receptive nature of "mere" sense and sense knowledge, is deeply ingrained in the philosophical tradition and has decisively determined the course of epistemology. The corrective reactions to this partisanship (they started with Hegel's *Phenomenology of the Spirit* and include Pragmatism as a determined and vocal cause) are in the natural danger of being provoked into opposite partisanship. The following limited observations take "action" in its primary sense of moving, i.e., moving one's body and through it other things; and since the "passive" in this context is represented by sense-affection, they can also be said to deal with the interrelation of sentience and motility.

Since Berkeley's classical *Essay towards a New Theory of Vision* (1709) it has become almost a commonplace in the theory of perception that visual data acquire their spatial (three-dimensional) meaning only by correlation with parallel tactual data; or more generally, that our object-perception and its spatial framework are the result of a mental integration of the deliverance of these two senses: sight and touch. The account is incomplete, however, so long as "touch" in this combination is taken as just another *sense,* only qualitatively different from sight, hearing, and smell. No mere superimposition of one set of qualities over another, no correlation of them as such, could conceivably yield the new property of space-in-depth. But when we include in "touch" the fact of its being an activity involving *motion,* then we go beyond "mere sensation" (an abstraction of analysis) and add to its "receptivity" that complement of action without which it would be barren of information. Note that the motion, to have this effect, must be my performance, i.e., "intentional" or "directed" motion: only as purposive act does movement vitally contribute to the organization of the perceptual world. Self-movement indeed may be called the spatial organizer in each sense-species, and the synthesizer of the several senses toward one common objectivity.

For the case of touch, the point has been made in the Essay: how, in exploring an object by feeling alone (e.g., in darkness), it is the direction of my own voluntary movements of limb, with my body as reference-system, that furnishes the framework of dimensional coordinates into which the successive contact sensations are integrated. We here merely repeat that without this kinesthetic side of the complex process no unification of the individual local data into a coherent series, and eventually no concrescence of them into a total simultaneous form, would come about in touch.

But what is obvious in the case of touch, seems at first inapplicable to the case of sight: that its cognitive feat should depend on movement. For was not the point of our Essay precisely that sight is the sense of the passive observer par excellence? That to look at things, at the world at large, is compatible with a state of complete rest, which even seems the optimal condition for visual attention and contemplation? Was not even the whole opposition of "theory versus practice," and hence of the *vita contemplativa* versus the *vita activa,* derived from this very aspect of vision? This still stands. Yet we should not be able to "see" if we had not previously moved. We should, e.g., not see the world arranged in depth, stretching away from us indefinitely, if we were not more than seeing creatures: if we were not creatures that also can move into space and have done so in the past.

The basic fact, of course, is that vision is the part-function of a whole body which experiences its dynamic involvement with the environment in the feeling of its position and changes of position. The "possession" of a body of which the eyes are a part is indeed the primal fact of our "spatiality": the body not merely as occupying a volume of space geometrically, but as always interacting with the world physically, even when at rest (e.g., by mere gravity). Without this background of nonvisual, corporeal feeling and the accumulated experience of performed motion, the eyes alone would not supply the knowledge of space, notwithstanding the immanent extension of the visual field.

This proposition can be argued on many levels. One might show that the reaching for and manipulating of things by the infant provides the elementary experience of the corporeality of seen objects and of an order of distances correlated to the sensations of sight. Or one might elaborate on the many neuromuscular adjustments participating in the optical act as such (turning of eyeballs, focusing of lens, etc.—involuntary small-scale motor activations), which help to imbue the optical sensation with objective reference. Or one might point to the built-in spatial orientation which the physical "directions" of the body provide with the organic sense of right and left,[1] front and back,[2] up and down—a sense always actualized

---

1. Cf. Kant's short essay "Of the first principle of the difference of directions in space" (further elaborated in "What is 'to orient oneself in thought'?"), where he points out that the distinction of identifiable direc-

in some rudiment of motion. The point I wish to comment upon is a further one: the dependence of optical *perspective* on *locomotion*.

It will be agreed that the knowledge of perspective includes an awareness of the potential visual displacements attendant upon a shift of the observer's position, i.e., upon his moving. The ability to preserve the identity of object distribution throughout a sequence of such apparent displacements is a necessary premise for the understanding of perspective distortion. It might seem, therefore, that what is required is the remembered experience of such displacement patterns in connection with motion, i.e., a past of variously having moved in space. But this is not the whole story. For how did motion itself come to be experienced as motion, if its evidence were just visual displacement? The epistemological circle is obvious. It is here where movement *qua performance* becomes crucial. A winged seed sailing on the wind, if it were endowed with eyes, would at most perceive a time sequence of two-dimensional visual manifolds continuously blending into their successors, shapes increasing and decreasing in size, changing in outline, opening and closing their ranks, overlapping and separating—a kaleidoscopic change with a definite but meaningless pattern, lacking reference to position and to dimensions defined thereby. Thus all its travels would not help it to gain a perception of space and to relate the passage of images to a space traversed. The difference between this imaginary case and the real one of the self-moving animal is that the latter changes its place by an exchange of mechanical action with the resisting medium, through or upon which it moves. The muscular effort required means that the relative motion is more than a shift of mutual geometrical position: through the interplay of force the geometrical becomes a dynamical situation which by this very character discloses the geometrical aspect as well. The proprioception of motor activity becomes a guide for the organism in the successive construction of spatial distance and direction out of the phases of the motion it actually performs.

Once in possession of the knowledge bequeathed by these motion-

---

tions in visual space is due to our feeling of a qualitative difference between the right and left sides of our bodies: if God between one night and the next changed the whole aspect of the starry sky into its mirror image, we should have no way of telling the difference without recourse to those qualitative body feelings—the purely geometrical evidence exhibiting no change.

2. Significantly, most free-moving animals (all vertebrates) have an axial direction of their body structure; in most cases this coincides with the main, i.e., forward direction of their locomotion. From the latter rule, man's upright posture is the significant exception (for its profound meaning cf. the excellent essay by Erwin Straus, "The Upright Posture," *The Psychiatric Quarterly*, 26 (1952), 529-61).

experiences, I can indeed view the world from my fixed standpoint and apprehend it in depth, in perspective, and in the order of its differently extending directions. I may then be the stationary and inactive observer who lets the spectacle of the world pass by his eyes as on a screen. But in this contemplative situation my former activity of actually moving through space, of directing myself toward some goal, of changing my direction, of correlating time used to distance covered, of measuring exertion against the visual results of change, all these and the always present possibility of performing the same acts again, underlie and impregnate that seemingly static presence of space which vision enjoys. We may therefore say that the possession of a body in space, itself part of the space to be apprehended, and that body capable of self-motion in counterplay with other bodies, is the precondition for a vision of the world. We have thus the paradox that it is something dynamic, a process, by which the framework of static experience is constituted, viz., a system of spatial coordinates (directions) with my own body at the "origin." And the example of the sense seemingy remotest from such involvement shows that motility, which itself requires sentience for its operation, in turn enters into the very constitution of sense where this is to be more than the mere registering of irritations from without: in other words, where sensation is to rise to perception.[3]

---

3. It follows, incidentally, that the Leibnizian monad, "mirroring" the universe "in perspective" from its "viewpoint" (note the visual model!) *without doing something* to this universe in the way of interaction, is a self-contradictory concept: the percipient, by the very nature of perception, *must* be also *agent.*—The last expression prompts a reference to Prof. John Macmurray's admirable Gifford Lectures of 1953 (published in 1957) on *The Self as Agent,* whose many striking agreements in viewpoint and conclusions with portions of the present volume came as a pleasant surprise to me when my attention was recently drawn to it. Especially his discussion of the relative claims of sight and touch, *op. cit.,* pp. 104 ff., finds close parallels in "The Nobility of Sight" (first published 1954). It is a coincidence of independent insight, which must be gratifying to either side. The publication of my corresponding views falls into about the same period or slightly before: "Causality and Perception," 1950; "Is God a Mathematician?", 1951; "Motility and Emotion" (now "To Move and to Feel"), 1953; "A Critique of Cybernetics" (now "Cybernetics and Purpose"), 1953; "The Nobility of Sight," 1954. (The First Essay of the present collection contains the opening of my lecture course on "The Problem of Life in the Theory of Being," given at the Hebrew University in Jerusalem in 1946/47). Prof. Macmurray was obviously as unaware of these pieces as I regrettably remained for years afterward of his work.

Image-making
and the Freedom of Man

The following is an essay in philosophical anthropology concerned with determining man's "specific difference" in the animal kingdom. For heuristic purposes I have assumed the situation of explorers on another planet who wish to ascertain the presence of "men" among the living creatures there. The situation is heuristically ideal because it is ideally rigorous, denying all support of morphological familiarity and with it the temptation to take accidentals of bodily type for essentials of a species of life. Detached from any particular zoology and from kinship relations, the term "man" can refer only to an analogy-of-essence that would justify assigning the name in the face of utter physical dissimilarity. What kind of minimum evidence would be conclusive, and what exactly would it be conclusive for?

Among the possible external clues that offer themselves as criteria, that one has philosophical preference which, in addition to being at once unequivocal and primitive, yields most for a definition of man's nature when interpreted in its internal implications. The argument presented here ought to be preceded by a discussion of the relative merits of various such clues—like tools, hearths, tombs. I start, however, where such a discussion has led me, foregoing the support of preparatory inventory and reasoned selection. The choice of image-making as particularly revealing is best justified by its results. Needless to say, no claim to exclusive validity is implied in the choice. A certain hermeneutic advantage, from which I wish to profit, lies in the relative simplicity of the phenomenon as compared, for example, with speech. The latter, though it is even more central to the nature of man (as it is certainly more comprehensive in bearing), is also much more complex in its constitution, its evidence accordingly more difficult to assess; besides, in the assumed situation, the question of its identification by outsiders—that is, the physical indifference of symbolic utterance as such, which is not its own evidence—would add a problem of recognition not germane to the issue itself; and finally, like "reason" and "thinking," the concept of "language" has become too controversial and uncertain in contemporary philosophy to serve the elementary enterprise here in mind. There is better hope for prior agreement on what a picture is than on what a word is. In fact, an understanding of the image faculty may contribute something to the understanding of the more elusive phenomenon of speech.

Our explorers enter a cave, and on its walls they discern lines or other configurations that must have been produced artificially, that have no structural function, and that suggest a likeness to one or another of the living forms encountered outside. The cry goes up: "Here is evidence of man!" Why? The evidence does not require the perfection of the Altamira paintings. The crudest and most childish drawing would be just as conclusive as the frescoes of Michelangelo. Conclusive for what? For the more-than-animal nature of its creator; and for his being potentially a speaking, thinking, inventing, in short "symbolical" being. And since it is not a matter of degree, as is technology, the evidence must reveal what it has to reveal by its formal quality alone.

What faculties and attitudes are involved in image-making? For our initial conviction that no mere animal would or could produce an image we may at this stage just adduce the biological uselessness of any mere representation. The artifacts of animals have a direct physical use in the promotion of vital ends, such as nutrition, reproduction, hibernation. A representation, however, changes neither the environment nor the condition of the organism itself. An image-making creature, therefore, is one that indulges in the making of useless objects, or has ends in addition to the biological ones, or can serve the latter in ways remote from the direct usefulness of instrumental things. Whichever it is (and it may be all three), in the pictorial representation the object is appropriated in a new, nonpractical way, and the very fact that the interest in it can shift to its *eidos* signifies a new object relation.

I

Before we proceed any further we must determine what an image is, or by what properties an object comes to be the image of another object.

1. The most obvious property is that of "likeness." An image is an object that bears a plainly recognizable, or at will discernible, likeness to another object.

2. The likeness is produced with intent: the object bearing it is in respect to that property an artifact. A natural resemblance between two objects does not constitute the one an image of the other.[1] The artificiality (and therewith intendedness) of the likeness in one of the two alike things must be as recognizable as the likeness itself. The external intention of the maker lives on as intrinsic "intentionality" in the product—the intentionality of representation, which communicates itself to the beholder. Thus, while likeness itself is mutual, the image relation using it is one-sided: the artificial thing is an image of the natural, not also the natural an image of the artificial.

3. The likeness is not complete. A duplication of all the properties of the original would result in the duplication of the object itself—in another instance of the same kind of object, not in an image. If I copy a hammer in every respect, I have another hammer and not an image of a hammer.

The incompleteness of the likeness must be perceptible, so as to qualify the likeness as "mere likeness." Else the beholder would suppose himself to be in the presence of the object and not of its image

---

1. This statement has to be qualified with respect to mirror images, shadows, and the like. A reflection in water is a natural, that is, nonartificial, resemblance, and it is an image of the object that is reflected, while the latter with all its likeness cannot be said to be an image of the former. But here the image is an accompaniment of the object and not an object by itself; and even if it is detachable, like the imprint of an animal form (a potential "image" for the later paleontologist), the likeness is the member of a cause-effect relation rather than a representation.

only. Such deception, a self-dissimulation of the image, defeats its true meaning which is to represent, not to simulate, the object. This is the difference between image and imitation. A likeness may indeed deceive me into taking it for the original. That it is only partial may not be obvious to the sense to which it is addressed—vision—because in terms of that sense alone it is deceptively complete. So long as I have not lifted the wax fruit from the bowl, it is for me not the likeness of an apple but an apple. Then the recognition, afforded by touch and smell, that the likeness is after all only partial, and contrived at that, transposes the object from one category to another: not in this case, however, to that of image but to that of fake.

For in this case the deception was intended. In the image it is not: its likeness is avowedly "superficial," in that it reproduces the surface appearance strictly as such and not as a pretense to a likeness also of the substance in which it is embodied. "Unsubstantial" in itself, the likeness concedes to the means of its embodiment their own substantiality. This confinement of the representative intention to the appearing surface is the most basic sense in which all image-likeness is incomplete, for it is constitutive for the genus "image" as such.[2] This incompleteness, then, which we may term the ontological one, is predecided with the image intention in general, and no longer a matter of choice in the particular case.

4. Beyond this basic condition, the "incompleteness" assumes degrees of freedom. Within the dimension constituted by the "ontological incompleteness," the image is again elliptic: much even of the surface appearance is omitted. Omission implies selection. In its positive aspect, then, the incompleteness of image-likeness means the selection of "representative" or "relevant" or "significant" features of the object, that is, of its appearance to the sense to which the image is addressed. The restriction to this one sense alone as the perceptual medium of representation is itself the first "selection" operative in image-making, and this is generically predetermined by the dominance of vision: man's nature has decided in advance for the visual aspect as representative of things. Confinement to two dimensions

---

2. Rather than being concealed, this kind of incompleteness may be emphasized in the extent to which the material's own quality is permitted to codetermine the appearance of the image.

introduces a further and more specific level of incompleteness which makes its own selective demands. But within the selective levels thus determined generically (visual representation in the solid, in the flat), there takes place a more arbitrary and particular selection of representative features, and the freedom here increases with the degree of incompleteness defining the generic levels as such: in the flat it is greater than in the solid, the one having inherently more of "abstraction" in it than the other.

At the moment it suffices to define as "representative" such elements as confer recognizability in the absence of completeness. The more successful the selection in this respect, the greater the incompleteness that the representation can afford. The advantage is one not only of economy (simplifying the task of representation) but also of expressiveness, emphasizing as it does the things that matter. Thus a "less" of completeness can mean a "more" of essential likeness. This aspect of incompleteness points to idealization, which need by no means go in the direction of beauty alone. Economy and idealization also put the image character as such beyond doubt: we shall hardly mistake the real object for an image of itself, for in its abundance of the accidental it lacks the symbolic concentration on the essential.

5. With these last remarks we have passed beyond the dimension of "incompleteness" to that of positive difference. Added to dissimilarity as a result of omitting and selecting, there is alteration of the selected features themselves, as a means of heightening the symbolic similitude, or in order to satisfy visual interests other than representation, or just as the result of inadequate ability. The dissimilarity may range all the way from slight displacements by way of emphasis to the most exaggerated caricature, and from unobtrusive harmonizing to complete assimilation of the "given" to a canon of style. Some such departure from the given is inseparable from the process of its "translation," in view of the human agency involved; and the tolerance allowed in this respect by the image category as such is indefinite. Choice or compulsion, mastery or the lack of it, each and all may have play within this tolerance. The involuntary oversimplifications and distortions of children's drawings, no less than the sovereign exercise of artistic intention, may leave only faint traces of likeness to the depicted object. Yet to artist and spectator alike, even such strained and imperfect likenesses are representations of the object in

question. There is almost no limit to the stretch of imagination that the capacity for symbolic understanding may command.

Carried by this capacity beyond the initial terms of image, the representational function may rest progressively less in real similitude than in the mere recognizability of the intention. At first an obvious degree of likeness is necessary to make the intention recognizable, and this is the province of image proper; but with the rise of a symbolic convention an increasing range of substitutions and graphical abbreviations becomes available, with increasing emancipation from "literalness." (One possible fruit of this development is ideographic script.) From the beginning, however, abstraction and stylization are present in the pictorial process as such, as the demands of economy are met by the freedom of transcription. And it is in the exercise of this freedom that the norm of the given object can be abandoned entirely for the creation of shapes never seen: the pictorial faculty opens the road to invention.

6. The object of representation is visual shape. Vision grants the greatest freedom to the mediacy of representation, not only by the wealth of data from which the latter can choose but also by the number of variables of which visual identities admit. There are many, equally recognizable, visual shapes to the same object, as a result of relative position and perspective: its "aspects"; each of these enjoys an independence from the variation of size due to distance; an independence from variations of color and brightness due to conditions of light; an independence from the completeness of detail, which can merge and disappear in the simultaneous wholeness of an object's view. Through all these variations of sense the form remains identifiable and continuously represents the same thing.

With such phenomenological traits, to which no other sense offers a full analogy, vision itself suggests the idea of representation and, as its means, an idea of "form" whose identity rests entirely in the proportion of its parts. In visual imagery, therefore, the large can be represented by the small, the small by the large, the solid by the plane, the colored by black and white, the continuous by the discrete and vice versa, the full by the mere outline, the manifold by the simple. Sight is the main perceptual medium of representation because it is not only the chief object-sense but also the home ground of abstraction.

7. The image is inactive and at rest, though it may depict move-

ment and action. These it can conjure into a static presence because the represented, the representation, and the vehicle of representation (the imaging thing, or physical carrier of the image) are different strata in the ontological constitution of the image. In spite of its embodiment, the likeness is unsubstantial, like a shadow or a mirror image. It can represent the dangerous without endangering, the harmful without harming, the desirable without satiating. What is represented in the mode of image is, in the image, removed from the causal commerce of things and transposed to a nondynamic existence that is the image existence proper—a mode of existence to be confounded neither with that of the imaging thing nor with that of the imaged reality. The last two both remain involved in the movement of becoming. As the imaged reality goes on in its course, the body of the image-thing, starting on its own history, continues to be part of the causal order in whose transactions it assumed its present condition; but considered in its imaging function it ceases to count in its own right. Its substantiality (whose sole requisite is to be stable, so as to preserve the image) is submerged in its symbolic aspect, and therewith is submerged its causal background—not only that of its natural prehistory (its past as a tree, a rock) but also that of becoming, under the artist's hands, its present self. The activity that went into its making is a matter of the past, of which the image-present keeps no record. That present has, as it were, renounced the status of effect, which still implies its cause: dissembling any past, it also presages no future—and out of this nontransient and timeless present the image meets the time-bound beholder in a presence that is as much detached from the process of its own genesis as from that of the beholder's life.[3]

A footprint is a sign of the foot that made it, and as effect tells the

---

3. This distinguishes image from pantomime and the symbolism of dance. The difference is similar to that between writing and speech. In miming representation (as in speech), the performer's own body in action is the carrier of the symbolism, which remains bound to the transient act itself. Thus the imagery, enacted in the space and time that actor and spectator share, remains merged with the common causal order in which things happen, interact, and pass. As a real event it has its allotted span within the common time, and is no more. It is indeed repeatable, and by this token its eidetic identity defies the uniqueness of real event; but it has to be repeated in order to be present, and it "is" only while being produced (as is the case with moving pictures).

story of its causation. A picture, apprehended as picture, is a sign not of the painter's motions but of the object depicted. In the image the causal nexus is cut. Free to depict any causal situation, including that of painting a picture, the image does not represent the causality of its own becoming.[4]

8. The difference between image and imaging thing, with the latter's self-effacement in the former, is matched by the difference between image and imaged object. The complete articulation is threefold. The substratum can be regarded by itself, the image by itself, the object of the image by itself: the image or likeness hovers as a third, ideal entity between the first and the last, both real entities, connecting them in the unique way of representation. It is this double distinction, or the threefold stratification, which makes it possible for the image to enjoy the described mode of a noncausal presence, exempt from the accidents of real event.

In particular, the difference between image and its physical carrier underlies the technical possibility of copying or reproducing in art. If a painting or a statue is accurately copied, we have in the copy not an image of an image but a duplication of one and the same image. The many prints of a snapshot, or of a plate throughout one book edition, are not so many additional images but one image, one representation so and so many times presented, despite the differences in the individual pieces of paper, dye chemicals, and other matter used to embody the likeness.

On the other hand, the difference between image and imaged object

---

4. It may, though, *betray* this causality in its visible technique (the stroke of the brush, the marks of the chisel), as a handwriting may betray the motor performance of the writer; and in both cases this effect can become intentional, that is, co-intended with the representational intention. In that case the image is charged with an expressive function superimposed on the representational one: which is to say that it is more than image. The image function by itself is strictly "objective", and as long as it is kept pure, the self-expression of the maker, which inevitably finds its way into it, remains unintentional and consequently unobtrusive—noticeable, if at all, to trained attention only. In subjectivist stages of civilization the maker's self-expression may become a goal and conspicuous by choice (as in the brushwork of baroque painters or of Van Gogh), and with this shift from the representational to the expressive the very role of image changes.

underlies the possibility of there being many different likenesses, and thus images, of the same object: as many as its aspects according to all the variables of visual appearance as such (see no. 6, above), and again, as many as the possible transcriptions of these aspects according to the variables of individual selection (no. 4) and alteration (no. 5). Thus, taking only one dimension out of many, that of "angle," we can on principle have an indefinite number of different shots of one person—of each of which we can have an indefinite number of prints.

A third possibility again derives from the ontological difference in question. Not only can one object be represented in an indefinite number of images, but also, and more typically, one image can represent an indefinite number of objects. A figure of *Pinus sylvestris* in a work on botany is a representation not of this or that individual fir tree but of any fir tree of that species. The antelope of the bushman drawing is every antelope remembered, anticipated, identifiable as *an* antelope; the figures of the hunters are every hunting party of bushmen in the past, present, or future. The representation, since it is through form, is essentially general. Image sensibly symbolizes generality poised between the individuality of the imaging thing and that of the imaged objects.

II

If these, then, are the properties of image, what properties are required in a subject for the making or beholding of images? The two, making and beholding, do not differ in the basic condition of their possibility. Making an image involves the ability to behold something as an image; and to behold something as an image and not merely as an object means also to be able to produce one. This is a statement of essence. It does not mean that he who appreciates a painting by Rembrandt is therefore able to produce its like. But it does mean that whoever can perceive a pictorial representation as such is the kind of being to whose nature the representational faculty belongs, regardless of special gifts, actual exercise, and degrees of proficiency attained. What kind of being is this?

The first requirement seems to be the ability to perceive likeness. But we must add forthwith: to perceive it in a certain way. Both man and bird perceive in the scarecrow (assuming its effect to rest on simulating something definite) a likeness to, say, a human figure. For the bird, however, this means mistaking the scarecrow for a man. Either it is so deceived or there is no relation at all: in between there can be only a state of indecision that must be resolved one way or the other. For the bird, this is a mere matter of sensory discrimination. Not so with man. It is not keener visual discrimination that protects man from confounding the likenss with the original, or poorer discrimination that lets him still accept as a likeness what the bird will dismiss altogether.[5] In fact, perceptiveness or visual discrimination has nothing to do with the matter. Increase of likeness would not, to human judgment, make the scarecrow anything but a better effigy; decrease would not, to the bird, make it pass into "mere effigy." When the deception breaks down, only straw, sticks, and rags remain. For the animal mere similitude does not exist. Where we perceive it, the animal perceives either sameness or otherness, but not *both in one,* as we do in the apprehension of similitude.

Likeness, then, must be perceived as "mere likeness," and this involves more than perception. Indeed, "image" is not a function of perceptual degree of likeness, but a conceptual dimension of its own within which all degrees of likeness can occur. The greatest degree still leaves the image an "image only"; the smallest can still constitute it an image of the object in question so long as the intended reference is recognizable. In all these degrees the image is, through the likeness relation, the image *of* something, of the imaged object, with which even the best likeness never merges.[6] The perceptual equation that underlies the experience of likeness must therefore be qualified by a distinction that is nonperceptual.

---

5. Or, in the latter case, should we have said, not that man is more easily satisfied with respect to likeness, but that he is more perceptive for it even in faint traces? But then it would have to be the bird that is the more perceptive in the first case—perceptive for likeness, not for difference.

6. Man can, of course, be deceived occasionally and confound an image with the real thing; but this merely means that for the moment he does not apply the image category at all, not that to him it has lost its meaning. Contrariwise, it may occur that he fails to perceive a likeness and the very intention of a likeness, and thus fails to recognize the perceptual object as an image; here again the image category simply does

That distinction, as we have found, is twofold: the image must be distinguished from its physical carrier; and the imaged object must be distinguished from both. With these distinctions likeness can be perceived as "likeness only." Through likeness as the intermediary the directly perceived object is apprehended not as itself but as standing for another object. It is there only to represent the other entity, and this is only represented; thus, paradoxically, the ideal link, the similitude or *eidos* as such, becomes the real object of apprehension.

The principle here involved on the part of the subject is the mental separation of form from matter. It is this that makes possible the vicarious presence of the physically absent at once with the self-effacement of the physically present. Here we have a specifically human fact, and the reason why we expect neither making nor understanding of images from animals. The animal deals with the present object itself. If it is sufficiently like another object, it is an object of the same kind. The likeness aids the recognition of the object-kind, but is not itself the object of recognition. Recognized is the present object alone as "one such," that is, as familiar in certain properties. These, spotlighted by activation of memory traces, call up in turn their former associates, which enter as expectations into the perceptual picture and, once recognition has taken place, form part of the "presence" of the object. Nothing but this is present, standing entirely for itself, though imbued with past experience. Only reality counts, and reality knows of no representation. In our search, therefore, for the conditions of image-making we are referred from the faculty of perceiving likeness to the more fundamental one of separating *eidos* from concrete reality, or form from matter.

III

To understand this faculty we have first to consider the givenness of reality itself, that is, we have to start from sense perception. *Eidos,* "appearance," is an object of sense, but not its whole object. In

---

not come into play, this time for lack of likeness, and the object is just taken for itself. This also does not mean that the difference between the vehicle of representation and the function of representation has become invalid for the observer.

perception external objects are apprehended not merely as "such," but also as "there." The qualitative data representing them ("forms" to Aristotle) are felt to be thrust upon the percipient, and in this thrust they convey the affective presence of the objects themselves. Perception is intrinsically awareness of such a self-giving presence— the experience of the reality of the object as co-existing with me here and now and on its own determining my sensory condition. This element of encounter—the self-communication of the object to my receptivity and its insistence on itself even while in my perceptive hold—is part of the internal evidence over and above the eidetic content of perception, when the latter is to be experience of real things.

But there is this paradox to sense perception: the felt affectiveness of its data, which is necessary for the experience of the "reality" of the real, as this is attested in the reality of my affectedness, must in part be canceled out again in order to permit the apprehension of its "objectivity." The element of encounter is balanced by one of abstraction, without which sensation would not rise to perception. First, in a somewhat stretched sense of the term, there is "abstraction" from the state of sensory stimulation itself in the very fact of one's perceiving the object instead of his own organic affection. Some sort of disengagement from the causality of the encounter provides the neutral freedom for letting the "other" appear for itself. (The organization of our senses assures this disengagement in advance.) In that appearance the affective basis ("stimulation," "irritation") is canceled, its record neutralized. Second, and in a more accepted sense, perception continuously "abstracts" from the immediate sensory content of affection in allowing the object its identity beyond the change of its views. We see not once this, once that, complex of data, but through both the same thing, "abstracting" as it were from the differences of successive sensations, or from the sense "material." This visual abstraction makes possible what Kant has called the synthesis of recognition.

Vision, of all senses, most conspicuously realizes in its normal performance this double feat of "abstraction": setting off the self-contained object from the affective condition of sensing, and upholding its identity and unity across the whole range of its possible transformations of appearance, each of which is in itself already an integrated simultaneous manifold. Recognition of the object as one previously known, or as like previously known ones, does not, therefore, require past sensations to be duplicated in present ones, recalled when so duplicated and found congruent with the present: in that case the same complex of simultaneous visual data, and the same succession of such compound "aspects," would have to be repeated in order to yield recognition of the same or the like, and this condition would rarely be fulfilled. What is equated in such acts of recognition is not similar sense-datum conglomerates but variant phases in the continuous transformation-series of a pattern or configuration. The phase sensibly available now may happen to be identical with one formerly experienced, but this would be the exception rather than the rule: the identity of the configuration as such is perceived across the whole scale of its *possible* visual transformations—and that multi-dimensional scale, governed by its structural and qualitative laws, itself forms a pattern of a higher order.[7] The several serial variabilities constituting this pattern are continuous, but recognition along each one's stretch, given sufficient familiarity with its law, can take place discontinuously; that is, the intermediate sequence need not be run through in actual experience.

An important observation follows. Within this comprehensive transformation pattern the single aspects (phases) do not stand for themselves, but each acts as a kind of "image"—one of the possible images—of the object. In this quality they allow recognition of the same object, or kind of object; that is, they allow it through a likeness that comprehends unlikeness. For not only are they like-unlike one another, but with none of them, nor with their serial totality, does the apprehended form of the object itself coincide. Thus each view alike represents the object "symbolically" (though *as* a symbol, one view may be superior to others and come to represent the object preferentially—for example, by being more familiar, or more informative, than others).

But did we not encounter these selfsame features before, when we

---

7. As indicated before, the pattern is in fact a multiple set of transformation patterns, which can operate singly, concurrently, and interdependently: variation with respect to size, to side, to perspective distortion, to illumination, and so on, forms each its own continuous series as one of the attributes of the complete visual schema.

analyzed the ontology of image? Thus it turns out that abstraction, representation, symbolism—*something* of the image function— already inheres in the performance of seeing, as the most integrative of the senses. This, in degrees, must then be credited even to some higher animals.

IV

What step then does the image faculty take in man when he proceeds to translate a visual aspect into a material likeness? We see at once that in this step a new level of mediacy is attained, beyond that which belongs to visual recognition of objects as such. The image becomes detached from the object, that is, the presence of the *eidos* is made independent of that of the thing. Vision involved a stepping back from the importunity of environment and procured the freedom of detached survey.[8] A stepping back of the second order takes place when appearance is comprehended *qua* appearance, distinguished from reality, and, with its presence freely commanded, is interposed between the self and the real whose presence is beyond command.

This free possession is first achieved in the internal exercise of imagination, by which, to the best of our knowledge, human *memory* is distinguished from animal recollection. The latter is joined to actual sensation. It may function on the occasion of a present perception in which a previous one is recognized by way of the quality "familiar" or "known" with which the present experience is imbued. Or, instead of accompanying repetitive perception as it occurs, recall may be evoked by appetite and projectively guide animal action toward a desired repetition ("remembering" the way to yesterday's feeding place), with "recall by familiarity" marking the successful progress of the action. But there is nothing to show that this kind of remembering enjoys an imaginary presence of its objects, and everything to argue against the assumption that, if it does, this presence is at the subject's command, to be summoned and dismissed at will. Appetitive need or actual perception governs the reactivation of past experience. Whether this is recalled *as* "past" and is not merely

---

8. For a more detailed and comprehensive analysis of vision and the "image" faculty inherent in it, see Sixth Essay, above.

superimposed on the present as a "knowledge" of what to expect or to do now, there is no way of telling with certainty. At any rate, the "recalling" is done not by the subject but by circumstances for the subject.

Human memory exceeds mere recollection of this kind by the freely reproductive faculty of imagination, which has the images of things at its call. That it can also alter them follows almost necessarily from having them in detachment from the actuality of sensation and thereby from the stubborn factuality of the object's own being. Imagination separates the remembered *eidos* from the occurrence of the individual encounter with it, freeing its possession from the accidents of space and time. The freedom so gained—to ponder things in imagination—is one of distance and control at once.

The remembered form can then be translated from internal imagination into an external image, which is again an object of perception —a perception, however, not of the original object but of its representation. It is externalized memory, and not a repetition of experience itself. To some extent it makes actual experience superfluous by making some of its essential content available without it. If the image is made directly "from nature" (probably a later development in pictorial history), memory is as it were anticipated and given in advance a permanent model for the repetitious renewal of its image. Thus externalized, the image defies time more effectively than in its precarious internal conservation. There, what had been saved from the flux of things was entrusted to the flux of self. Externalized again, it abides in itself, its presence independent of the moods and stimulations that rule over the working of memory, and even outlasting the shortness of its maker's life.

In the external representation the image is also made sharable, the common property of all who look at it. It is an objectification of individual perception comparable to that which is achieved in verbal description; like the latter, it serves communication and, at the same time, benefits perception itself, or *knowledge*. For in the process of depicting the simultaneous appearance part for part, as in the process of describing it, vision is forced to discern and correlate what it first had all in one. The artist sees more than the nonartist, not because he has a better vision, but because he does the artist's work, namely, remaking the things he sees: and what one makes he knows.

As the remaker of things "in their likeness," pictorial man submits to the standard of truth. An image may be more or less true to the object. The intention to depict things acknowledges them as they are and accepts the verdict of their being on the adequacy of the pictorial homage. The *adaequatio imaginis ad rem,* preceding the *adaequatio intellectus ad rem,* is the first form of theoretical truth—the precursor of verbally descriptive truth, which is the precursor of scientific truth. (See Appendix to this Essay.)

But the remaker of things is potentially also the maker of new things, and the one power is not different from the other. The freedom that chooses to render a likeness may as well choose to depart from it. The first intentionally drawn line unlocks that dimension of freedom in which faithfulness to the original, or to any model, is only one decision: transcending actual reality as a whole, it offers its range of infinite variation as a realm of the *possible,* to be made true by man at his choice. The same faculty is reach for the true and power for the new.

And still another power is implied in the pictorial faculty. Images after all have to be made, not merely conceived. Thus their external existence as a result of human activity reveals also a physical aspect of the power that the image faculty wields: the kind of command that man has over his body. This command, whether it terminates in the production of an image, of a thing, or of any other physical action, is itself governed by "image." Indeed, this is but the bodily side of the very image faculty itself, of which we have discussed so far the mental side alone. The envisaged form is not embodied by the wish, and the inner command of the *eidos,* with all its freedom of mental drafting, would remain ineffective had it not also the power to guide the subject's body in execution. Of this translation of an eidetic pattern into movement of limb, writing is the most familiar example; dance (by designed choreography) is another; and the use of our hand throughout exhibits this motor translation of form in its widest practical range as the condition of all technology. What we here have is a trans-animal, uniquely human fact: eidetic control of motility, that is, muscular action governed not by set stimulus-response pattern but by freely chosen, internally represented and purposely projected *form.* The eidetic control of motility, with its freedom of external execution, complements the eidetic control of imagination, with its freedom of internal drafting. Without the latter, there would be no rational faculty, but without the former, its possession would be futile. Both together make possible the freedom of man. Expressing both in one indivisible evidence, *homo pictor* represents the point in which *homo faber* and *homo sapiens* are conjoined—are indeed shown to be one and the same.

I return once more to the mental side. The Bible tells us (Genesis 2:19) that God created the beasts of the field and the fowls of the air, but left it to Adam to name them. A Haggada to this passage (Genesis Rabba XVII.5) states that God praised the wisdom of Adam before the angels, saying that in giving names to all creatures, to himself, and even to God, Adam had done what the angels could not do. The giving of names to objects is here regarded as the first feat of newly created man and as the first distinctively human act. It was a step beyond creation. He who did it demonstrated by it his superiority over his fellow creatures and foreshadowed his coming mastery over nature. In giving names to "every living creature" created by God, man created species names for the plurality into which each would multiply. The name, becoming general, would preserve the archetypal order of creation in the face of individual multiplicity. Its use in each individual case would renew the original act of creation in its formal aspect. Thus the symbolic duplication of nature by names is at the same time an ordering of nature according to its generic patterns. Each horse is the original horse, each dog the original dog.

The generality of the name is the generality of the image. The early hunter drew not this or that bison but *the* bison—every possible bison was conjured, anticipated, remembered thereby. The drawing of the image is analogous to the act of calling by name, or rather is the unabridged version of this act, because it spells out in a sensible presence that inner image of which the phonetic sign is an abbreviation and through whose generality alone the sign can relate to the many individuals. Image-making each time re-enacts the creative act that is hidden in the residual name: the symbolic making-over-again of the world. It exhibits what the use of names takes for granted: the availability of the *eidos* as an identity over and above the particulars, for human apprehension, imagination, and discourse.

V

Thus our explorers, chancing upon pictorial representation, whether accomplished or poor, can be sure of more than having discovered creatures with a certain peculiarity of behavior ("species S with habits a, b, c . . . , among which is picture-making"). They can be sure of having discovered, in the makers of those likenesses, creatures who enjoy the mental and corporeal freedom we term human; who also give names to things, that is, have language. They can be sure of the possibility of communicating with them. And as a possibility, they can anticipate that the abstraction shown in those likenesses will lead in time to the abstraction of geometrical form and rational concept; and that the motile control implied in their making will, in conjunction with that abstraction, lead in time to technology. The actuality of such developments is unforeseeable, dependent as they are on the accidents of history, but their potentiality is given with that kind of being of which the pictorial activity is the first visible and unmistakable sign.

The encountering of artificial likenesses, then, is the heuristic experience we have been looking for, and in its inner implications this external criterion points to the differentia of man. We note that the criterion does not demand reason but is content with potential reason (as with potential geometry and the like). The potentiality resides in something that is not itself reason (and so on), and may never happen to advance to it. But if it does it will be an advance within the level constituted by that basic "something" that operates in the earliest attempts at representation. The level of man is the level of the possibilities that are indicated (not defined, and certainly not assured) by the pictorial faculty: the level of a nonanimal mediacy in the relation to objects, and of a distance from reality entertained and bridged by that mediacy at the same time. The existence of images, which shows form wrested from fact, is a witness to this mediacy, and in its open promise alone suffices as evidence of human freedom.

Former speculation demanded more concerning what should be regarded as conclusive evidence for Homo sapiens: at some time, nothing less than figures exemplifying geometrical propositions would suffice. This surely is an unfailing, but also an overexacting criterion. Where would it leave the bushman? The criterion of attempted sensible likeness is more modest, but also more basic and comprehensive. It is full evidence for the transanimal freedom of the makers. This freedom, in both theoretic and practical respects, of which reason is a more specific development, is distinctive of man. To see the differentia fulfilled in the crudest likeness of an antelope as much as in the figure of the Pythagorean theorem is not to scale down the stature of man. For the gap between animal world-relation and the crudest attempt at representation is infinitely wider than that between the latter and any geometrical construction. It is a metaphysical gap, compared with which the other is one only of degree.

APPENDIX (p. 172)
On the Origins of the Experience of Truth

In the Essay, pictorial representation has been related to truth; image-making is thus placed in the larger class of man's efforts for truth. It is indeed among the first forms in which this effort becomes thematic, but it is not the original locus for the experience of truth itself. This lies on a more primitive, less freely chosen level. To supplement the treatment of the pictorial sphere, something should be said of that original locus and the relation in which the pictorial truth effort stands to it.

1. The sense in which one can speak of an experience of truth may be illustrated by the situation in which one feels moved to exclaim "So this is what it *really* is!"—such exclamation containing a submerged, if not explicit, "and *not* this!" The illustration is to convey the at once emphatic and antithetical character of the truth-experience, i.e., that it stands out from the normal flow of acceptance of phenomena and *against* the background of error and falsehood: this background being itself an "experience" only realized in the act of supersedure by its opposite. In short, we wish to indicate that the experience of truth, as simultaneous exposure of untruth, includes an element of *negation*. Hence follows, as a first proposition, that the capacity for truth presupposes the capacity to negate, and that therefore only a being that can entertain negativity, that can say "no," can entertain truth. And since the power of negation is a part of freedom, indeed a defining ingredient of it, the proposition is that freedom is a prerequisite of truth, and that the experience of truth itself is the evidence and exercise of a certain kind of freedom.

2. Falsehood in its simplest form is encountered in two types of occasion: in errors of perception and in the lying of men (I omit, as a no longer "simple" source, mistake of reasoning). In both cases we are

misled—in the one by the appearance of things, in the other by words about things. In either case, then, the character of falsehood is that of *deception,* with the important difference between natural deceptiveness and contrived deceiving: the one proceeding from the objects of deception themselves, the other from an intermediary between the objects and myself; the one from their presence, the other in their absence. But in both cases the deception does proceed from something other than myself and as it were waylays me: I am the victim and not the agent of it, led into error rather than committing error.

Hence follows a second proposition, viz., that the negation first operative in the experience of truth is defensive rather than offensive: it is concerned to parry a thrust of the world, not to harry its reserve—a reaction to positive feigning, not to mere withholding, to the occasional lying rather than the habitual hiding on the part of things. If so, the truth-event has at first the character of un-deceiving (oneself), and only much later also that of "un-concealing" or "unveiling" (the veiled things: the latter is Heidegger's formula for the initial meaning of truth). Simulation, not opaqueness, is the initial stumbling block; delusion, not ignorance, the first object of the "No" in discovery. Deception is a particular and positive act. Not reticence but talking makes the liar: more than holding back the truth, he puts something else in its place to pass for it, and he does it credibly. Similarly it is the suggestiveness, the persuasive likenesses, the manifold make-believe of things *as perceived* that we are prey to, long before we are plagued by their secretiveness and our curiosity: they too "talk" to us in many tongues, and time and again are found out to have "lied" by "pretending" to be what they are not.

Their "reticence," in an altogether different respect, as a general condition—the reconditeness masked in *all* their appearing as such, "true" no less than "false"—is discovered on a higher plane of wonder and curiosity, where appearance, already secured on its own plane according to the distinction of spurious and genuine, invites no longer rectification *qua* appearance but penetration "behind" appearance—to a truth different from it in kind. Then truth as *by nature* hidden confronts appearance that by nature hides it. To this later, universal distinction the earlier, more naïve one transmits its style of straight negation native to the primitive shock-experience of truth, but not necessarily fitting the new field.

3. Of the two occasions for the primitive truth-encounter—deceptive appearing to the senses, intentional deceiving by the use of symbols—the first, being a fact of direct "seeing," is obviously more elementary and "prior" to the other, mediated one. Hence follows the further proposition that the original locus of falsehood and truth is *perception,* and that

therefore, if the power to negate is a condition for the experience of truth (prop. 1), it must be a particular trait of *human* perception, embodying that freedom, which fits it for the experience of falsehood and truth. Thus the nature of human perception, and what distinguishes it from the merely animal kind, becomes an integral part of any investigation into the origin of the truth experience.[1]

4. Once reared in the involuntary encounters of perception, the "experience of truth" can free itself from the contingencies for corrective reaction and, rather than be provoked by false likeness, provide its own object in purposely produced true likeness, in which the chosen content of perception is enshrined for continuous affirmative recognition. This happens in pictorial representation, the subject of our Essay, where the positive component in the truth-experience comes to the fore. That of critical negation still survives in the selections and rejections which mark the process of execution, but that of affirmation and enhanced appropriation motivates the process from the outset, insisting on its own satisfaction. Hence follows a fourth proposition, viz., that the *image-making* of early man represents a pristine form of active truth-effort, in its closeness to the perceptual soil preceding that of thought in "theory"; and that the power it employs—to contemplate images (forms) abstracted from actual presence—first exemplifies the positive freedom which must complement that of negation for the experience of truth to come fully into its own.

5. Finally, instead of staying with perception (i.e., the "given") and abiding by its verdict, both image-faculty and faculty of negation can be geared to will or desire, with the result either of supplanting the evidence of perception by what one would have it to be (wishful thinking), or of opposing it by what one would make it to be (projective thinking). Thus the power to negate and to picture is also employed in the service of falsehood, where only a second negation will restore truth; or in the service of innovation, where action is called in to transform potential into actual truth. Although these voluntaristic exercises of the negative-posi-

---

1. It should be made clear that we are dealing with the origins of the experience of *truth,* not with those of the experience of *knowing:* the latter is the wider phenomenon, for not all knowledge is concerned with truth, though all truth is contained in knowing. For instance, getting to know how things are done, e.g., a pot made, a fire kindled, a house built—i.e., learning how to do it—is not the same as finding out what things are. (Cf. also: knowing how to behave and to conduct oneself.) There are interesting relations between the two kinds of knowing, that concerned with doing and that concerned with truth: some of them are dealt with in the Eighth Essay.

tive freedom we are considering in the context of the truth-experience are of supreme importance in the affairs of man—the source both of illusory belief and of creative utopia—they are here merely mentioned to indicate the larger horizons behind our more limited theme. In what follows, we shall somewhat elaborate the "original locus" we have indicated. Its critical phenomenon is error or falsehood exposed.

The possibility of error arises with higher sense-perception as such (i.e., prior to man) and with it also possible rectification of error. An animal may *mistake* one object for another and then find out about its mistake. It may also be uncertain about the true nature of a perceived x that suggests several things as possibilities, and finally become sure what it really is. But neither of these cases raises for the animal the issue of truth or falsehood. There is indecision of response, or replacement of one response by another which is now found to be the suitable one, as one perception has been replaced by another which now rules the situation. The distinction between truth and falsehood, and therefore the idea of knowledge, arises only where the "wrong" perception is not simply supplanted by the "right" one but *survives* to be confronted *as falsified* with the right one; or more generally, where two terms are available for comparison, and one of them is accepted as the standard by which the other is judged. What I just called rectification of error in animals, the revision of a sensation in the light of subsequent sensation, merely relinquishes the former impression but does not hold it up against the new one to establish in what it fell short of truth. For this to happen, the past must stay available in the strangely noncommittal way which not memory as such, but only the detachment of appearance from reality in conjunction with memory provides: we then can compare without being alternately captives to the phenomenal presences as they jostle each other in our mental beholding. The image situation is a case in point. Where likeness is considered, the question of agreement and disagreement can be asked and can lead to the question: Is this a *true* likeness, and in what respect is it not? Several conditions must be fulfilled for the asking and answering of this question. And the first condition, necessary to arm us against the inherent compulsion of the merely given, is the distinction between pretension and authenticity. This distinction is thrust upon us in the experience of falsehood.

It is obvious that perception, especially sight, offers that experience. A perceptual aspect is taken to be that of a certain object, that is, something is taken *for* something. That which is thus taken is before me: that for which it is taken is in me from previous acquaintance. It may be argued that there is a submerged *judgment* in this perceptual recognition of something as something, and indeed this was Descartes' view; but this implies an atomic view of perception as first consisting of single, neutral "ideas" of sense, to which affirmation, negation, and relation are super-added in secondary acts. In this view, there can be perception *without* integration of the data into wholes, without completion of the given by the not-given, and without the collaboration of memory. If this were so, then even to take the sensually "given" for an *object* at all would be an extraneous addition to the primarily sensed and could be called, by some stretch of terminology, an implicit judgment. In that case, of course, we should have to say that animals perform judgments continually through-out their perceptual lives and that only verbal explicitness distinguishes human from animal "judgment." But apart from the semantic disadvan-tage of thus attenuating the meaning of a term, the idea of a perceiving which does *not* in the very act relate the present content to a wider range of experience, is a mere abstraction. To perceive *is* to admit the sense-content into a total of experience in which it exhibit such cognitive qualities as known, familiar, vaguely familiar, puzzling, startling. Even the experience of absolute novelty which leaves the percipient entirely at a loss as to what he is perceiving is possible only with reference to the accustomed wherein he is perceptually at home. Thus perception as such, as it constitutes itself in each instance on the background of past experi-ence, also points forward to future validation or invalidation: the next perception may confirm, amplify, correct, or cancel it (though it cannot of course cancel the previous sensation in itself). The essentially frag-mentary nature of any particular "view," which cannot possibly stand on itself, calls for continuous integration in the exercise of the visual faculty itself, and this integration is done in the light of past experience and through such integrative means as Gestalt psychology has shown to oper-ate in sensation itself. To call all this by the name of "judgment" serves only to confuse the issue. But it does involve the possibilities of confirma-tion and disappointment and thus has a reference to the question of truth and falsehood.

Of the alternative just mentioned, disappointment is the more critical for the emergence of the problem of truth. Confirmation, as a rule, passes unnoticed as a matter of course and is specifically experienced only after doubt, i.e., where the first perception left the subject uncertain, though inclined in the right direction. The disappointment of a wrong anticipa-tion is by far the more forceful and epistemologically relevant experience. The crouching animal over there turns out to be a bush. Is a judgment here corrected by a judgment? This would be the case only if the taking for an animal had been a matter of consciously guessing on insufficient evidence. But if it was thrust upon me with the immediate perception, indistinguishable from the perceiving itself, we should speak of deceptive appearance, not of error of judgment: not that I committed something but that the object lied to me. The fact that the world can play false to us, i.e., to our senses and to the acquired standards of our perceptual experience, is the pre-logical, pre-linguistic, pre-symbolical basis for the phenomenon of truth. "It was not truly an animal, in truth there is a bush there": it is only in this opposition to exposed falsehood that the idea of truth can arise, and when it does, "truth" is at first a character not of myself (as it would be as the truth of judgment) but of the world confronting me. The world was untruthful when the thirsty wanderer discovers the spring he has sighted to be salty, when seemingly solid ground becomes quagmire beneath the feet, when gold turns out to be fool's gold. In all these cases things themselves looked like things they were not, were perceived as these, to unmask themselves afterward. To be true, then, means first of all to be genuine and reliable and undisguised. The "true" well is that which does not disappoint. But genuineness itself comes to be discovered only with the experience of its opposite, which furthermore must be retained in the mind for comparison and contrast: the mere "explosion" of an impression by a subsequent corrective impression is not enough.

If we put the experiences we described into propositional form we should have statements like these: "An animal is crouching over there"; "It is not an animal, it is a bush." The second statement *retains* the first in the *negative* mode, as part of its own complete content. Its meaning is not fulfilled by now beholding just the bush. The past taking—now discovered to be a mis-taking—of the appearance for an animal qualifies the new recognition as a true recognition which stands out from the normal acceptance of phenomena. But this new quality can be apprehended as such only if reference is made to the falsified phenomenon, and this can be done only if it is still available in memory.

This leads us back to the consideration of the image-function. Suppose the issue is not between a crouching animal and a bush, where the "explosion" of the former impression through the later is complete and results in total revision. Suppose the issue to be between two fairly similar species of animals. The scout of a hunting tribe has come back with the message that he has spotted a herd of antelope; members of the hunting crew, upon approaching the scene, contend that these are buffaloes. If this turns out to be the case, or if an argument develops about it, the scout may explain his original impression by pointing out that such and such features discerned by him led him to his version of what he saw, and others will point out that if he had remembered certain other features of antelopes, he would have found that these are not antelopes; and if in addition he had remembered certain features of buffalo, he would have recognized the creatures for what they were. In other words, *forms* are compared, in this case of general images rather than of concrete individuals, and only in such a comparison is the wholeness of overall perception analyzed into distinct features of component detail and of proportion that can be isolated for mutual confrontation.

Herewith we have returned to the subject of the Essay. For what in our example was done by verbal discourse (with either direct pointing to the objects or recourse to memory), is in essence also achieved by the drawing, recognition, acceptance or rejection of a representative likeness; and this goes to show that the verbal sphere is not the exclusive and necessary locus of the phenomenon of truth and knowledge. Pictorial representation, closer to the perceptual terms than the abstract symbolism of language, and less concerned with the practical ends of communication, is a fundamental exercise of man's truth-effort in relation to the visible world. Every portrayal of things conserves a knowledge of them and itself comes under the criteria of knowledge. An image is either true or partially true or false. It has, as long as it is not considered aesthetically, no other *raison d'être* than the truth-reference, i.e., the reference of adequateness, to the object represented. As we put it in the Essay: what the schoolmen expressed, in the definition of truth, as *adaequatio intellectus ad rem,* appears here in the more elementary form of *adaequatio imaginis ad rem.*

All this refers to the concept of *theoretical* truth and its origins in experience. A different matter altogether is moral truth which means truthful dealing with one's fellow men. This, and not what the Heidegger school says, was the first meaning of *a-lēthēs* and *a-lētheuein:* not to feign and dissimulate one's designs, e.g., in the crafty verbal dealings of Greek communal life: to speak one's mind and not to hide it: to be frank and open—predicated of persons as relating to persons, not of things related to persons, and least of persons related to things. And as a matter of linguistic fact, the verb *alētheuein* never meant, transitively, to "undeceive" or "un-conceal"; in its pretheoretical use it always meant, intransitively, to abstain from concealing and deceiving, becoming transitive only in the sense of "making true" one's promise or someone's hope, or predicting truly what was to happen.[2]—The appropriation of this morally

---

2. Even in its later, theoretical use the transitive power of the verb *alētheuein* was confined to the internal object "statement" ("making true discourse"), with the addition of "about . . ." or "in respect of . . ." (*kata tinos*): it still meant "speaking truthfully," with the difference that the

weighted term into the theoretical sphere was indeed of supreme importance, but it was a secondary development brought about in the philosophical schools. It is a moot question how much of the earlier associa-
tions (of not-dissembling, etc.) survived in the new setting.

---

speech is now meant to be "true," not to the speaker's thoughts, but to the
things thought and spoken about; and, of course, there being no reason,
in theoretical discourse, for wishing to hide the latter (while there may be
good reasons, in practical discourse, for hiding the former), the "not
hiding" aspect of etymological yore had lost its possible application, quite
apart from probably being long forgotten by that time anyway. But as to
"un-hiding," the pet interpretation of the School: never did grammar
permit the Greeks to alētheuein the things themselves (ta pragmata, as
direct object), i.e., to "bring them out of their hiding into the light of
truth." (They need no saving, but the thinker does: the logos alēthēs
resolves an aporia, i.e., a difficulty that has arisen in discourse itself.)
Much philological nonsense has been written on that score to underpin
philosophical profundity.

From Philosophy of the Organism to the Philosophy of Man

Since with the last Essay we have passed the borderline between the physical and the mental sphere and will henceforth move in the latter alone, it may be appropriate to recapitulate the stages by which this threshold was reached from metabolism upward.

The separation of *eidos* from reality with which we met in the phenomena of "image" and "truth" signifies the passage to a new, critical level of mediacy in the relation of organism to environment. The growth of such mediacy can be observed throughout organic evolution. Metabolism itself, and therefore plant life already, is mediated identity and continuity (Third Essay). On the animal level, representing a decisive step beyond the relative immediacy of vegetative existence, mediacy has the three aspects of motility, perception, emotion (Fourth and Fifth Essays). All three imply *distance:* across it, and *through* the modes of perceiving, striving, acting, "world" is constituted and replaces the mere environment of the plant. "World" confronts the subject with discrete, self-contained objects, whereas the plant-environment consists of adjacent matter and impinging forces. Direct chemical commerce with the environment is the vegetative mode of outwardness, and it remains the basis for all organic existence. But in animal life this vegetative level is served deviously through the organism's relations to objects out in space which are perceived, desired, reached, and acted upon externally before entering

into the organic commerce of the metabolizing system. Thus the freedom of the animal level is that of external adjustments made in
actions distinct from the end to be achieved and therefore coming
under the alternative of correct-incorrect, of success and failure. By
the very dialectic of life, this superimposed level of mediacy, in spite
of its instrumental role for mere organic survival, constitutes its own
scale of concerns which reverse the relation of ends and means as
between vegetative and animal function. The feelings of pleasure and
pain that accompany animal experience as intrinsic rewards and
punishments of conduct, to which must be added the excitement of
action itself, are clear indications of the endowment of animal functions with values and ends of their own. What seems not to be found
yet in animals is that *perception* by itself becomes imbued with pleasure and assumes the status of an experience sought for its own
sake.

In the sphere of perception we note in particular the contribution
of the distance senses to the pattern of mediacy. Among these, sight
represents in the purest manner the setting apart of organism and
world, and their recombination in a secondary relation (Sixth Essay).
The object seen is interposed between the organism and its direct
organic dealings with the environment. These dealings are henceforth
initiated, directed, and controlled by the information concerning
things that are distant, i.e., outside the organic range itself. The arc of
this detour of satisfaction is the locus for the freedom and risk of
animal life. In the span between the self and the distant object (as yet
unengaged), which long-range vision sets up, emotion can make its
choice and long-range locomotion can take its course. But sight, as
the Sixth Essay has shown, contains trans-animal potentialities of
beholding and attitude which a higher mental faculty can actualize.

In the image-faculty of man a further degree of mediacy is reached,
and the distance between organism and environment widened by a
further step (Seventh Essay). This new degree lies in the ideative
extension of *perception* and at first hardly affects the human versions
of animal emotion and motility (though it does so later on). The new
mediacy consists in the interposition of the abstracted and mentally
manipulable *eidos* between sense and actual object, just as on the
level of animal mediacy the perception of objects was interposed
between the organism and its primary environment-relation. Imaging

and speaking man ceases to see things directly: he sees them through the screen of representations of which he has become possessed by his own previous dealings with objects, and which are evoked by the present perceptual content, impregnating it with their *symbolic* charge, and added to by the new experience itself. Their greatest role, however, lies in between experiences, when the actual object is not present for direct perception: then the abstracted images that are at the command of the subject provide in themselves the material for an "experience" at a remove—symbolic experience, in which the world is taken hold of without imposing its presence. The very phenomenon of truth, as that of falsehood, is located in this mediacy of the third degree.

Yet even this is the threshold to a further mediation. The fateful freedom of objectification, which confronts the self with the potential sum total of the "other," the "world," as an indefinite realm for possible understanding and action, can and eventually must turn back, with its burden of mediacy, upon the subject itself and make *it* in turn the object of a relation which again takes the detour via the *eidos.* The "form" here involved is different in kind from those of the whole realm of outwardness, for it concerns the self's *relation* to all outwardness. The new dimension of *reflection* unfolds, where the *subject* of all objectification appears *as such* to itself and becomes objectified for a new and ever more self-mediating kind of relation. With the first asking of the question, What is man's, what is my place and part in the scheme of things?, the self becomes engulfed in the distantness in which all things are kept by man and from which they have to be retrieved in acts of eidetic intentionality. Although this is another exercise of the eidetic faculty, it is by no means automatically given with its outward exercise exemplified by pictorial representation. True man emerges when the painter of the bull and even of its hunter turns to concerning himself with the unpaintable image of his own conduct and the state of his self. Over the distance of this wondering, searching, and comparing perception there is constituted the new entity, "I." This is of all the greatest venture in mediacy and objectification. We use the term "image" deliberately. Man models, experiences, and judges his own inner state and outward conduct after the image of what is man's. Willingly or not he lives the idea of man—in agreement or in conflict, in acceptance or in defiance, in compliance or in repudiation, with good or with bad conscience. The image of man never leaves him, however much he may wish at times to revert to the bliss of animality. To be created in the image of God means to have to live with the image of man. That image is worked out and entertained in the verbal intercommunication of society, and thus the individual finds it ready-made and thrust upon him. As he learns from others to see things and to speak about them, so he learns from them to see himself and to express what he sees there "in the image and likeness" of the established pattern. But learning this, learning to say "I," he potentially discovers his own identity in its solitary uniqueness. A private objectivity of the self is thus in constant rapport with the public image of man and through its own exteriorization contributes to the continuous remaking of the latter—the anonymous share of each self in the history of all. In complete accommodation it may let itself be absorbed into the general model; in defeated nonconformity it may withdraw into its own solitude; in rare cases it may assert itself to the point of setting itself up as a new image of man and impose it on society, to replace the prevailing image.

In reflection upon self the subject-object split which began to appear in animal evolution reaches its extreme form. It has extended into the center of feeling life, which is now divided against itself. Only over the immeasurable distance of being his own object can man "have" himself. But he does have himself while no animal does. The vital concern of feeling which is at the bottom of life's venture and toil, and which is always for the enjoyment of selfness in the meeting with otherness, has here by a daring detour found its true and, in a way, original object. As in all achievements of life, the price is high. As human satisfaction is different from animal and far surpassing its scope, so is human suffering, though man also shares in the animal range of feelings. But only man can be happy and unhappy, thanks to the measuring of his being against terms that transcend the immediate situation. Supremely concerned with what he is, how he lives, what he makes out of himself, and viewing himself from the distance of his wishes, aspirations, and approvals, man and man alone is open to despair. The German word *Verzweiflung* somehow renders the connection of despair with the twofoldness, the division of the self, that has come about with the transfer of the subject-object split to the realm of the subject itself, making it the quivering product of ever-mediating relation instead of an immediate possession. Suicide, this unique privilege of man, shows the ultimate manner in which man can become the object of himself.

It is in the gulf opened by this confrontation of oneself with oneself, and in the exercise of the relation which in some way or other always has to span the gulf, that the highest elations and deepest dejections of human experience have their place. As are the data of his external senses, so are the findings of his reflection the mere material for continuous synthesis and integration into a total image. This work goes on as long as man is alive as man. *Quaestio mihi factus sum,* "a question have I become unto me": religion, ethics, and metaphysics are attempts, never completed, to meet and answer the question within an interpretation of total reality.

With the emergence of this possibility, history succeeds to evolution, and biology cedes the field to a philosophy of man.

The Practical Uses of Theory

I

In his commentary to Aristotle's *On the Soul,* Thomas Aquinas wrote as follows:

"All knowledge is obviously good because the good of any thing is that which belongs to the fulness of being which all things seek after and desire; and man as man reaches fulness of being through knowledge. Now of good things some are just valuable, namely, those which are useful in view of some end—as we value a good horse because it runs well; whilst other good things are also honourable: namely, those that exist for their own sake, for we give honour to ends, not to means. Of the sciences some are practical, others speculative; the difference being that the former are for the sake of some work to be done, while the latter are for their own sake. The speculative sciences are therefore honourable as well as good, but the practical are only valuable."[1]

About three and a half centuries later, Francis Bacon wrote in *The Great Instauration* as follows:

---

1. A. M. Pirotta, ed., *Sancti Thomae Aquinatis in Aristotelis Librum de Anima Commentarium, Lectio* I, 3. The above English quotation is from the translation by K. Foster and S. Humphries, *Aristotle's De Anima in the Version of William of Moerbeke and the Commentary of St. Thomas Aquinas,* p. 45.

"I would address one general admonition to all: that they consider what are the true ends of knowledge, and that they seek it not either for pleasure of the mind, or for contention, or for superiority to others . . . but for the benefit and use of life, and that they perfect and govern it in charity. . . . [From the marriage of the Mind and the Universe] there may spring helps to man, and a line and race of inventions that may in some degree subdue and overcome the necessities and miseries of humanity. . . . For the matter in hand is no mere felicity of speculation, but the real business and fortunes of the human race, and all power of operation. . . . And so those twin objects, *human knowledge* and *human power,* do really meet in one."[2]

Here are two opposing statements of the aim and very meaning of knowledge and, consequently, of its relation to possible use, or to "works." On this old theme the present discourse attempts to offer some comments unavailable to the original contestants but available to us in the light of the new "necessities and miseries of humanity," which are besetting us, so it seems, precisely as a concomitant of that use of knowledge which Bacon envisaged as the remedy for humanity's old necessities and miseries.

Aquinas and Bacon obviously speak of two different things. In assigning different ends to knowledge, they speak in fact of different kinds of knowledge, having also different kinds of things for their subject. Taking Aquinas first, who of course speaks for Aristotle, the "speculative" (that is, theoretical) sciences of his statement are about things unchangeable and eternal—the first causes and intelligible forms of Being—which, being unchangeable, *can* be contemplated only, not involved in action: theirs is *theoria* in the strict Aristotelian sense. The "practical sciences," on the other hand, are "arts," not "theory"—a knowledge concerning the planned changing of the changeable. Such knowledge springs from experience, not from theory or speculative reason. The guidance that theory *can* provide

---

2. From the Preface of Francis Bacon to *The Great Instauration.* The four sentences of the quotation occur in the text in that order, but widely scattered. An additional quotation from the Preface may instance Bacon's direct criticism of classical theory: "And for its value and utility it must be plainly avowed that that wisdom which we have derived principally from the Greeks is but the boyhood of knowledge, and has the characteristic property of boys: it can talk, but it cannot generate; for it is fruitful of controversies but barren of works."

with regard to the arts consists not in promoting their invention and informing their procedures, but in informing their user (if he partakes in the theoretical life) with the wisdom to use those arts, like all things, wisely, that is, in proper measure and for proper ends. This may be called a practical benefit of theory through the enlightening effect which it has on the whole person of its votaries beyond its immediate actuality. But this benefit is not in the nature of a "use" made of theory as a means, and is anyway a second best in response to the necessities of man: the best is the sustained activity of pure thought itself, where man is most free.

So far Aristotle and Aquinas. It is the "necessities of humanity" which assume first place in Bacon's scheme: and since art is man's way of meeting and conquering necessity, but has not hitherto enjoyed the benefit of speculative reason (mainly by the latter's fault), Bacon urges that the two be brought into a new relationship in which their former separation is overcome. This involves a revision of both, but first, in causal order, of speculative science, which has so long been "barren of works." Theory must be so revised that it yields "designations and directions for works," even has "the invention of arts" for its very end, and thus becomes itself an art of invention. Theory it is nonetheless, as it is discovery and rational account of first causes and universal laws (forms). It thus agrees with classical theory in that it has the nature of things and the totality of nature for its object; but it is such a science of causes and laws, or a science of such causes and laws, as then makes it possible "to command nature in action." It makes this possible because from the outset it looks at nature *qua* acting, and achieves knowledge of nature's laws of action by itself engaging nature in action—that is, in experiment, and therefore on terms set by man himself. It yields directions for works because it first catches nature "at work."

A science of "nature at work" is a mechanics, or dynamics, of nature. For such a science Galileo and Descartes provided the speculative premises and the method of analysis and synthesis. Giving birth to a theory with inherently technological potential, they set on its actual course that fusion of theory and practice which Bacon was dreaming of. Before I say something more of that kind of theory which lends itself to technical application, and indeed has intrinsic reference to this kind of use, I must say something about use as such.

I I

What is use for? The ultimate end of all use is the same as the end of all activity, and this is twofold: preservation of life, and betterment of life, that is, promotion of the good life. Put negatively, as suggested by Bacon's pair "necessities and miseries," the twofold end is to ward off extinction and to overcome misery. We note the emergency aspect that Bacon gives to human endeavor, and thus to knowledge as part of that endeavor. He speaks of lifting or lessening an adverse and pressing condition, whereas Thomas, with Aristotle, speaks positively of attaining "fulness of being," or perfection. Bacon's negative emphasis invests the task of knowledge with a kind of physical and moral urgency altogether strange and novel in the history of theory, but increasingly familiar since his time.

The difference in emphasis admits, however, of common ground: assuming mere preservation (which takes precedence in both cases) to be assured in its basic conditions, misery means denial of a good life; its removal then means betterment, and therefore by both accounts, that of Aristotle and that of Bacon, the ultimate aim of all doing beyond that minimum necessary for survival is the good life or human happiness. Leaving the term "happiness" in all the ambiguity it must have until we determine what happiness may consist in, we may thus state as the ground common to Bacon and Aristotle that the "what for" of all use, including that of knowledge, is happiness.

Whose happiness? If, as Bacon holds, knowledge is to do away with the miseries of mankind, it is the happiness of mankind which the pursuit of knowledge has for its aim. If, as Aristotle holds, man as man reaches fullness of being through, or rather in, knowledge, it is the happiness of the knower which the pursuit of pure knowledge achieves. In both cases there is, then, a supreme "use" to theoretical knowledge. To Aristotle it consists in the good that knowledge works in the soul of the knower, that is, in the condition of knowing itself as the perfection of the knower's being.

Now, to claim this ennobling effect for knowledge makes sense only when theory is knowledge of the noblest, that is, most perfect, objects. There being such objects is indeed the condition of there being "theory" in the classical sense of the word; and conversely, failing such objects the contemplative ideal of classical philosophy becomes pointless. Assuming the condition as given, then theory, as intellectual communion with those objects—and through such communion modifying the subject's own condition—does not merely promote but in its actuality constitute happiness: a happiness termed "divine," and therefore but briefly obtainable in the lives of mortals. Hence in this case possession and use of theory are the same. If there is a further "use" of it beyond its own activity—and therefore a contribution to happiness of a more "human" (as distinct from "divine") kind—it consists, as we have seen, in the wisdom it confers on the person for the conduct of his life in general, and in the comprehension which, from the summit of speculation, transfuses his understanding of all things, including common things. But although theory through wisdom may deliver its possessor from the spell of common things, and thereby increase his moral freedom from their necessity, it does not increase his physical control over and use of them (rather tends to limit the latter), and leaves the realm of necessity itself unaffected.

Since Bacon's time it has been the other alternative that matters. To him and those after him, the use of knowledge consists in the "fruits" it bears in our dealing with the common things. To bear that fruit the knowledge itself must be knowledge of common things—not derivatively so, as was classical theory, but primarily and even before becoming practical. This is indeed the case: the theory that is thus to be fruitful is knowledge of a universe which, in the absence of a hierarchy of being, consists of common things entirely. Since freedom can then no longer be located in a cognitive relation to the "noblest objects," knowledge must deliver man from the yoke of necessity by meeting necessity on its own ground, and achieves freedom for him by delivering the things into his power. A new vision of nature, not only of knowledge, is implied in Bacon's insistence that "the mind may exercise over the nature of things the authority which properly belongs to it." The nature of things is left with no dignity of its own.[3]

---

3. "For as all works do show forth the power and skill of the workman, and not his image; so it is of the works of God, which do show the omnipotency and wisdom of the maker, but not his image: and therefore therein the heathen opinion differeth from the sacred truth; for they supposed the world to be the image of God, and man to be an extract or compendious image of the world; but the Scriptures never vouchsafe to attribute to the world that honour, as to be the image of God, but only *the*

All dignity belongs to man: what commands no reverence can be commanded, and all things are for use. To be the master of nature is the right of man as the sole possessor of mind, and knowledge, by fitting him to exercise this right, will at last bring man into his own. His own is "the kingdom of man," and it consists in his sovereign use of things. Sovereign use means more use—not merely potential but actual and, strange to say, even necessary use. Control, by making ever more things available for more kinds of uses, enmeshes the user's life in ever more dependencies on external objects. There is no other way of exercising the power than by making oneself available to the use of the things as they become available. Where use is forgone the power must lapse, but there is no limit to the extension of either. And so one master is exchanged for another.

Even the laying hold of power in the first place is not quite so free as the appeal to man's legitimate authority suggests. For not only is man's relation to nature one of power, but nature herself is conceived in terms of power. Thus it is a question of either ruling or being ruled; and to be ruled by a nature not noble or kindred or wise means slavery and hence misery. The exercise of man's inherent right is therefore also the response to a basic and continuous emergency: the emergency of a contest decreed by man's condition. The attack of knowledge, being a defense against necessity, is itself a function of necessity and retains this aspect throughout its career, which is a continuous response to the new necessities created by its very progress.

III

For knowledge to be beneficial to man's estate it must be "perfected and governed in charity." This is to say that whoever administers the course and the use of theory must take the necessities and miseries of

---

work of his hands; neither do they speak of any other image of God, but man" (Bacon, *The Advancement of Learning,* Book II: *Works,* ed. J. Spedding and R. L. Ellis, III, pp. 349 f. [=*The Philosophical Works,* ed. J. M. Robertson, p. 91]). Leo Strauss adduces this passage in support of the statement: "The division of philosophy into natural and human philosophy is based on the systematic distinction between man and world, which Bacon makes in express controversy against ancient philosophy" (*The Political Philosophy of Hobbes,* p. 91, n. 1).

humanity to heart. The blessings of knowledge are not in the first place for the knower but for his not-knowing fellow men—and for himself only insofar as he is one of them. Unlike the magician, the scientist does not acquire in his own person the power that springs from his art. He hardly even acquires, and certainly does not own, the knowledge itself in his own person: since this knowledge is a collective enterprise, his fractional contribution goes into the common stock, of which the scientific community is the depository and society as a whole should be the beneficiary. Among the benefits that knowledge grants through power over things is relief from toil: leisure then, but not the scientist's own, is here a fruit of knowledge. The classical pattern was the opposite: leisure was a condition of theory, antecedently assured to make theory possible, not something to be achieved by its exertions. Modern theoretical activity, far from being use of leisure, is itself a toil and part of the common toil of humanity, however gratifying to the toiler. This alone shows that modern theory does not, in human terms, take the place of classical theory.

Furthermore, the need for charity or benevolence in the use of theory stems from the fact that power can be for evil as well as for good. Now, charity is not itself among the fruits of theory in the modern sense. As a qualifying condition of its use—which use theory itself does not specify, let alone assure—it must spring from a source transcendent to the knowledge that the theory supplies.

Here a comparison with the classical case is instructive. Though Plato does not call it by that name, the responsibility that compels the philosopher to return to the "cave" and help his fellow men imprisoned there is an analogue to Bacon's charity or pity. But also how different! In the first place, since of theory in the Platonic sense the activity as well as the object is noble, it will itself be the source of benevolence in its adepts for whatever part they may take in the active life. Nonbenevolent action would be inconsistent with the light they partake of through the highest knowledge. No such contradiction obtains between the insights of science and their potential nonbenevolent use. Second, though in Plato's scheme the "descent" into the active life is not by inclination but by duty, and this duty is proximately enforced by the state, its ultimate sanction emanates from the object of contemplation itself, namely, "the good," which is not envious and impels its own communication; thus no additional and heterogenic principle is required to provide the ground of responsibility. Finally, the returning philosopher's action in the cave is concerned, not with the managing of things, but with the ordering of lives; in other words, it is not technical but political, informed by the vision of order in the intelligible world. Thus it is an "application" that derives its motive, its model, and its standard of what is beneficial from the one and self-sufficient theory. Such "application" can be exercised only in person by the authentic adepts of theory; it cannot be delegated, as can and must be the application of the "know-how" of technical science.

By contrast, modern theory is not self-sufficiently the source of the human quality that makes it beneficial. That its results are detachable from it and handed over for use to those who had no part in the theoretical process is only one aspect of the matter. The scientist himself is by his science no more qualified than others to discern, nor even is he more disposed to care for, the good of mankind. Benevolence must be called in from the outside to supplement the knowledge acquired through theory: it does not flow from theory itself.

Why is this so? One answer is commonly expressed in the statement that science is "value-free" (*wertfrei*), with the corollary that values are not objects of knowledge, or at any rate of scientific knowledge. But why is science divorced from value, and value considered nonrational? Can it be because the validation of value requires a transcendence whence to derive it? Relation to an objective transcendence lies today outside theory by its rules of evidence, whereas formerly it was the very life of theory.

"Transcendence" (whatever else the term comprises) implies objects higher than man, and about such was classical theory. Modern theory is about objects lower than man: even stars, being common things, are lower than man. No guidance as to ends can be derived from them. The phrase "lower than man," implying a valuation, seems to contradict the asserted "value-freedom" of science. But this value-freedom means a neutrality as much of the objects as of the science: of the objects, their neutrality (indifference) toward whatever value may be "given" them. And that which lacks intrinsic value of its own is lower than that by reference to which alone it may receive value, namely, man and human life, the only remaining source and referent of value.

What then about the sciences of man, like psychology or sociology? Surely it cannot be said of them that the objects of science are lower than man? Their object *is* man. Is it not true that with them value re-enters the universe of science? And can there not spring from them, as dealing with source and reference of all value, a valid theory of value? But here we have to distinguish: Valuation as a fact of human behavior indeed becomes known in the human sciences—but not value itself. And facetious as it may sound: insofar as they are *sciences* their object too is "lower than man." How so? For a scientific theory of him to be possible, man, including his habits of valuation, has to be taken as determined by causal laws, as an instance and part of nature. The scientist does take him so—but not himself while he assumes and exercises his freedom of inquiry and his openness to reason, evidence, and truth. Thus man-the-knower apprehends man-*qua*-lower-than-himself and in doing so achieves knowledge of man-*qua*-lower-than-man, since all scientific theory is of things lower than man the knower. It is on that condition that they can be subjected to "theory," hence to control, hence to use. Then man-lower-than-man explained by the human sciences—man reified—can by the instructions of these sciences be controlled (even "engineered") and thus used.

Charity then, or even love (as love of mankind rather than person), in trying to make such use a charitable or beneficent one, does not correct but rather confirm the lower status. And as the use of what is lower-than-man can only be for what is lower and not for what is higher in the user himself, the knower and user becomes in such use, if made all-inclusive, himself lower than man. And all-inclusive it becomes when it extends over the being of one's fellow men and swallows up the island-kingdom of the person. Inevitably the manipulator comes to see himself in the same light as those his theory has made manipulable; and in the self-inclusive solidarity with the general human lowliness amidst the splendor of human power his charity is but self-compassion and that tolerance which springs from self-contempt: we are all poor puppets and cannot help being what we are. Benevolence then degenerates to condoning and conniving.

Even when of a purer and less ambiguous kind, benevolence alone is insufficient to insure beneficial use of science. As a disposition to refrain from harming, it is of course as indispensable in this context as it is in the fellowship of men in general. But in its positive aspect good will is *for* the good and must therefore be informed by a conception of what is the good. Whence such a conception can derive and whether it can be raised to the rank of "knowledge" must here be left undecided. If there is a knowledge of it, not science can supply it. Mere benevolence cannot replace it—nor even love, if love without reverence; and whence can reverence come except from a knowledge of what is to be revered? But even if a guiding knowledge of the good, that is, true philosophy were available, it might well find its counsel to be of no avail against the self-generated dynamics of science in use. To this theme I shall return at the end. Now I must say something more about the specifically modern practice-theory relation itself and the ways it works, rather than what it works for.

I V

We speak of *using* when we apply something as a means toward an end. As the end is distinct from the means, so normally is the means distinct from its application. That is to say, the means has a prior existence of its own and would continue to be what it is even if never so applied at all. Whether this holds fully for theory too, or for every theory, we have reason to doubt. But in speaking of uses of theory that much is conceded that theory, however used, is also something by itself.

Being something by itself is not necessarily to be neutral to possible use. Use may be essential, or it may be accidental, to that which can serve as a means. Some things, though having a substantive being of their own once they exist, do so *as* means from the outset. A tool, for example, owes its very being to the purpose beyond itself for which it was designed. If not put to such service it misses its *raison d'être*. To other things use comes as it were as an afterthought on the part of a user: for them, being used is accidental, extraneous to the being they have in their own independent right. In the first category are mainly man-made things, like hammers or chairs, in the second mainly natural ones, like horses or rivers. Theory is certainly man-made, and it has uses; but whether use is essential or accidental to it may well depend on the kind of theory one considers, as also on the kind of use. Mathematics, for example, differs in this respect from physics. My thesis is that to modern theory in general, practical use is no accident but is integral to it, or that "science" is technological by its nature.

Practical is a use which involves external action, resulting in a change in the environment (or preventing a change). External action requires the use of external, physical means, and moreover some degree of information, which is an internal, nonphysical thing. But all action which is not strictly routine, and not purely intuitive, requires more than that, namely, deliberation, and this can be as to ends and as to means: as to ends—for example, whether desirable, and whether generally possible; as to means—for example, which as such suitable, and which here and now available. In all these respects, *knowledge* (if not necessarily theory) enters into the conditions and conduct of action and is made use of.

Obviously it is a different kind of knowledge that has to do with the desirability of ends, and a different kind that has to do with feasibility, means, and execution. Again, within the latter kind, the knowledge which pronounces on possibility in principle is different from the one which maps, still in the abstract, possible ways of realization, and this from the discernment of the course of action most practicable in the given circumstances. We have here a scale descending from the general to the particular, from the simple to the complex, and at the same time from theory to practice, which is complexity itself. The knowledge of possibility rests on the universal principles of the field, its constitutive laws (the terminal points of what Galileo called the "resolutive method"); that of typical ways of coming-to-be on more complex and more specific causal patterns, embodying the first principles and providing models for rules of action ("compositive method"); the knowledge, finally, of what to do now is entirely particular, placing the task within the context of the whole, concrete situation. The first two steps are both within theory, or rather, they each *can* have their developed theory. The theory in the first case we may call science proper, such as theoretical physics; the theory in the second case, derivative from it in logic, if not always in fact, we may call technological or applied science—which, it must be remembered, is still "theory" in respect to action itself, as it offers the specific rules of action as parts of a reasoned whole and without making a decision. The particular execution itself has no theory of its own and can have none. Though applying the theory, it is not simply derivative of it but involves decision based on *judgment;* and there is no science of judgment (as little as there is one of decision)—that is, judgment cannot be replaced by, or transformed into, science, much as it can avail itself of the findings and even of the intellectual discipline of science and is itself a kind of knowledge, a cognitive faculty. Judgment, says Kant, is the faculty of subsuming the particular under the universal; and since reason is the faculty of the universal, and science the operation of that faculty, judgment as concerned with particulars is necessarily outside science and strictly the bridge between the abstractions of the understanding and the concreteness of life.

In the first stage, that of pure science, the form of propositions is categorical: A is P, B is P, . . . In the applied stage, the form is hypothetical: if P is to be, then either A or B . . . must be provided. In the deliberations of practical judgment, the propositional form is problematical: particulars f, g, . . . available in the situation, do perhaps (not, partially) fit the demands of universal A, or B, . . . ; may therefore be (not, more, less) suitable for bringing about P. Invention is typically such a combination of concrete judgment with abstract science.

It is in this realm of concrete judgment and choice that the practical use of theory comes about. Whence it follows that the use of theory does not itself permit of a theory: if it is enlightened use, it receives its light from deliberation, which may or may not enjoy the benefits of good sense. But this knowledge of use is different not only from the knowledge of the theory used in the case but from that of any theory whatsoever, and it is acquired or learned in ways different from those of theory. This is the reason why Aristotle denied there being a science of politics and practical ethics; the *where, when, to whom* . . . cannot be reduced to general principles. Thus there is theory and use of theory, but no theory of the use of theory.

At the opposite end of the scale is the knowledge concerning ends repeatedly alluded to—of which today we do not know whether it admits of theory, as once it was held eminently to do. This knowledge alone would permit the valid discrimination of worthy and unworthy, desirable and undesirable uses of science, whereas science itself only permits discrimination of its correct or incorrect, adequate or inadequate, effectual or ineffectual use. But it is with this very science which is not in doubt that we must now concern ourselves, asking what features intrinsically fit this type of theory for use in the world of things.

V

Of theory formation one of its nineteenth-century masters, Heinrich Hertz, had this to say: "We form images or symbols of the external objects; the manner in which we form them is such that the *logically* necessary consequences of the images are invariably the images of the *materially* necessary consequences of the corresponding objects."[4]

This is an elliptic statement. For the "images or symbols" formed and used are not of the immediate external objects such as rocks and trees, or even of whole classes or general types of such, but symbols for the residual products of a speculative analysis of the given objects and their states and relations—residues which admit of none but symbolic representation, yet by hypothesis are presumed to underlie the objects and are thus treated as "external objects" themselves in substitution for the original objects.

The key term here is "analysis." Analysis has been the distinctive feature of physical inquiry since the seventeenth century: analysis of *working* nature into its simplest dynamic factors. These factors are framed in such identical quantitative terms as can be entered, combined, and transformed in equations. The analytical method thus implies a primary *ontological reduction* of nature, and this precedes mathematics or other symbolism in its application to nature. Once left to deal with the residual products of this reduction, or rather, with their measured values, mathematics proceeds to reconstruct from them the complexity of phenomena in a way which can lead beyond the data of the initial experience to facts unobserved, or still to come, or to be brought about. That nature lends itself to this kind of reduction was the fundamental discovery, actually the fundamental anticipation, at the outset of mechanical physics.

With this reduction, "substantial forms," that is, wholeness as an

---

4. H. Hertz, *Prinzipien der Mechanik*, p. 1, taken from H. Weyl, *Philosophy of Mathematics and Natural Science*, p. 162.

autonomous cause with respect to its component parts, and therefore the ground of its own becoming, shared the fate of final causes. In Newtonian physics the integral wholeness of form, on which classical and medieval ontology was based, is broken up into elementary factors for which the parallelogram of forces is a fitting graphic symbol. The presence of the future, formerly conceived as potentiality of becoming, consists now in the calculability of the operation of the forces discernible in a given configuration. No longer something original in its own right, form is the current compromise among the basic actions of aggregate matter. The falling apple is not so much elevated to the rank of cosmic motion as the latter is brought down to the level of the falling apple. This establishes a new unity of the universe, but of a different complexion from the Greek one: the aristocracy of form is replaced by the democracy of matter.

If, according to this "democracy," wholes are mere sums, then their seemingly genuine qualities are due to the quantitatively more or less involved combination of some simple substrata and their dynamics. Generally complexity and degrees of complexity supplant all other ontological distinctions. Thus for purposes of explanation the parts are called upon to account for the whole, and that means that the primitive has to account for the more articulated, or, in older parlance, *the lower for the higher.*

With no hierarchy of being but only distributions of a uniform substratum, all explanation has to start from the bottom and in fact never leaves it. The higher is the lower in disguise, where the disguise is provided by complexity: with the latter's analysis, the disguise dissolves, and the appearance of the higher is reduced to the reality of the elemental. From physics this schema of explanation has penetrated all provinces of knowledge, and it is now as much at home in psychology and sociology as in the natural sciences where it originated. No longer is the realm of passion characterized by the absence of reason, but reason is characterized as a disguise and servant of passion. The transcendental philosophy of a society is but the ideological superstructure to (and thus a disguise of) its vital interests, which reflect organic needs, which depend on physical constitution. The rat in the maze tells us what we are. Always the lower explains the higher and in the course of analysis emerges as its truth.

Now this ontological analysis has *per se* technological implication prior to any application in fact. The latter is possible only because of the manipulative aspect inherent in the theoretic constitution of modern science as such. If it is shown how things are made up of their elements, it is also shown, on principle, how they can be made up out of such elements. Making, as distinct from generating, is essentially putting together pre-existing materials or rearranging pre-existing parts. Similarly, scientific cognition is essentially analysis of distribution, that is, of the conditions in which elements are interrelated, and is not burdened with the task of comprehending the essence of those elements themselves. Not what they are but how they function under such specified conditions, that is, in such combinatorial relations, is the theme that science can and does pursue. This restriction is basic to the modern conception of knowledge; for, unlike substantial natures, distributions of conditions can be reconstructed, even freely constructed, in mental models and so allow of understanding. Again, unlike "natures," they may be actually repeated or modified in human imitation of nature, that is in technique, and so allow of manipulation. Both understanding and making are here concerned with relations and not with essences. In fact, understanding of this sort is itself a kind of imaginary making or remaking of its objects, and this is the deepest cause for the technological applicability of modern science.

Early in the eighteenth century, Vico enunciated the principle that man can understand only what he has made himself. From this he reasoned that not nature, which as made by God stands over against man, but history, which is of man's own making, can be understood by man. Only a *factum*—what has been made—can be a *verum*. But in opposing this principle to Cartesian natural science, Vico overlooked the fact that, if only "has been made" is widened to "can be made," the principle applies to nature even better than to history (where in fact its validity is doubtful). For according to the mechanistic scheme the knowledge of a natural event deals, as we have seen, not with the God-created part of the situation—the intrinsic nature of the substances involved—but with the variable conditions which, given those substances, determine the event. By re-enacting those conditions, in thought or in actual manipulation, one can reproduce the event without producing the substratum. To understand the substratum itself is as much beyond man's powers as to produce it. But the latter is beyond the powers even of nature, which, once created in its substantial entities, goes on "creating" only by manipulating them, that is, by the shift of relations. Conditions and relations are the vehicle for created nature's noncreative productions, just as they are the vehicle for created man's cognition of nature and also for his technical imitation of nature's ways of production. This was the meaning of Bacon's famous maxim that nature can be commanded only by being obeyed. Nature's quasi-technical modes of making—or nature as its own artificer and artifact—is the at once knowable and imitable aspect of it, whereas essences in themselves are unknowable because unmakeable. The metaphor of "nature's workshop," into which science is to pry in order to learn her procedures, popularly expresses the point that the distinction between natural and artificial, so basic to classical philosophy, has lost its meaning. "I do not," wrote Descartes, "recognize any difference between the machines made by craftsmen and the diverse bodies put together by nature alone . . . all the rules of mechanics belong to physics, so that all things which are artificial are thereby natural" (*Principles* IV, art. 203).[5] In the same vein, Descartes could say "Give me matter and motion, and I shall make the world once more"—a saying impossible in the mouth of a premodern thinker. To know a thing means to

---

5. But do "all the rules of mechanics" equal "*all* the rules of physics"? The readily conceded truth that the former "belong to" physics may serve to cover the very different subreption that they exhaust the book of rules of physics (i.e., of nature). The complete passage in the *Principles,* from which the above quotation is taken, is of capital importance as the enunciation of a really new principle, which has since dominated natural science and natural philosophy. Its technological implications are obvious. The new doctrine of a uniform nature, here emerging from the ruins of the medieval edifice, naïvely assumes an identity of macro- and micromodes of operation, which more recent physics has found wanting. But even apart from any later discoveries, one could have objected at the outset on logical grounds that from the fact of machines working by natural principles entirely it does not follow that they work by the entire natural principles, or, that nature has no other modes of operation than those which man can utilize in his constructions. But this very view of nature (not the innocent one of human mechanics) was Descartes' true conviction: its spirit alone, going far beyond a mere experiment with Occam's razor, accounts for the supreme confidence of the next statement quoted in the text.

know how it is or can be made and therefore means being able to repeat or vary or anticipate the process of making. It does not matter whether man can always actually, with the forces at his command, provide the factors making up the required conditions and, therefore, himself produce their result. Man cannot reproduce a cosmic nebula, but assuming he knows how it is produced in nature, he would on principle be able to produce one too if he were sufficiently large, powerful, and so on, and this is what to know a nebula means. To put it in the form of a slogan, the modern knowledge of nature, very unlike the classical one, is a "know-how" and not a "know-what," and on this basis it makes good Bacon's contention that knowledge is power.

This, however, is not the whole story of the technological aspect inherent in scientific theory. Theory is an internal fact and internal action. But its relation to external action may be not only that of means to end by way of application, but also the reverse: that is, action may be employed in the service of theory as theory may be employed in the service of action. Some complementarity of these two aspects suggests itself from the outset: it may be that only that theory which has grown out of active experience can be turned to the active changing of experience; or only that theory can become a means to practice which has practice among its own means. That this is the case becomes obvious when we consider the role of experiment in the scientific process.

The alliance contemplated by Bacon between knowing and changing the world is indeed much more intimate than the mere delegation of theoretical results to practical use, that is, the *post factum* application of science, would make it. The procedure of science itself, if it is to yield practically relevant results, has to be practical, namely, experimental. We must "close with nature" and do something to it in order to make it yield its secrets through the response we have elicited, "seeing," as Bacon says, "that the nature of things betrays itself more readily under the vexations of art than in its natural freedom." Thus in two different respects modern science is engaged in the active changing of things: on the small scale of the experiment it effects change as a necessary means of knowing nature, that is, it employs practice for the sake of theory; the kind of theory gained in this way lends itself to, and thus invites, the large-scale changes of its technical application. The latter, in turn, becomes a source of theoretical insights not to be gained on the laboratory scale—in addition to furnishing the tools for more effective laboratory work itself, which again in turn yields new increments of knowledge, and so on in a continuous cycle. In this way the fusion of theory and practice becomes inseparable in a way which the mere terms "pure" and "applied" science fail to convey. Effecting changes in nature as a means and as a result of knowing it are inextricably interlocked, and once this combination is at work it no longer matters whether the pragmatic destination of theory is expressly accepted (for example by the "pure" scientist himself) or not. The very process of attaining knowledge leads through manipulation of the things to be known, and this origin fits of itself the theoretical results for an application whose possibility is irresistible—even to the theoretical interest, let alone the practical, whether or not it was contemplated in the first place.

V I

At the same time the question as to what is the true human end, truth or use, is entirely left open by the fact of the union as such and is in essence not affected by the conspicuous preponderance of the practical element. The answer is determined by the image of man, of which we are uncertain. Certain it is from what we have learned that if "truth" be the end it cannot be the truth of pure contemplation. The modern discovery that knowing nature requires coming to grips with nature—a discovery bearing beyond the field of natural science—has permanently corrected Aristotle's "contemplative" view of theory. More, of course, was involved in the ideal of the contemplative life than a conception merely of theoretical method: more than the latter's correction must also be involved in a legitimate farewell to the ideal—a farewell the more bidden with a heavy heart the more understood in its necessity.

It was Aristotle's contention that we act in order to intuit and not intuit in order to act—on which the favorite modern comment is that it reflects nothing but the attitude of a leisure class in a slave society. Rarely in our pragmatic climate is the trouble taken to ask whether Aristotle, socially biased or not, might not be right. He was, after all, not deaf to the demands of "reality." That the necessities of life have to be taken care of first he explicitly states, this being the task allotted to civilization; only he considered this task to be finite, not infinite, or interminable, as it is likely to appear to modern thought on the basis of different attitudes and experiences. Even with these it is well to consider the Greek reasoning in the matter, so as to put the contemporary dynamism of the active life in its proper perspective. Some simple considerations will still be found pertinent. Thus Aristotle's reasoning that we make war in order to have peace is unanswerable, and the generalization that we toil in order to find rest is at least eminently reasonable.[6] Clearly, then, the rest to be found must not consist in suspension of activity but must itself be a kind of life, that is, have its content in an activity of its own—which to Aristotle was "thought." Now, when full due is given to the sanity and appeal of this classical stance, it must be said that it implies views both of civilization and of thought which, rational as they are, have in the light of modern experience become questionable concerning civilization, and untenable concerning thought.

As to civilization, Aristotle takes for granted that once it has reached a working equilibrium between legitimate wants and means for their satisfaction it can devote its surplus to making possible the philosophical life, the life of thought, the true goal of man. Today we have good reason for disbelief in the very attainment of such an equilibrium. We therefore see no better use (in fact, no choice) for the "surplus" than to be fed back into the active process for that adjustment of its constantly generated disequilibrium which results in progress—a self-feeding automatism in which even theory is of necessity involved as factor and function at once, and to which we cannot see (let alone set) a limit. But, if infinite, then the process of civilization calls for the constant care of the best minds—that is: for their constant employment in the "cave."

And as for "thought" itself, the modern adventure of knowledge has corrected the Greek view of it in yet another respect than that of its possible detachment from practice, and for all we know as definitively. To the Greeks, be it Plato or Aristotle, the number of the truly knowable things is finite, and the apprehension of first principles, whenever obtained, is definitive—subject to intermittent renewal but

---

6. *Nicomachean Ethics*, X, 7, 1177 b 4 f.

not to obsolescence through new discovery and better approximation. To the modern experience of knowledge it is inconceivable that any state of theory, including the conceptual system of first principles governing it, should be more than a temporary construct to be superseded by the next vista to which it opens itself the way when all its implications are matched against all the facts. In other words, the *hypothetical* character of modern science *ipso facto* qualifies each of its explanatory and integrating attainments as setting a new problem rather than granting the object for ultimate beholding.

At the root of this difference is, of course, the difference between modern nominalism, with its understanding of the tentative nature of symbolism, as against classical realism. To the latter, concepts reflect and match the self-existing forms of being, and these do not change; to the former, they are products of the human mind, the endeavor of a temporal entity and therefore subject to change. The element of infinity in Greek *theoria* concerned the potential infinity of satisfaction in beholding the eternal, that which never changes; the element of infinity in modern theory concerns the interminableness of the process by which its tentative hypotheses are revised and absorbed into higher symbolical integrations. Thus the idea of potentially infinite progress permeates the modern ideal of knowledge with the same necessity as it permeates the modern ideal of technical civilization;[7] and so, even apart from the mutual involvement of the two, the contemplative ideal has become invalid, nay, illogical, through the sheer lack of those presumed ultimates, the abiding "noblest objects," in whose apprehension knowledge would come to rest and turn from search into contemplation.

VII

It seems, then, that practice and theory conspire to commit us to unceasing dynamism, and with no abiding present our life is ever into the future. What Nietzsche has called "sovereign becoming" is upon us, and theory, far from having where to stand beyond it, is

---

7. And as it permeates the modern idea of nature or reality itself: the very doctrine of being, not merely that of knowledge and of man, has become engulfed in the symbolism of process and change.

chained to its chariot, in harness before it or dragged in its tracks—which, it is hard to tell in the dust of the race, and sure it is only that not theory is the charioteer.

There are those who cheer the surge that sweeps them along and disdain to question "whither?"; who hail change for its own sake, the endless forward thrust of life into the ever new, unknown, the dynamism as such. Yet, surely, for change to be valuable it is relevant *what* entity changes (if not toward what), and this underlying whatness must in some way be definable as that nature of "man as man" which qualifies the endless consummation of its possibilities in change as a worthwhile enterprise. Some image then is implied in the affirmation of change itself. But, if an image, then a norm, and if a norm, then also the freedom of negation, not only the surrender of affirmation; and this freedom itself transcends the flux and points to another sort of theory.

That theory would have to take up the question of ends which the radical vagueness of the term "happiness" leaves open, and on which science, committed to provide the means for happiness, cannot pronounce. The injunction to use it in the interest of man, and to the best of his interest, remains empty as long as it is not known what the best interest of man is.

Faced with the threat of catastrophe we may feel excused from inquiring into ends, since averting catastrophe is a nondebatable first end, suspending all discussion of ultimate ends. Perhaps we are destined to live for long with such pressing emergencies of our own making that what we can do is shoring-up and short-term remedy, not planning for the good life. The former surely needs no philosophy; to meet the recurrent emergency that kind of knowledge would seem competent which has helped to create it—technological science, for it did help create it in each instance by successfully meeting its predecessor.

But if ever we entrust or resign ourselves wholly to the self-corrective mechanics of the interplay of science and technology, we shall have lost the battle for man. For science, with its application governed solely by its own logic, does not really leave the meaning of happiness open: it has prejudged the issue, in spite of its own value-freedom. The automatism of its use—insofar as this use carries beyond the recurrent meeting of the recurrent emergency created by itself—has set the goal of happiness in principle: indulgence in the use of things. Between the two poles of emergency and indulgence, of resourcefulness and hedonism, set up by the ever-expanding power over things, the direction of all effort and thereby the issue of the good tends to be predecided. But we must not let that issue be decided by default.

Thus even with the pressure of emergencies upon us we need a view beyond them to meet them on more than their own terms. Their very diagnosis (wherever it is not a case of extremity) implies at least an idea of what would not be an emergency, as that of sickness implies the idea of health; and the anticipation of success inherent in all struggle against danger, misery, and injustice must face the question of what life befits man when the emergency virtues of courage, charity, and justice have done their work.

VIII

Whatever the insights of that "other" theory called philosophy, and whatever its counsels, there is no stopping the use of scientific theory which propels us into the flux, for stopping its use means stopping theory itself; and the course of knowledge must not be stopped—if not for its gains, then in spite of its costs.

Nor is a return to the classical position open to honesty and logic. Theory itself has become a process, and one, as we have seen, which continuously involves its own use; and it cannot be "possessed" otherwise. Science is, therefore, theory and art at once. But whereas in other arts having the skill and using it are different, so that its possessor is free to use it or not, and to decide when, the skill of science as a collective property begets its use by its own momentum, and so the hiatus between two stages, where judgment, wisdom, freedom can have their play, is here dangerously shrinking: the skill possesses its possessor.

Theory itself has become a function of use as much as use a function of theory. Tasks for theory are set by the practical results of its preceding use, their solutions to be turned again to use, and so on. Thus theory is thoroughly immersed in practice.

With this mutual feedback mechanism theory has set up a new realm of necessity, or what may be called a second nature in place of the first nature from whose necessity theory was to liberate man. To this second nature, no less determinative for being artificial, man is as subject as he was to original nature, and theory itself is under it while constantly engaged in its further making.

If we equate the realm of necessity with Plato's "cave," then scientific theory leads not out of the cave; nor is its practical application a return to the cave: it never left it in the first place. It is entirely of the cave and therefore not "theory" at all in the Platonic sense.

Yet its very possibility implies, and its actuality testifies to, a "transcendence" in man himself as the condition for it. A freedom beyond the necessities of the cave is manifest in the relation to truth, without which science could not be. This relation—a capacity, a commitment, a quest, in short, that which makes science humanly possible—is itself an extrascientific fact. As much, therefore, as science is of the cave by its objects and its uses, by its originating cause "in the soul" it is not. There is still "pure theory" as dedication to the discovery of truth and as devotion to Being, the content of truth: of that dedication science is the modern form.

To philosophy as transscientific theory the human fact of science can provide a clue for a theory of man, so that we may know again about the essence of man—and through it, perhaps, even something of the essence of Being. Whenever such knowledge will again be with us, it can provide a basis for the supremely useful and much-needed knowledge of ends. Pending that event, unforeseeable today as to when and if, we have to live with our poverty—comforted perhaps by the recollection that once before the "I know that I know not" has proved as a beginning of philosophy.[8]

---

8. Three comments, by professors Solomon E. Asch, Erich Hula, and Adolph Lowe, followed the delivery of this paper at the twenty-fifth anniversary celebration of the Graduate Faculty, New School for Social Research, in April, 1959. The comments were published with the paper in *Social Research*, 26/2 (1959), pp. 151-166, and reprinted in M. Natanson, *Philosophy of the Social Sciences: A Reader* (New York: Random House, 1963), pp. 142-157.

Gnosticism, Existentialism, and Nihilism

In this essay I propose, in an experimental vein, to draw a comparison between two movements, or positions, or systems of thought widely separated in time and space, and seemingly incommensurable at first glance: one of our own day, conceptual, sophisticated, and eminently "modern" in more than the chronological sense; the other from a misty past, mythological, crude—something of a freak even in its own time, and never admitted to the respectable company of our philosophic tradition. My contention is that the two have something in common, and that this "something" is such that its elaboration, with a view to similarity and difference alike, may result in a reciprocal illumination of both.

In saying "reciprocal," I admit to a certain circularity of procedure. My own experience may illustrate what I mean. When, many years ago, I turned to the study of Gnosticism, I found that the viewpoints, the optics as it were, which I had acquired in the school of Heidegger, enabled me to see aspects of gnostic thought that had been missed before. And I was increasingly struck by the familiarity of the seemingly utterly strange. In retrospect, I am inclined to believe that it was the thrill of this dimly felt affinity which had lured me into the gnostic labyrinth in the first place. Then, after long sojourn in those distant lands returning to my own, the contemporary philosophic scene, I found that what I had learned out there made me now better understand the shore from which I had set out. The extended discourse with ancient nihilism proved—to me at least—a help in discerning and placing the meaning of modern nihilism: just as the latter had initially equipped me for spotting its obscure cousin in the past. What had happened was that Existentialism, which had provided the means of a historical analysis, became itself involved in the results of it. The fitness of its categories to the particular matter was something to ponder about. They fitted as if made to measure: *were* they, perhaps, made to measure? At the outset, I had taken that fitness as simply a case of their presumed general validity, which would assure their utility for the interpretation of any human "existence" whatsoever. But then it dawned on me that the applicability of categories in the given instance might rather be due to the very kind of "existence" on either side—that which had provided the categories and that which so well responded to them.

It was the case of an adept who believed himself in possession of a key that would unlock every door: I came to this particular door, I tried the key, and lo! it fitted the lock, and the door opened wide. So the key had proved its worth. Only later, after I had outgrown the belief in a universal key, did I begin to wonder *why* this one had in fact worked so well in this case. Had I happened with just the right kind of key upon the right kind of lock? If so, *what* was there between Existentialism and Gnosticism which made the latter open up at the touch of the former? With this turnabout of approach, the solutions in the one became questions to the other, where at first they had just seemed confirmations of its general power.

Thus the meeting of the two, started as the meeting of a method with a matter, ended with bringing home to me that Existentialism, which claims to be the explication of the fundamentals of human existence as such, is the philosophy of a particular, historically fated situation of human existence: and an analogous (though in other respects very different) situation had given rise to an analogous response in the past. The object turned object-lesson, demonstrating both contingency and necessity in the nihilistic experience. The issue posed by Existentialism does not thereby lose in seriousness; but a proper perspective is gained by realizing the situation which it reflects and to which the validity of some of its insights is confined.

In other words, the hermeneutic functions become reversed and reciprocal—lock turns into key, and key into lock: the "existential-ist" reading of Gnosticism, so well vindicated by its hermeneutic success, invites as its natural complement the trial of a "gnostic" reading of Existentialism.

I

More than two generations ago, Nietzsche said that nihilism, "this weirdest of all guests, . . . stands before the door."[1] Meanwhile, the guest has entered and is no longer a guest, and, as far as philosophy is concerned, existentialism is trying to live with him. Living in such company is living in a crisis. The beginnings of the crisis reach back into the seventeenth century, where the spiritual situation of modern man takes shape.

Among the features determining this situation is one which Pascal was the first to face in its frightening implications and to expound with the full force of his eloquence: man's loneliness in the physical universe of modern cosmology. "Cast into the infinite immensity of spaces of which I am ignorant, and which know me not, I am fright-ened."[2] "Which know me not": more than the overawing infinity of cosmic spaces and times, more than the quantitative disproportion, the insignificance of man as a magnitude in this vastness, is it the "silence," that is, the indifference of this universe to human aspira-tions—the not-knowing of things human on the part of that within which all things human have preposterously to be enacted—which constitutes the utter loneliness of man in the sum of things.

As a part of this sum, as an instance of nature, man is only a reed, liable to be crushed at any moment by the forces of an immense and blind universe in which his existence is but a particular blind acci-dent, no less blind than would be the accident of his destruction. As a thinking reed, however, he is no part of the sum, not belonging to it, but radically different, incommensurable: for the *res extensa* does not

---

1. *Der Wille zur Macht,* (1887), §1.
2. *Pensées,* ed. Brunschvicg, fr. 205.

think, so Descartes had taught, and nature is nothing but *res extensa* —body, matter, external magnitude. If nature crushes the reed, it does so unthinkingly, whereas the reed—man—even while crushed, is aware of being crushed.[3] He alone in the world thinks, not because but in spite of his being part of nature. As he shares no longer in a meaning of nature, but merely, through his body, in its mechanical determination, so nature no longer shares in his inner concerns. Thus that by which man is superior to all nature, his unique distinction, mind, no longer results in a higher integration of his being into the totality of being, but on the contrary marks the unbridgeable gulf between himself and the rest of existence. Estranged from the community of being in one whole, his consciousness only makes him a foreigner in the world, and in every act of true reflection tells of this stark foreignness.

This is the human condition. Gone is the *cosmos* with whose immanent *logos* my own can feel kinship, gone the order of the whole in which man has his place. That place appears now as a sheer and brute accident. "I am frightened and amazed," continues Pascal, "at finding myself here rather than there; for there is no reason whatever why here rather than there, why now rather than then." There had always been a reason for the "here," so long as the cosmos had been regarded as man's natural home, that is, so long as the world had been understood as "cosmos." But Pascal speaks of "this remote corner of nature" in which man should "regard himself as lost," of "the little prison-cell in which he finds himself lodged, I mean the (visible) universe."[4] The utter contingency of our existence in the scheme deprives that scheme of any human sense as a possible frame of reference for the understanding of ourselves.

But there is more to this situation than the mere mood of homelessness, forlornness, and dread. The indifference of nature also means that nature has no reference to ends. With the ejection of teleology from the system of natural causes, nature, itself purposeless,

---

3. *Op. cit.,* fr. 347 "A reed only is man, the frailest in the world, but a reed that thinks. Unnecessary that the universe arm itself to destroy him: a breath of air, a drop of water are enough to kill him. Yet, if the All should crush him, man would still be nobler than that which destroys him: for he knows that he dies, and he knows that the universe is stronger than he; but the universe knows nothing of it."

4. *Op. cit.,* fr. 72.

ceased to provide any sanction to possible human purposes. A universe without an intrinsic hierarchy of being, as the Copernican universe is, leaves values ontologically unsupported, and the self is thrown back entirely upon itself in its quest for meaning and value. Meaning is no longer found but is "conferred." Values are no longer beheld in the vision of objective reality, but are posited as feats of valuation. As functions of the will, ends are solely my own creation. Will replaces vision; temporality of the act ousts the eternity of the "good in itself." This is the Nietzschean phase of the situation in which European nihilism breaks the surface. Now man is alone with himself.

> The world's a gate
> To deserts stretching mute and chill.
> Who once has lost
> What thou hast lost stands nowhere still.

Thus spoke Nietzsche (in *Vereinsamt*), closing the poem with the line, "Woe unto him who has no home!"[5]

Pascal's universe, it is true, was still one created by God, and solitary man, bereft of all mundane props, could still stretch his heart out toward the transmundane God. But this God is essentially an unknown God, an *agnostos theos,* and is not discernible in the evidence of his creation. The universe does not reveal the creator's purpose by the pattern of its order, nor his goodness by the abundance of created things, nor his wisdom by their fitness, nor his perfection by the beauty of the whole—but reveals solely his power by its magnitude, its spatial and temporal immensity. For extension, or the quantitative, is the one essential attribute left to the world, and therefore, if the world has anything at all to tell of the divine, it does so through this property: and what magnitude can tell of is power.[6] But

---

5. Die Welt—ein Tor
Zu tausend Wüsten stumm und kalt!
Wer das verlor,
Was du verlorst, macht nirgends Halt.

(The translation offered in the text was supplied by a friend who wishes to be anonymous.)

6. Cf. Pascal, *loc. cit.* "In short, it is the greatest sensible sign of God's omnipotence that our imagination loses itself in this thought (*sc.* of the immensity of cosmic space)."

a world reduced to a mere manifestation of power also admits toward itself—once the transcendent reference has fallen away and man is left with it and himself alone—nothing but the relation of power, that is, of mastery. The contingency of man, of his existing here and now, is with Pascal still a contingency upon God's will; but that will, which has cast me into just "this remote corner of nature," is inscrutable, and the "Why?" of my existence is here just as unanswerable as the most atheistic existentialism can make it out to be. The *deus absconditus,* of whom nothing but will and power can be predicated, leaves behind as his legacy, upon departing the scene, the *homo absconditus,* a concept of man characterized solely by will and power—the will for power, the will to will. For such a will even indifferent nature is more an occasion for its exercise than a true object.[7]

The point that particularly matters for the purpose of this discussion is that a change in the vision of nature, that is, of the cosmic environment of man, is at the bottom of that metaphysical situation which has given rise to modern existentialism and to its nihilistic implications. But if this is so, if the essence of existentialism is a certain dualism, an estrangement between man and the world, with the loss of the idea of a kindred *cosmos*—in short, an anthropological acosmism—then it is not necessarily modern physical science alone which can create such a condition. A cosmic nihilism as such, begotten by whatever historical circumstances, would be the condition in which some of the characteristic traits of existentialism might evolve. And the extent to which this is found to be actually the case would be a test for the relevance which we attribute to the described element in the existentialist position.

There is one situation, and one only that I know of in the history of Western man, where—on a level untouched by anything resembling modern scientific thought—that condition has been realized and lived out with all the vehemence of a cataclysmic event. That is the gnostic movement, or the more radical ones among the various

---

7. The role of Pascal as the first existentialist, which I have here very roughly sketched as a starting point, has been more fully expounded by Karl Löwith in his article on "Man Between Infinities," in *Measure, A Critical Journal* (Chicago), Vol. 1 (1950), 297-310.

gnostic movements and teachings, which the deeply agitated first three centuries of the Christian era proliferated in the Hellenistic parts of the Roman Empire and beyond its eastern boundaries. From them, therefore, we may hope to learn something for an understand-of that disturbing subject, nihilism, and I wish to put the evidence before the reader as far as this can be done in the space of a brief chapter, and with all the reservations which the experiment of such a comparison calls for.

II

The existence of an affinity or analogy across the ages, such as is here alleged, is not so surprising if we remember that in more than one respect the cultural situation in the Greco-Roman world of the first Christian centuries shows broad parallels with the modern situation. Spengler went so far as to declare the two ages "contemporaneous," in the sense of being identical phases in the life cycle of their respective cultures. In this analogical sense we would now be living in the period of the early Caesars. However that may be, there is certainly more than mere coincidence in the fact that we recognize ourselves in so many facets of later post-classical antiquity, far more so, at any rate, than in classical antiquity. Gnosticism is one of those facets, and here recognition, difficult as it is rendered by the strangeness of the symbols, comes with the shock of the unexpected, especially for him who does know something of Gnosticism, since the expansiveness of its metaphysical fancy seems ill to agree with the austere disillusion-ment of existentialism, as its religious character in general with the atheistic, fundamentally "post-Christian" essence by which Nietzsche identified modern nihilism. However, a comparison may yield some interesting results.

The gnostic movement—such we must call it—was a widespread phenomenon in the critical centuries indicated, feeding like Christianity on the impulses of a widely prevalent human situation, and therefore erupting in many places, many forms, and many languages.[8] First among the features to be emphasized here is the radi-

---

8. For a complete treatment of Gnosticism see my German work *Gnosis and spätantiker Geist* (Göttingen, 1954 and 1964) and the shorter

cally dualistic mood which underlies the gnostic attitude as a whole and unifies its widely diversified, more or less systematic expressions. It is on this primary human foundation of a passionately felt experience of self and world, that the formulated dualistic doctrines rest. The dualism is between man and the world, and concurrently between the world and God. It is a duality not of supplementary but of contrary terms; and it is one: for that between man and world mirrors on the plane of experience that between world and God, and derives from it as from its logical ground—unless one would rather hold conversely that the transcendent doctrine of a world-God dualism springs from the immanent experience of a disunion of man and world as from its psychological ground. In this three-term configuration—man, world, God—man and God belong together in contraposition to the world, but are, in spite of this essential belonging-together, in fact separated precisely by the world. To the Gnostic, this fact is the subject of revealed knowledge, and it determines gnostic eschatology: *we* may see in it the projection of his basic experience, which thus created for itself its own revelatory truth. Primary would then be the feeling of an absolute rift between man and that in which he finds himself lodged—the world. It is this feeling which explicates itself in the forms of objective doctrine. In its theological aspect this doctrine states that the Divine is alien to the world and has neither part nor concern in the physical universe; that the true God, strictly transmundane, is not revealed or even indicated by the world, and is therefore the Unknown, the totally Other, unknowable in terms of any worldly analogies. Correspondingly, in its cosmological aspect it states that the world is the creation not of God but of some inferior principle whose law it executes; and, in its anthropological aspect, that man's inner self, the *pneuma* ("spirit" in contrast to "soul" = *psyche*) is not part of the world, of nature's creation and domain, but is, within that world, as totally transcendent and as unknown by all worldly categories as is its transmundane counterpart, the unknown God without.

That the world is created by some personal agency is generally taken for granted in the mythological systems, though in some an

English version *The Gnostic Religion* (Boston: Beacon Press, 2nd ed. 1963).

almost impersonal necessity of dark impulse seems at work in its genesis. But whoever has created the world, man does not owe him allegiance, nor respect to his work. His work, though incomprehensibly encompassing man, does not offer the stars by which he can set his course, and neither does his proclaimed wish and will. Since not the true God can be the creator of that to which selfhood feels so utterly a stranger, nature merely manifests its lowly demiurge: as a power deep beneath the Supreme God, upon which even man can look down from the height of his god-kindred spirit, this perversion of the Divine has retained of it only the power to act, but to act blindly, without knowledge and benevolence. Thus did the demiurge create the world out of ignorance and passion.

The world, then, is the product, and even the embodiment, of the negative of *knowledge*. What it reveals is unenlightened and therefore malignant force, proceeding from the spirit of self-assertive power, from the will to rule and coerce. The mindlessness of this will is the spirit of the world, which bears no relation to understanding and love. The laws of the universe are the laws of this rule, and not of divine wisdom. *Power* thus becomes the chief aspect of the cosmos, and its inner essence is ignorance (*agnosia*). To this, the positive complement is that the essence of man is knowledge—knowledge of self and of God: this determines his situation as that of the potentially knowing in the midst of the unknowing, of light in the midst of darkness, and this relation is at the bottom of his being alien, without companionship in the dark vastness of the universe.

That universe has none of the venerability of the Greek *cosmos*. Contemptuous epithets are applied to it: "these miserable elements" (*paupertina haec elementa*), "this puny cell of the creator" (*haec cellula creatoris*).[9] Yet it is still *cosmos,* an order—but order with a vengeance, alien to man's aspirations. Its recognition is compounded of fear and disrespect, of trembling and defiance. The blemish of nature lies not in any deficiency of order, but in the all too pervading completeness of it. Far from being chaos, the creation of the demiurge, unenlightened as it is, is still a system of law. But cosmic law, once worshiped as the expression of a reason with which man's reason can communicate in the act of cognition, is now seen only in

---

9. Marcion: Tertullian, *Contra Marcionem,* I. 14.

its aspect of compulsion which thwarts man's freedom. The cosmic *logos* of the Stoics, which was identified with providence, is replaced by *heimarmene,* oppressive cosmic fate.

This *fatum* is dispensed by the planets, or the stars in general, the personified exponents of the rigid and hostile law of the universe. The change in the emotional content of the term *cosmos* is nowhere better symbolized than in this depreciation of the formerly most divine part of the visible world, the celestial spheres. The starry sky—to the Greeks since Pythagoras the purest embodiment of reason in the sensible universe, and the guarantor of its harmony—now stared man in the face with the fixed glare of alien power and necessity. No longer his kindred, yet powerful as before, the stars have become tyrants—feared but at the same time despised, because they are lower than man. "They (says Plotinus indignantly of the Gnostics), who deem even the basest of men worthy to be called brothers by them, insanely deny this title to the sun, the stars in the heavens, nay, to the world-soul, our sister, herself!" (*Enn.* II.9.18). Who is more "modern," we may ask—Plotinus or the Gnostics? "They ought to desist (he says elsewhere) from their horror-tales about the cosmic spheres. ... If man is superior to the other animate beings, how much more so are the spheres, which not for tyranny are in the All, but to confer upon it order and law" (*ibid.,* 13). We have heard how the Gnostics felt about this law. Of providence it has nothing, and to man's freedom it is inimical. Under this pitiless sky, which no longer inspires worshipful confidence, man becomes conscious of his utter forlornness. Encompassed by it, subject to its power, yet superior to it by the nobility of his soul, he knows himself not so much a part of, but unaccountably placed in and exposed to, the enveloping system.

And, like Pascal, he is frightened. His solitary otherness, discovering itself in this forlornness, erupts in the feeling of dread. Dread as the soul's response to its being-in-the-world is a recurrent theme in gnostic literature. It is the self's reaction to the discovery of its situation, actually itself an element in that discovery: it marks the awakening of the inner self from the slumber or intoxication of the world. For the power of the star spirits, or of the cosmos in general, is not merely the external one of physical compulsion, but even more the internal one of alienation or self-estrangement. Becoming aware of itself, the self also discovers that it is not really its own, but is rather the involuntary executor of cosmic designs. Knowledge, *gnosis,* may liberate man from this servitude; but since the *cosmos* is contrary to life and to spirit, the saving knowledge cannot aim at integration into the cosmic whole and at compliance with its laws, as did Stoic wisdom, which sought freedom in the knowing consent to the meaningful necessity of the whole. For the Gnostics, on the contrary, man's alienation from the world is to be deepened and brought to a head, for the extrication of the inner self which only thus can gain itself. The world (not the alienation from it) must be overcome; and a world degraded to a power system can only be overcome through power. The overpowering here in question is, of course, anything but technological mastery. The power of the world is overcome, on the one hand, by the power of the Savior who breaks into its closed system from without, and, on the other hand, through the power of the "knowledge" brought by him, which as a magical weapon defeats the force of the planets and opens to the soul a path through their impeding orders. Different as this is from modern man's power relation to world-causality, an ontological similarity lies in the formal fact that the countering of power with power is the sole relation to the totality of nature left for man in both cases.

I I I

Before going any further, let us stop to ask what has here happened to the old idea of the *cosmos* as a divinely ordered whole. Certainly nothing remotely comparable to modern physical science was involved in this catastrophic devaluation or spiritual denudation of the universe. We need only observe that this universe became thoroughly demonized in the gnostic period. Yet this, together with the transcendence of the acosmic self, resulted in curious analogies to some phenomena which existentialism exhibits in the vastly different modern setting. If not science and technology, what caused, for the human groups involved, the collapse of the cosmos piety of classical civilization, on which so much of its ethics was built?

The answer is certainly complex, but at least one angle of it may be briefly indicated. What we have before us is the repudiation of the classical doctrine of "whole and parts," and some of the reasons for this repudiation must be sought in the social and political sphere. The doctrine of classical ontology according to which the whole is prior to the parts, is better than the parts, and is that for the sake of which the parts are, and wherein they find the meaning of their existence—this time-honored axiom had lost the social basis of its validity. The living example of such a whole had been the classical *polis,* the city-state, whose citizens had a share in the whole and could affirm its superior status in the knowledge that they, the parts, however passing and exchangeable, not only were *dependent* on the whole *for* their being but also *maintained* that whole *with* their being: just as the condition of the whole made a difference to the being and possible perfection of the parts, so their conduct made a difference to the being and perfection of the whole. Thus this whole, making possible first the very life and then the good life of the individual, was at the same time committed to the individual's care, and in surpassing and outlasting him was also his supreme vindication.

Now this justifying complement of the primacy of the whole in sociopolitical terms—the part's vital and self-fulfilling function in the whole—had lapsed in the conditions of later antiquity. The absorption of the city-states into the monarchies of the Diadochi and finally into the Roman Empire deprived the *polis* intelligentsia of its constructive function. But the ontological principle survived the conditions of its concrete validation. Stoic pantheism, and generally the physicotheology of post-Aristotelian thought, substituted for the relation between citizen and city that between the individual and the cosmos, the larger living whole. By this shift of reference the classical doctrine of whole and parts was kept in force even though it no longer reflected the practical situation of man. Now it was the *cosmos* that was declared to be the great "city of gods and men,"[10] and to be a citizen of the universe, a *cosmopolites,* was now considered to be the goal by which otherwise isolated man could set his course. He was asked, as it were, to adopt the cause of the universe as his own, that is, to identify himself with that cause directly, across all intermedi-

---

10. It is characteristic, however, that the treatise "On the Cosmos," in elaborating the comparison between the universe and a commonwealth, uses the model of monarchy rather than of republic; see in ch. 6 the circumstantial treatment of the rule of the Persian Great King and its parallel in the divine rule of the universe.

aries, and to relate his inner self, his *logos,* to the *logos* of the whole.

The practical side of this identification consisted in his affirming and faithfully performing the *role* allotted to him by the whole, in just that place and station in which cosmic destiny had set him. Wisdom conferred inner freedom in shouldering the tasks, composure in facing the whims of fortune besetting their execution, but did not set or revise the tasks themselves. "To play one's part"—that figure of speech on which Stoic ethics dwells so much—unwittingly reveals the fictitious element in the construction. A role played is substituted for a real function performed. The actors on the stage behave "as if" they acted their choice, and "as if" their actions mattered. What actually matters is only to play well rather than badly, with no genuine relevance to the outcome. The actors, bravely playing, are their own audience.

In the phrase of playing one's part there is a bravado that hides a deeper, if proud, resignation, and only a shift in attitude is needed to view the great spectacle quite differently. Does the whole really care, does it concern itself in the part that is I? The Stoics averred that it does by equating *heimarmene* with *pronoia,* cosmic fate with providence. And does my part, however I play it, really contribute, does it make a difference to the whole? The Stoics averred that it does by their analogy between the cosmos and the city. But the very comparison brings out the tenuousness of the argument, for—in contrast to what is true in the *polis*—no case can be made out for my relevance in the cosmic scheme, which is entirely outside my control and in which my part is thus reduced to a passivity which in the *polis* it did not have.

To be sure, the strained fervor by which man's integration in the whole was maintained, through his alleged affinity to it, was the means of preserving the dignity of man and thereby of saving a sanction for a positive morality. This fervor, succeeding that which had formerly been inspired by the ideal of civic virtue, represented a heroic attempt on the part of the intellectuals to carry over the life-sustaining force of that ideal into fundamentally changed conditions. But the new atomized masses of the Empire, who had never shared in that noble tradition of *arete,* might react very differently to a situation in which they found themselves passively involved: a situation in which the part was insignificant to the whole, and the whole alien to the parts. The aspiration of the gnostic individual was not to "act a part" in this whole, but—in existentialist parlance—to "exist authentically." The law of empire, under which he found himself, was a dispensation of external, inaccessible force; and for him the law of the universe, cosmic destiny, of which the world state was the terrestrial executor, assumed the same character. The very concept of law was affected thereby in all its aspects—as natural law, political law, and moral law.

This brings us back to our comparison.

I V

The subversion of the idea of law, of *nomos,* leads to ethical consequences in which the nihilistic implication of the gnostic acosmism, and at the same time the analogy to certain modern reasonings, become even more obvious than in the cosmological aspect. I am thinking of gnostic antinomianism. It is to be conceded at the outset that the denial of every objective norm of conduct is argued on vastly different theoretical levels in Gnosis and Existentialism, and that antinomian Gnosis appears crude and naïve in comparison with the conceptual subtlety and historical reflection of its modern counterpart. What was being liquidated, in the one case, was the moral heritage of a millennium of ancient civilization; added to this, in the other, are two thousand years of Occidental Christian metaphysics as background to the idea of a moral law.

Nietzsche indicated the root of the nihilistic situation in the phrase "God is dead," meaning primarily the Christian God. The Gnostics, if asked to summarize similarly the metaphysical basis of their own nihilism, could have said only "the God of the cosmos is dead"—is dead, that is, as a god, has ceased to be divine for us and therefore to afford the lodestar for our lives. Admittedly the catastrophe in this case is less comprehensive and thus less irremediable, but the vacuum that was left, even if not so bottomless, was felt no less keenly. To Nietzsche the meaning of nihilism is that "the highest values become devaluated" (or "invalidated"), and the cause of this devaluation is "the *insight* that we have not the slightest justification for positing a beyond, or an 'in itself' of things, which is 'divine,' which is morality in person."[11] This statement, taken with that about the death of God, bears out Heidegger's contention that "the names God and Christian God are in Nietzsche's thought used to denote the transcendental (supra-sensible) world in general. God is the name for the realm of ideas and ideals" (*Holzwege,* p. 199). Since it is from this realm alone that any sanction for values can derive, its vanishing, that is, the "death of God," means not only the actual devaluation of highest values, but the loss of the very possibility of obligatory values as such. To quote once more Heidegger's interpretation of Nietzsche, "The phrase 'God is dead' means that the supra-sensible world is without effective force" (*ibid.,* p. 200).

In a modified, rather paradoxical way this statement applies also to the gnostic position. It is true, of course, that its extreme dualism is of itself the very opposite of an abandonment of transcendence. The transmundane God represents it in the most radical form. In him the absolute beyond beckons across the enclosing cosmic shells. But this transcendence, unlike the "intelligible world" of Platonism or the world lord of Judaism, does not stand in any positive relation to the sensible world. It is not the essence or the cause of it, but its negation and cancellation. The gnostic God, as distinct from the demiurge, is the totally different, the other, the unknown. Like his inner-human counterpart, the acosmic self or *pneuma,* whose hidden nature also reveals itself only in the negative experience of otherness, of nonidentification and of protested indefinable freedom, this God has more of the *nihil* than the *ens* in his concept. A transcendence withdrawn from any normative relation to the world is equal to a transcendence which has lost its effective force. In other words, for all purposes of man's relation to the reality that surrounds him this hidden God is a nihilistic conception: no *nomos* emanates from him, no law for nature and thus none for human action as a part of the natural order.

On this basis the antinomian argument of the Gnostics is as simple as, for instance, that of Sartre. Since the transcendent is silent, Sartre argues, since "there is no sign in the world," man, the "abandoned" and left-to-himself, reclaims his freedom, or rather, cannot help taking it upon himself: he "is" that freedom, man being "nothing but his

---

11. *Wille zur Macht,* §§ 2-3.

own project," and "all is permitted to him."[12] That this freedom is of a desperate kind, and, as a compassless task, inspires dread rather than exultation, is a different matter.

In this connection we sometimes meet in gnostic reasoning the *subjectivist* argument of traditional moral skepticism: nothing is naturally good or bad, things in themselves are indifferent, and "only by human opinion are actions good or bad." Spiritual man in the freedom of his knowledge has the indifferent use of them all (Iren. *adv. haer.* I.25.4-5). While this reminds one of nothing more than the reasoning of certain classical Sophists, a deeper gnostic reflection upon the *source* of such "human opinions" transforms the argument from a skeptical to a metaphysical one, and turns indifference into opposition: the ultimate source is found to be not human but demiurgical, and thus common with that of the order of nature. By reason of this source the law is not really indifferent but is part of the great design upon our freedom. Being law, the moral code is but the psychical complement to the physical law, and as such the internal aspect of the all-pervading cosmic rule. Both emanate from the lord of the world as agencies of his power, unified in the double aspect of the Jewish God as creator and legislator. Just as the law of the physical world, the *heimarmene,* integrates the individual bodies into the general system, so the moral law does with the souls, and thus makes them subservient to the demiurgical scheme.

For what is the law—either as revealed through Moses and the prophets or as operating in the actual habits and opinions of men—but the means of regularizing and thus stabilizing the implication of man in the business of the world and worldly concerns; of setting by its rules the seal of seriousness, of praise and blame, reward and punishment, on his utter involvement; of making his very will a compliant party to the compulsory system, which thereby will function all the more smoothly and inextricably? Insofar as the principle of this moral law is justice, it has the same character of constraint on the psychical side that cosmic fate has on the physical side. "The angels that created the world established 'just actions' to lead men by such precepts into servitude" (*op. cit.,* I.23.2-3). In the normative law man's will is taken care of by the same powers that control his body.

---

12. J. P. Sartre, *L'existentialisme est un humanisme,* pp. 33 f.

He who obeys it has abdicated the authority of his self. Here we have, beyond the mere indifference of the "subjectivist" argument and beyond the merely permissive privilege of freedom, a positive metaphysical interest in repudiating allegiance to all objective norms and thus a motive for their outright violation. It is the double interest in asserting the authentic freedom of the self by daring the Archons and in injuring their general cause by individually thwarting their design.

As to the assertion of the authentic freedom of the self, it is to be noted that this freedom is a matter not of the "soul" (*psyche*), which is as adequately determined by the moral law as the body is by the physical law, but wholly a matter of the "spirit" (*pneuma*), the indefinable spiritual core of existence, the foreign spark. The soul is part of the natural order, created by the demiurge to envelop the foreign spirit, and in the normative law the creator exercises control over what is legitimately his own. Psychical man, definable in his natural essence, for instance as rational animal, is still natural man, and this "nature" can no more determine the pneumatic self than in the existentialist view any determinative essence is permitted to prejudice the freely self-projecting existence.

Here it is pertinent to compare an argument of Heidegger's. In his *Letter on Humanism,* Heidegger argues, against the classical definition of Man as "the rational animal," that this definition places man within animality, specified only by a *differentia* which falls within the genus "animal" as a particular quality. This, Heidegger contends, is placing man too low.[13] I will not press the point whether there is not a verbal sophism involved in thus arguing from the term "animal" as used in the classical definition.[14] What is important for us is the

---

13. Heidegger, *Über den Humanismus* (Frankfurt, 1949), p. 13.

14. "Animal" in the Greek sense means not "beast" or "brute," but any "animated being," including demons, gods, the ensouled stars—even the ensouled universe as a whole (cf. Plato, Timaeus 30 c): no "lowering" of man is implied in placing him within this scale, and the bogy of "animality" in its modern connotations is slipped in surreptitiously. In reality, the lowering to Heidegger consists in placing "man" in *any* scale, that is, in a context of *nature* as such. The Christian devaluation of "animal" to "beast," which indeed makes the term usable only in contrast to "man," merely reflects the larger break with the classical position—that break by which Man, as the unique possessor of an immortal soul, comes to stand outside "nature" entirely. The existentialist argument takes off from this

rejection of any definable "nature" of man which would subject his sovereign existence to a predetermined essence and thus make him part of an objective order of essences in the totality of nature. In this conception of a transessential, freely "self-projecting" existence I see something comparable to the gnostic concept of the transpsychical negativity of the *pneuma*. That which has no nature has no norm. Only that which belongs to an order of natures—be it an order of creation, or of intelligible forms—can have a nature. Only where there is a whole is there a law. In the deprecating view of the Gnostics this holds for the *psyche,* which belongs to the cosmic whole. Psychical man can do no better than abide by a code of law and strive to be just, that is, properly "adjusted" to the established order, and thus play his allotted part in the cosmic scheme. But the *pneumaticos,* "spiritual" man, who does not belong to any objective scheme, is above the law, beyond good and evil, and a law unto himself in the power of his "knowledge."

V

But what is this knowledge about, this cognition which is not of the soul but of the spirit, and in which the spiritual self finds its salvation from cosmic servitude? A famous formula of the Valentinian school thus epitomizes the content of *gnosis:* "What makes us free is the knowledge who we were, what we have become; where we were, wherein we have been thrown; whereto we speed, wherefrom we are redeemed; what is birth and what rebirth."[15] A real exegesis of this programmatic formula would have to unfold the complete gnostic myth. Here I wish to make only a few formal observations.

First we note the dualistic grouping of the terms in antithetical pairs, and the eschatological tension between them, with its irreversible direction from past to future. We further observe that the terms throughout are concepts not of being but of happening, of movement.

---

new basis: the play on the semantic ambiguity of "animal," while scoring an easy point, conceals this shift of basis of which that ambiguity is a function, and fails to meet the classical position with which it ostensibly argues.

15. Clemens Alex., *Exc. ex Theod.,* 78.2.

The knowledge is of a history, in which it is itself a critical event. Among these terms of motion, the one of having "been thrown" into something strikes our attention, because we have been made familiar with it in existentialist literature. We are reminded of Pascal's "Cast into the infinite immensity of spaces," of Heidegger's *Geworfenheit,* "having been thrown," which to him is a fundamental character of the *Dasein,* of the self-experience of existence. The term, as far as I can see, is originally gnostic. In Mandaean literature it is a standing phrase: life has been thrown into the world, light into darkness, the soul into the body. It expresses the original violence done to me in making me be where I am and what I am, the passivity of my choiceless emergence into an existing world which I did not make and whose law is not mine. But the image of the throw also imparts a dynamic character to the whole of the existence thus initiated. In our formula this is taken up by the image of speeding toward some end. Ejected into the world, life is a kind of trajectory projecting itself forward into the future.

This brings us to the final observation I wish to make apropos of the Valentinian formula: that in its temporal terms it makes no provision for a *present* on whose content knowledge may dwell and, in beholding, stay the forward thrust. There is past and future, where we come from and where we speed to, and the present is only the moment of *gnosis* itself, the peripety from the one to the other in a supreme crisis of the eschatological *now.* There is this to remark, however, in distinction to all modern parallels: in the gnostic formula it is understood that, though thrown into temporality, we had an origin in eternity, and so also have an aim in eternity. This places the innercosmic nihilism of the Gnosis against a metaphysical background which is entirely absent from its modern counterpart.

To turn once more to the modern counterpart, let us ponder an observation which must strike the close student of Heidegger's *Sein und Zeit,* that most profound and still most important manifesto of existentialist philosophy. Heidegger there develops a "fundamental ontology" according to the modes in which the self "exists," that is, constitutes its own being in the act of existing, and with it originates, as the objective correlates thereof, the several meanings of Being in general. These modes are explicated in a number of fundamental categories which Heidegger prefers to call "existentials." Unlike the objective "categories" of Kant, they articulate primarily structures not of reality but of realization, that is, not cognitive structures of a world of objects given, but functional structures of the active movement of inner time by which a "world" is entertained and the self originated as a continuous event. The "existentials" have, therefore, each and all, a profoundly temporal meaning. They are categories of internal or mental time, the true dimension of existence, and they articulate that dimension in its tenses. This being the case, they must exhibit, and distribute between them, the three horizons of time—past, present, and future.

Now if we try to arrange these "existentials," Heidegger's categories of existence, under those three heads, as it is possible to do, we make a striking discovery—at any rate one that struck me very much when, at the time the book appeared, I tried to draw up a diagram, in the classical manner of a "table of categories." It is the discovery that the column under the head of "present" remains practically empty—at least insofar as modes of "genuine" or "authentic" existence are concerned. I hasten to add that this is an extremely abridged statement. Actually a great deal is said about the existential "present," but not as an independent dimension in its own right. For the existentially "genuine" present is the present of the "situation," which is wholly defined in terms of the self's *relation* to its "future" and "past." It flashes up, as it were, in the light of decision, when the projected "future" reacts upon the given "past" (*Geworfenheit*) and in this meeting constitutes what Heidegger calls the "moment" (*Augenblick*): moment, not duration, is the temporal mode of *this* "present" —a creature of the other two horizons of time, a function of their ceaseless dynamics, and no independent dimension to dwell in. Detached, however, from this context of inner movement, by itself, mere "present" denotes precisely the renouncement of genuine future-past relation in the "abandonment" or "surrender" to talk, curiosity, and the anonymity of "everyman" (*Verfallenheit*): a failure of the tension of true existence, a kind of slackness of being. Indeed, *Verfallenheit,* a negative term which also includes the meaning of degeneration and decline, is *the* "existential" proper to "present" as such, showing it to be a derivative and "deficient" mode of existence.

Thus our original statement stands that all the relevant categories of existence, those having to do with the possible authenticity of selfhood, fall in correlate pairs under the heads of either past or future: "facticity," necessity, having become, having been thrown, guilt, are existential modes of the past; "existence," being ahead of one's present, anticipation of death, care, and resolve, are existential modes of the future. No present remains for genuine existence to repose in. Leaping off, as it were, from its past, existence projects itself into its future; faces its ultimate limit, death; returns from this eschatological glimpse of nothingness to its sheer factness, the unalterable datum of its already having become this, there and then; and carries this forward with its death-begotten resolve, into which the past has now been gathered up. I repeat, there is no present to dwell in, only the crisis between past and future, the pointed moment between, balanced on the razor's edge of decision which thrusts ahead.

This breathless dynamism held a tremendous appeal for the contemporary mind, and my generation in the German Twenties and early Thirties succumbed to it wholesale. But there is a puzzle in this evanescence of the present as the holder of genuine content, in its reduction to the inhospitable zero point of mere formal resolution. What metaphysical situation stands behind it?

Here an additional observation is relevant. There is, after all, besides the existential "present" of the moment, the presence of things. Does not the co-presence with them afford a "present" of a different kind? But we are told by Heidegger that things are primarily *zuhanden,* that is, useable (of which even "useless" is a mode), and therefore related to the "project" of existence and its "care" (*Sorge*), therefore included in the future-past dynamics. Yet they can also become neutralized to being merely *vorhanden* ("standing before me"), that is, indifferent objects, and the mode of *Vorhandenheit* is an objective counterpart to what on the existential side is *Verfallenheit,* false present. *Vorhanden* is what is merely and indifferently "extant," the "there" of bare nature, there to be looked at outside the relevance of the existential situation and of practical "concern." It is being, as it were, stripped and alienated to the mode of mute thinghood. This is the status left to "nature" for the relation of theory—a deficient mode of being—and the relation in which it is so objectified is a deficient mode of existence, its defection from the futurity of care into the spurious present of mere onlooking curiosity.[16]

---

16. I am speaking here throughout of *Sein und Zeit,* not of the later Heidegger, who is certainly no "Existentialist."

This existentialist depreciation of the concept of nature obviously reflects its spiritual denudation at the hands of physical science, and it has something in common with the gnostic contempt for nature. No philosophy has ever been less concerned about nature than Existentialism, for which it has no dignity left: this unconcern is not to be confounded with Socrates' refraining from physical inquiry as being above man's understanding.

To look at what is there, at nature as it is in itself, at Being, the ancients called by the name of contemplation, *theoria*. But the point here is that, if contemplation is left with only the irrelevantly extant, then it loses the noble status it once had—as does the repose in the present to which it holds the beholder by the presence of its objects. *Theoria* had that dignity because of its Platonic implications—because it beheld eternal objects in the forms of things, a transcendence of immutable being shining through the transparency of becoming. Immutable being is everlasting present, in which contemplation can share in the brief durations of the temporal present.

Thus it is eternity, not time, that grants a present and gives it a status of its own in the flux of time; and it is the loss of eternity which accounts for the loss of a genuine present. Such a loss of eternity is the disappearance of the world of ideas and ideals in which Heidegger sees the true meaning of Nietzsche's "God is dead": in other words, the absolute victory of nominalism over realism. Therefore the same cause which is at the root of nihilism is also at the root of the radical temporality of Heidegger's scheme of existence, in which the present is nothing but the moment of crisis between past and future. If values are not beheld in vision as being (like the Good and the Beautiful of Plato), but are posited by the will as projects, then indeed existence is committed to constant futurity, with death as the goal; and a merely formal resolution to be, without a *nomos* for that resolution, becomes a project from nothingness into nothingness. In the words of Nietzsche quoted before, "Who once has lost what thou hast lost stands nowhere still."

V I

Once more our investigation leads back to the dualism between man and *physis* as the metaphysical background of the nihilistic situation.

There is no overlooking one cardinal difference between the gnostic and the existentialist dualism: Gnostic man is thrown into an antagonistic, antidivine, and therefore antihuman nature, modern man into an indifferent one. Only the latter case represents the absolute vacuum, the really bottomless pit. In the gnostic conception the hostile, the demonic, is still anthropomorphic, familiar even in its foreignness, and the contrast itself gives direction to existence—a negative direction, to be sure, but one that has behind it the sanction of the negative transcendence to which the positivity of the world is the qualitative counterpart. Not even this antagonistic quality is granted to the indifferent nature of modern science, and from that nature no direction at all can be elicited.

This makes modern nihilism infinitely more radical and more desperate than gnostic nihilism ever could be for all its panic terror of the world and its defiant contempt of its laws. That nature does not care, one way or the other, is the true abyss. That only man cares, in his finitude facing nothing but death, alone with his contingency and the objective meaninglessness of his projecting meanings, is a truly unprecedented situation.

But this very difference, which reveals the greater depth of modern nihilism, also challenges its self-consistency. Gnostic dualism, fantastic as it was, was at least self-consistent. The idea of a demonic nature against which the self is pitted, makes sense. But what about an indifferent nature which nevertheless contains in its midst that to which its own being does make a difference? The phrase of having been flung into indifferent nature is a remnant from a dualistic metaphysics, to whose use the nonmetaphysical standpoint has no right. What is the throw without the thrower, and without a beyond whence it started? Rather should the existentialist say that life—conscious, caring, knowing self—has been "thrown up" by nature. If blindly, then the seeing is a product of the blind, the caring a product of the uncaring, a teleological nature begotten unteleologically.

Does not this paradox cast doubt on the very concept of an indifferent nature, that abstraction of physical science? So radically has anthropomorphism been banned from the concept of nature that even man must cease to be conceived anthropomorphically if he is just an accident of that nature. As the product of the indifferent, his being, too, must be indifferent. Then the facing of his mortality would simply warrant the reaction "Let us eat and drink for tomorrow we die." There is no point in caring for what has no sanction behind it in any creative intention. But if the deeper insight of Heidegger is right— that, facing our finitude, we find that we care, not only whether we exist but how we exist—then the mere fact of there being such a supreme care, anywhere within the world, must also qualify the totality which harbors that fact, and even more so if "it" alone was the productive cause of that fact, by letting its subject physically arise in its midst.

The disruption between man and total reality is at the bottom of nihilism. The illogicality of the rupture, that is, of a dualism without metaphysics, makes its fact no less real, nor its seeming alternative any more acceptable: the stare at isolated selfhood, to which it condemns man, may wish to exchange itself for a monistic naturalism which, along with the rupture, would abolish also the idea of man as man. Between that Scylla and this her twin Charybdis, the modern mind hovers. Whether a third road is open to it—one by which the dualistic rift can be avoided and yet enough of the dualistic insight saved to uphold the humanity of man—philosophy must find out.

Heidegger and Theology

Prefatory Note. This essay was delivered, in slightly abridged form, to a conference of theologians concerned with the subject of "Non-Objectifying Thinking and Speaking in Contemporary Theology."[1] To the conferees that title had one concrete and topical meaning: the use of the later thought of Martin Heidegger for Protestant theology. In view of the circumstances of its conception and delivery, and the echo it has provoked then and afterward,[2] I thought that I should

---

1. *Second Consultation on Hermeneutics,* convened by the Graduate School of Drew University, April 9-11, 1964. The paper was the opening address, preceded by the reading of a number of "theses" which Martin Heidegger had sent to serve as a basis for the consultation.

2. The following published comments have come to my notice: Robert W. Funk, "Logic and the Logos," *The Christian Century* (Sept. 23, 1964), 1175-1177; *id.,* "Colloquium on Hermeneutics," *Theology Today* (Oct., 1964), 287-306 (both articles report on the Consultation as a whole); Eugene B. Borowitz, "Bonhoeffer's World comes of Age," *Judaism: A Quarterly Journal* 14/1 (Winter, 1965), 81-87 (deals with the Drew Consultation and this paper on pp. 81 f.); William J. Richardson, S.J., "Heidegger and God—and Professor Jonas," *Thought: Fordham University Quarterly* 40/156 (Spring, 1965), 13-40. The last-named, extensive critique by the author of *Heidegger: Through Phenomenology to Thought* (The Hague, 1963), and a participant at the Drew Consultation, was first propounded as the annual Suarez Lecture delivered at Fordham University, April 27, 1964, a few weeks after the occasion which pro-

leave the essay its original character of a speech that addresses an audience.

I

The problem of objectification, and with it that of reversing or partially unmaking it, was bequeathed to Western theology from its origin in the mating of the Biblical word with the Greek *logos*. It is thus as old as Christian theology itself, and even slightly older. Which side of the double parentage would be dominant and which recessive in the offspring was demonstrated in the very first encounter of the two in Philo Judaeus. A telling symbol of what happened to the Biblical word through him and his successors is unwittingly supplied by an allegory which he evolves from an etymology of the name "Israel." The name is taken to mean "He who sees God," and Jacob's acquiring this name is said to represent the God-seeker's progress from the stage of hearing to that of seeing, made possible by the miraculous conversion of ears into eyes. The allegory falls into the general pattern of Philo's views on "knowing God." These rest on the Platonic supposition that the truest relation to being is intuition, beholding. This eminence of sight, when extended into the religious sphere, determines also the highest and most authentic relation to God—and with it also to the *word* of God.[3] To this Philo indeed

---

voked it. A rejoinder to this able countercritique by a devoted and thoroughly informed student of Heidegger's thought must be left for another occasion.—My paper was published in *The Review of Metaphysics* 18/2 (Dec., 1964), 207-223, and is here reprinted with a few minor changes in agreement with the German version, "Heidegger und die Theologie," *Evangelische Theologie* 24/12 (Dec., 1964), 621-642.

3. "Seeing with the eyes is the fairest of all the senses . . . but seeing with the ruling principle of the soul excels all other faculties: this is the insight (*phronesis*), the vision of the mind. He who has succeeded not only to gain science of all that exists in nature but also to behold the Father and Creator of the All, has attained to the summit of blessedness, for higher than God there is nothing; and whoever has reached Him thus with the intending eye of his soul may pray for this stage to persist and last" (*De Abrahamo*, 57 f.). (References to Philo Judaeus are according to the paragraph numbering in the standard Greek edition by L. Cohn and P. Wendland, which the Loeb Classical Library reproduces; translations are mine.) Note how God is here ranked, as the highest being, in the

assigns a nature which makes vision, i.e., intellectual contemplation, and not audition, its genuine criterion. Referring to the phrase in Exodus, "All the people saw the voice" (20:18), he comments:

---

rank order of all being; and this inclusion, even if by way of culmination, is precisely the ontological correlate to the visual approach. Under the terms set by this approach the statement that God is "the being one" assumes a definite meaning which cannot but clash with the equally emphasized claim that he transcends all ontological determination. This meaning of God's "being" becomes manifest in Philo's calling him "the most perfect good" (*teleiotaton agathon,* e.g., in *De Confusione Linguarum,* 180). Platonically understood, the good (or "the good itself") is the highest category of being hypostasized into a representation of the beingness of all beings as such. Although "beyond essence" (for essence pertains to specific being), it is yet the essence of all essence, or the form of forms—and as such the terminal *object* of the intuiting eros which in it reaches its goal: an impersonal, indeed structural ontological principle, lifted out of the evidence of being as a whole in metaphysical vision, it is by its very nature the correlate of *theoria* and nowhere to be found but in pure theory. So Plato. Now when *Philo* declares his *God* to be "the most perfect good" (which Plato did not) and thus makes *him* the culmination of the hierarchy of all being, he stays in line with the original Greek, "visual" approach and with the ontology determined by it. But what does that mean for man's relation to God, i.e., for the life of piety? The perfect good is the end-good, the final goal of a desire for possession. We may venture the statement that wherever God is defined as the *summum bonum* (e.g., by Augustine), then he is also understood as the final object of an appetition, i.e., as the potential ultimate satisfaction of a desire for a presence: and then the most valid relation of piety must be vision, which grants the purest mode of the object's presence. Accordingly, Philo conceives the way of piety, being the way toward God, as a progress of perfection, in which the passage from hearing to seeing marks a decisive point. Typologically, Ishmael, the handmaid's son, the "merely hearing" type, is contrasted with Israel, the true-born, as the seeing type. (Cf. *De Fuga et Inventione,* 208.) And the elevation of Jacob himself to the grade of Israel is a change-over from the condition of hearing to that of seeing: "Jacob is the name for learning and progressing, i.e., for the powers that depend on hearing; but Israel is the name for perfection, for it means 'seeing God'—and what could be more perfect in the realm of truth than to see the truly existent one?" (*De Ebrietate,* 82; cf. also *De Migratione Abrahami,* 47 ff.). The transition takes place through the conversion of ears into eyes: "By a divine breath the Logos converts the ears of Jacob (the "ascetic" who wrestles with the angel) into eyes, thereby transforming him into a new type called Israel, the seeing one" (*De Somniis,* I, 129).

"Highly significant, for human voice is to be heard, but God's voice is in truth to be seen. Why? Because that which God speaks is not words but works, which the eye discriminates better than the ear" (*De Decalogo*, 47).[4] "Works," finished realities, are what God "speaks," i.e., what he, either by his being or by his acting, puts before our eyes. And the finished or perfected is objectively present and can only be looked at; it presents itself in its *eidos*. But Biblically understood, the word of God is primarily call and command, and commands are not looked at but heard—and obeyed or disobeyed. Now it is obvious that this is not the antithesis Philo has in mind. The logos *he* contrasts with the seen one as "merely" heard is the apophantic (not the imperative) logos which pronounces on objects, i.e., on "visibles" in the widest sense, and thus calls indeed for a seeing to fulfill and redeem its symbolic intention. Such logos about a state of things, which substitutes for authentic presence by meaningful signs, is received by a provisional "mere hearing" which by its own sense strains toward its completion in the seeing of the signified content. A more perfect, archetypal logos, exempt from the human duality of sign and thing and therefore not bound to the forms of speech, would not require the mediation of hearing but is immediately beheld by the mind as the truth of things. In other words, the antithesis of seeing and hearing argued by Philo lies as a whole within the realm of "seeing"—that is to say, it is no real antithesis but a difference of degree relative to the ideal of immediate, intuitive presence of the object. It is with a view to this ideal that the "hearing" here opposed to "seeing" is conceived, namely, as its deputizing, provisional mode, and not as something authentic, basically other than seeing. Accordingly, the turn from hearing to seeing here envisaged is merely a progress from a limited to an adequate knowledge of the same and within the same project of knowledge. But we have the

---

4. Cf. *De Migratione Abrahami*, 47 ff. "Scripture teaches that, whereas the voice of mortal creatures has for its criterion the sense of hearing, the words (statements, *logoi*) of God are seen in the manner of light; for it says 'all the people saw the voice. . . .' For the speech divided into noun and verb and all the members of the sentence is audible . . . but the voice of God which is beheld by the eye of the soul is visible. . . . Therefore God's statements have the soul's sense of sight for their criterion. The divine communication is of pure, unmixed *logos* which a pure soul beholds by acuteness of sight."

right to take Philo's parable of perfection through the conversion of ears into eyes on our part as a parable for that turn from hearing to seeing which he himself and after him Christian theology (not to speak of Gnosticism) underwent in their primary constitution—the turn from the original hearing of the call of the living, nonworldly God is to the theoretical will for vision of the supernatural, divine truths. In this sense the "conversion of ears into eyes" can be considered a symbol of the first rank.

Taking a cue from Philo we may ask: If the adoption of the "seeing" approach from Greek philosophy was a misfortune for theology, does the repudiation or overcoming of that approach in a contemporary philosophy provide a conceptual means for theology to reform itself, to become more adequate to its task? Can it thus lead to a new alliance between theology and philosophy after, e.g., the medieval one with Aristotelianism has broken down? The question assumes that some use of philosophy, i.e., of the elucidation of the nature of reality by secular thought, and of the nature of thinking about reality in secular thought, is desirable and even necessary for theology. This assumption must be granted, since theology, as the logos about things divine, is by definition the discursive, in some sense scientific, elucidation of the contents of faith (not, of course, of the internal *structure* of faith, which would be phenomenology) and thus, for one thing, comes under the rules and norms of elucidation and discourse as such; and since the contents of faith comprise the dealings of God with the world and with man, the elucidation of the mundane and human side of this polarity must be informed by a knowledge of what world and man are, and philosophy is supposed to provide such knowledge. It would then follow that that philosophy is most adequate to theology which is most adequate to being, i.e., which is most nearly true—by the criteria of philosophy itself, i.e., by the criteria of secular reason. But since for a decision on this the theologians cannot wait for the consensus of philosophers, nor even necessarily trust its authority, they may be guided in their choice by the appeal of affinity, the lessons of past experience with philosophical liaisons, the present needs of their discipline, and by appraising which philosophy is most helpful to the discharge of theology's task, or least dangerous to its own trust, to its own genuineness, least seductive, least alienating—by any or all of these considerations, but as little as possible by fashion. On all these counts the theologian would do well to exercise a great deal of caution and mistrust. And especially in the face of tempting similarity: what theology needs in this relationship is the otherness of philosophy, not its similarity. However, the experiment of relationship itself is inescapable, and the one choice closed is abstention. Thus, the openness to contemporary thought shown by theology in the present experiment—as it was shown at all times—is to be welcomed.

I I

First, then, on the count of affinity, the appeal of Heidegger's thought, at least of his language, to the Christian theologian cannot be denied. He brings to the fore precisely what the philosophical tradition had ignored or withheld—the moment of call over against that of form, of mission over against presence, of being grasped over against surveying, of event over against object, of response over against concept, even the humility of reception over against the pride of autonomous reason, and generally the stance of piety over against the self-assertion of the subject. At last, to resume the Philonic cue, the suppressed side of "hearing" gets a hearing after the long ascendancy of "seeing" and the spell of objectification which it cast upon thought; and Christian thought may turn its eyes, no longer blinded by the metaphysical vision, to this quarter to have them reconverted into ears and so to hear, and perhaps make heard, its own message anew.

Or so it seems to some. And on the *prima facie* evidence it must be granted that evangelical theology hears there familiar sounds and can feel more at home with this than with some other varieties of modern or traditional thought. But isn't it perhaps too much at home there? Are the familiar sounds legitimate there? Is theology perhaps lured by them onto alien ground made all the more dangerous by the mysterious masking, the inspirational tone, which make its paganism so much more difficult to discern than that of straightforward, identifiably secular philosophy?

Let us ask what the *prima facie* affinity here really means. To take a well-known example, Heidegger holds that "thinking" is a "thanking" for the favor of being. He asserts this of "primal" (*anfänglich*) or "essential" thinking, which he opposes to the "secondary," derivative (*abkünftig*) thinking of metaphysics and science. Whereas the language of the last two is that of objectifying discourse, the language of essential thinking has the quality of thanksgiving. The Biblical or generally religious ring of these statements is unmistakable. But does this consonance on the philosopher's part arise from independent philosophical reflection, or was the Biblical model itself a factor in the reflection? I think there can be no doubt that the latter is the case. We are simply in the presence of the well-known and always known fact that there is much secularized Christianity in Heidegger's thought. This was evident from the beginning, from *Sein und Zeit* on; and notwithstanding the strenuous assertion by Heidegger and by others on his behalf that such concepts as guilt, care, anxiety, call of conscience, resolution, *Verfallenheit,* authenticity-unauthenticity, have a purely ontological meaning with no ontic (e.g., psychological) connotation, and least of all are meant morally, the reasonable observer, without entering into the question of subjective honesty, will not let such disclaimers keep him from giving tradition its due. He will then acknowledge, to repeat, that Heidegger's secular thinking does embody elements from Christian thought. But does that justify saying that there is an autonomous parallel between the two? a correspondence or correlation? that therefore the one can offer aid and comfort to the other, the side of knowledge to that of faith? In the case of Moses and Plato—the case of Philo—there *could* have been an independent and therefore relevant correlation, or complementation, or mutual confirmation; but in the case of dependence with which we deal here the situation is logically different, and the invocation of concordance is spurious, even falsifying. Such invocation seems to be a temptation for some theologians. For theology, too, not to be outdone, now wishes to be "primal" thinking,[5] though by its very nature, being derivative from a revelation, it ought not even to entertain such a wish. But since Heidegger, too, speaks of revelation,

---

5. Cf. Heinrich Ott, *Denken und Sein: Der Weg Martin Heideggers und der Weg der Theologie* (Zürich, 1959), p. 171: "We start from the premise that theology is surely a thinking in the initial and essential sense, *qua* thinking unsurpassable, not to be exceeded by any other kind of thought. . . . It thus follows that theology itself is the primal and essential thinking."

or what sounds suspiciously like it, viz., the self-unveiling of being
(*Entbergung*), these two—revelation-dependent and "primal" thinking—seem to be compatible, even identical. Does not, as one theologian argues in support of such concordance,[6] Anselm of Canterbury
pray as follows: "Teach me to seek thee and *show thyself* to me as I
seek; for I am not able to seek thee unless thou teachest, nor to find
thee unless thou showest thyself" (*Proslogion*, Chap. I)? Does not
theology's relation to God as here described by Anselm precisely
correspond to thinking's relation to being as seen by Heidegger? Is
not the "fate-laden" (*geschicklich*) character of thinking, as response
to the unveiling of being that is given to it to think, here adequately
stated in the analogous terms of theological thinking[7]—a special and
applied case as it were of what has now philosophically been shown
to be the general nature of "essential thought"? To speak thus is the
temptation indicated, to which some theologians succumb. But isn't
this putting things upside down? Shouldn't one say at best that thinking's relation to being as seen by Heidegger corresponds to theology's
relation to God? And that characteristics of the latter could not be
transposed into philosophical, i.e., unbelieving terms better than was
done in Heidegger's doctrine of the fate-laden character of thinking . . .
response . . . unveiling of being? Whether even this would be a true
statement remains to be seen. But the turning around of the relationship as such is by no means a matter of indifference (as one might
say "correspondence is correspondence from whatever end I start"),
for it reverses the whole locus of the standard of adequacy—of what
has to be measured by what. For once, up to *this* point, the situation
is not, as so often, theology's trying to appropriate from the domain
of philosophy and in the process being appropriated by it, but philos-

---

6. H. Ott, "Theologie als Gebet und Wissenschaft," *Theologische Zeit-
schrift* 14 (1958), 120 ff.

7. Thus Ott's compliment to Anselm as reproduced by James M.
Robinson in his instructive report "The German Discussion of the later
Heidegger" in *New Frontiers in Theology: Discussion among German
and American Theologians*, ed. J. M. Robinson and J. B. Cobb, Vol. I:
The Later Heidegger and Theology (New York: Harper & Row, 1963),
p. 47. This volume, an excellent record of the German-American discussion on the subject, was frequently referred to in the address because it
was well known to the participants of the Drew Consultation. It is henceforth quoted as *Robinson-Cobb*.

ophy's appropriating from the domain of theology and coming into its debt—whatever *that* may do to philosophy. This is the philosopher's concern and need not trouble the theologian. But neither must he lose sight of the true interdependence of things. I am sorry, as a mere child of the world, to have to say this to theologians: instead of theology's finding validation or corroboration for itself in what has been borrowed from itself, the real case is that philosophy must examine the philosophical validity of Heidegger's borrowing from theology. This is not our present task, and although its result may considerably lessen the theoretical prestige of those elements which the theologian wishes to reappropriate, it may still leave them the usefulness of the conceptual articulation which they have received under philosophical treatment. But the theologian must ask, before he reimports his own original product: what have you done with my little ones? in what company did you bring them up? are they still my uncorrupted children? can I take them back from you? and what, *if* I take them, will I take *with* them? Now, though the crucial question "Can I take them back from you?" is a question of decision, the other questions, especially the last: "What, if you decide to take them, will you have to take with them?" is a question of fact and logical necessity, and can be considered and answered by the philosopher who has a knowledge, albeit a merely objective one, of both sides. And here I may provisionally point to at least one modest virtue of objectifying speech, viz., that it will bring to light incompatibilities and thus enable theology to speak of heresy.

Now, if we first ask how Heidegger came to adopt the Judaeo-Christian vocabulary in the first place, the vocabulary of guilt and conscience and call and voice and hearing and response and mission and shepherd and revelation and thanksgiving, we could of course not take seriously the claim—if it were made—that it was simply suggested by the phenomena themselves and represents the result of their unprejudiced analysis. No mere analysis will ever yield those concepts and that language (and we shall deal later with the fact that not even Heidegger's account of thinking hails from an "analysis" of thinking as it is so often called in the American discussion). At any rate the Biblical ring is no mere coincidence compelled by the independent linguistic demands of the subject matter and at best counting in favor of the ancient predecessor. But this answer would in any case not be

Heidegger's own and would not fit in with his very conception of thinking. In accord with the fate-laden character of thinking as the self-unveiling history of being itself, *he* might rather say that the Christian speech, and the disclosure of being laid down in it, are via our tradition an integral part of the fate to which our thinking must respond, and that therefore the language is genuine as *his* thinking response to the task as *conditioned* by history. Some such answer probably comes close to the truth of the matter, even though it underplays the role of free choice; and to some extent philosophy has gained from this opening of its universe to features which it has all too long ignored. But the theologian has no cause to rejoice in this endorsement of his cherished heirlooms by an influential thinker. As I understand it—and of course it is somewhat awkward for me to act as spokesman for, or defender of, the cause of Christian theology— the theologian should resist the attempt to treat his message as a matter of historic fate, and thus as part of a comprehensive becoming, and thus as one element among others in a tradition, and as itself something divisible, assimilable in part and left in part, ready for the pickings of the unbeliever. He must ask whether one can take half of his story without falsifying the whole—as he will in time have to ask conversely whether Heidegger's philosophy can be assimilated in part without taking in the whole. But most of all he must resist the idea of fate itself. And herewith I come to Heidegger's doctrine.

I I I

Let us start with the idea of fate.[8] It looms large in Heidegger's thinking, and in his idea of thinking. Thinking's lot is cast by being. Being speaks to thought, and what it speaks is thought's lot. But what, how, and when it speaks is decreed by the *history* of being and *is* this history as the history of its own unveiling or concealing. And as this is not at the thinker's command, thinking about being—which as *genitivus subjectivus* is at the same time also the thinking of being

---

8. Heidegger's German term is *Geschick* in preference to the more common *Schicksal:* by this derivative form from the root-word *schicken,* he wishes to rescue the element of "sending" from that of mere "decree" or brute force, which predominates in the average usage of the more common term.

itself, namely its self-clearing taking place in man—has a fatelike character (or, is "fate-laden": *geschicklich*). The fateful nature of thought is its dependence upon what is sent to it, and the sending issues from the history of being. Now on this the secular philosopher (a redundant expression) will comment that thinking is precisely an effort not to be at the mercy of fate, an effort to save or achieve the freedom of insight (once called "reason") in the face of the pressure of being and of our own condition—an effort enjoying the chance of at least partial success. Heidegger himself, not quite consistent, at times seems to appeal to precisely this aspect of the power, nobility, and self-responsibility of thought—as when he holds that genuine philosophy must arise in a new openness to being (like that of the pre-Socratics!), an openness we can only achieve as we *free ourselves* from the distorting conceptualizations imposed on our vision by our fateful history.[9] Although contradictions count for little in the shelter of primal thinking, those committed to the uncomfortable exactions of objective thought must raise here a number of questions. Is this "freeing ourselves," which presumably is taking place, e.g., in Heidegger's own thought, an action that itself is free from fate and not itself *of* fate? Is fate overcome, transcended, abolished in the *"self-freeing"* from the impositions of past fate? Or is it itself a gift of fate—and then to our chosen generation, because the time was fulfilled? because the chances withheld from all generations since the fall from pristine Greek grace are fatefully granted to us? because emerging at last from the long forgetfulness of being decreed by the self-concealing of being, which again is its own fate, we are at last favored with its unveiling—an event again not *of* being only but also happening *to* being as much as to us? The latest turn in its fate? In this case we—we of all people!—would be in a state of grace, whose advent in the emergence of primal thinking ushers in a new apostolic age. Or is this possibility of laying hold of the truth—some tiny corner of it—open to every generation and attempted in each, with changing success? and the element of fate is only how helpful or hindering the historical situation is—and of course the incalculable chance of there arising a great thinker: things futile to meditate on instead of tackling the task as best one can? In that view we are in principle no better off

---

9. Cf. Cobb's comments in *Robinson-Cobb,* p. 188.

than other ages nor worse: it is up to us as it was up to them. And we
are hardly the proper judges as to whether we have succeeded better.
I notice I have slipped into a language which knows of no history of
being but only of a history of finite human attempts to get at being—
a knowledge always provisional, revocable, imperfect. However, so
far I must not move outside the Heideggerian frame of reference if I
am to stay in discourse with its theological devotees. If, then, it is to
be fate, are we—as a last variety—to deify history as working out its
own destiny, using human minds as its organs—if not in the Hegelian
sense, where our present state of grace would equal the phase of the
Absolute Spirit, then by some other logic or illogic of determination?

All these are questions for the philosopher. But as regards the
theologian—or should I rather say the believer—may I for a moment
speak on his behalf? Then it seems to me that the Christian, and
therefore the Christian theologian, must reject any such idea of fate
and history as extending to the status of his own mandate. For one
thing the Christian is said to be saved from the power of fate. So I
remember reading in the early books. Second and more so, that which
saved him was, by the understanding of faith as distinct from the
understanding of the world, not an event of the world and thus not an
event of fate, nor destined ever to become fate or part of fate itself,
but an event invalidating all dicta of fate and overruling the words
which fate speaks to man, *including the words of self-unveiling being.*
Nor is it, third, itself a mere unveiling or showing-itself: the cruci-
fixion, I should say, was not in the first place an event of language.
Must I say this to Christian theologians? It seems so. For I read:
"[The words], as answer to the word of being, are in a fate-like
manner determined on the part of being. It is . . . fate that they speak
as they do. This is true of theology as well. . . . Our answer to the call
of revelation is linguistic. . . . Existence itself [is] essentially linguistic. . . . The speech of our faith . . . is our essential answer to the
call of God's revelation, not merely the inadequate *expression* of our
answer."[10] And since the call, itself speechless, gains speech only in
our answer, there ensues the parallel: "Just as one encounters being
in this or that historic fate-laden conceptualization, just so Christian
language is . . . the historic, fate-laden medium in which God's word

---

10. H. Ott, *Denken und Sein,* pp. 190 f.

speaks to us. . . . Existence is itself essentially linguistic and faith takes place within our language, which is our answer to God" (*Robinson-Cobb,* p. 55). Accordingly, and quite consistently, the Bible itself is taken as one linguistic record of such *answer,* "the Biblical answer to the word of God" (*ibid.,* p. 54). But full as the Bible may be of it—is it the *speaking* answer of man that the revelation is really after? And answer to what? I hear *questions* to man as the doer of deeds, not the speaker of words: "Adam, where are you?" (Gen. 3:9); "Cain, where is Abel your brother? (Gen. 4:9): this is not the voice of being; and the "clearing" in which it places the addressed one is that of his guilt; and the reminder calls the memory of his hardened will, not of his forgetful thought: "He has told you, O man, what is good and what the Lord requires of you: what else but to do justice, and to love mercy, and to walk humbly with your God?" (Mic. 6:8). This requires more than a linguistic answer.

But as to Heidegger's being, it is an occurrence of unveiling, a fate-laden happening upon thought: so was the Führer and the call of German destiny under him: an unveiling of something indeed, a call of being all right, fate-laden in every sense: neither then nor now did Heidegger's thought provide a norm by which to decide how to answer such calls—linguistically or otherwise: no norm except depth, resolution, and the sheer force of being that issues the call. But to the believer, ever suspicious of this world, depth may mean the abyss, and force, the prince of this world. As if the devil were not part of the voice of being! Heidegger's own answer is, to the shame of philosophy, on record and, I hope, not forgotten.[11] But quite apart from this personal fact (whose philosophical significance, however, is immense), the theologian cannot, if he keeps faith with himself, accept *any* system of historical fate or reason or eschatology as a frame to

---

11. The record is collected in Guido Schneeberger, *Nachlese zu Heidegger: Dokumente zu seinem Leben und Denken* (Bern, 1962). The following quotation from a proclamation by Heidegger (then Rector) to the students of the University of Freiburg in November, 1933, serves as an example: "Not doctrines and 'ideas' be the rules of your being. The Führer himself and alone is the present and future German reality and its law. Learn ever deeper to know: that from now on each and every thing demands decision, and every action, responsibility. Heil Hitler!" (*op. cit.,* pp. 135 f.).

integrate his trust into—be it Hegel's or Comte's or Marx's or Spengler's or Heidegger's—for the simple reason that it is about "this world,"
ὁ κόσμος οὗτος, and its truth at best the truth of this world: and of
this world the Christian has learned that it certainly does have its law
(be it reason or fate) and its being and its power and its voice, or
voices rather, as the plural "the archons of this world" suggests; and
so he can indeed learn from those doctrines, and the more so the
truer they are, what he has to contend with—the nature of the princi-
palities and powers—and what he himself is subject to, insofar as he
too is a creature and citizen of this world. But adopt their vista for
the understanding of his subject matter? No. This must be the radically other to it. It must be clearly and unambiguously understood
that the "being" of Heidegger is, *with* the "ontological difference,"
inside the bracket with which theology must bracket in the totality of
the created world. The being whose fate Heidegger ponders is the
quintessence of this world, it is *saeculum*. Against this, theology
should guard the radical transcendence of its God, whose voice comes
not out of being but breaks into the kingdom of being from without.

My theological friends, my Christian friends—don't you see what
you are dealing with? Don't you sense, if not see, the profoundly
pagan character of Heidegger's thought? Rightly pagan, insofar as it
is philosophy, though not every philosophy must be so devoid of
objective norms; but more pagan than others from your point of view,
not in spite but because of its, also, speaking of call and self-revealing
and even of the shepherd. Consider these two statements where objectification helps to show up what is irreconcilable. "The world is
God's handiwork"; "being reveals itself." However objectifying, and
therefore not to be taken literally, the first statement may be—in even
the most demythologized sense it most certainly excludes the (equally
objectifying) statement that Being—i.e., the Being of the beings—
reveals itself, by *its initiative,* in experience, in the encounter of
beings (human) with beings (things); i.e., that revelation is immanent in the world, nay, belongs to its nature; i.e., that the world is
divine. Quite consistently do the gods appear again in Heidegger's
philosophy. But where the gods are, God cannot be. That theology
should admit this foe—no mean foe, and one from whom it could
learn so much about the gulf that separates secular thinking and

faith—into its inner sanctum, amazes me. Or, to express myself reverently: it passes my understanding.

IV

In order to show that I have not overstated the essential immanentism of Heidegger's thought, let us have one brief look at his own exposition of the groundwork for a natural theology. It occurs in his *Letter on Humanism* and belongs to those loci from which the friends of religion can prove that Heidegger is not an atheist. Surely he is not—we have heard of the return of the gods in his world-view. But then the real opposite to the Christian and Jewish view is not atheism, which contemplates a neutral world and thus does not pre-empt divinity for what is not divine, but paganism which deifies the world. This is what Heidegger says: "Only from the truth of *being* can the essence of the *holy* be thought. Only from the essence of the holy is the essence of *deity* to be thought. Only in the light of the essence of deity can that be thought and said which the word 'God' should name."[12] ". . . the holy, which as yet is but the space for the essence of deity, which itself in turn only provides the dimension for the gods and the God. . . ."[13] Now this is absolutely in the philosophical or metaphysical tradition, though surely not in its language. One need only remember Socrates' discussion of the holy and its relation to the gods in the *Euthyphro*. The ascent of thought from being to God: the analysis of being yielding the holy and the divine, the holy and the divine belonging to the structure of reality as such, the divine affording the ontological dimension for gods and God to exist or not to exist—I need not elaborate. If this is not a draft for the ontological procedure of a natural theology, whose remote ancestors are Plato and Aristotle, I do not know what is. I, as an old friend of metaphysics, have no quarrel with that. But shouldn't the theologian?

Lest this remain a merely rhetorical question, let us now examine what really happens in a meeting of Heideggerian thought and theology. As a point of departure I take a statement by Ott. "The *being of God* signifies, according to the way we have understood 'being' thus

---

12. Martin Heidegger, *Platons Lehre von der Wahrheit. Mit einem Brief über den "Humanismus"* (Bern, 1947), p. 102 (italics added).

13. M. Heidegger, *op. cit.* pp. 85 f.

far, an *event of unveiling* (un-hiding: *Entbergung*): that God unveils himself to thinking as He who He is; that He himself befalls thought as a fate and imposes himself on it as subject-to-be-thought" (Ott, *op. cit.*, p. 148). We ask: is it "being" that unveils itself, or beings? If the former, which is Heidegger's stance, then God, who is *a* being (again Heidegger's stance), does not "unveil himself" (though, in Biblical terms, he may "reveal" himself), but Being unveils itself through him, and his imperious self-revealing may even stand in the way of the unveiling of Being—he may, so to speak, block the view of being. Or vice versa, depending on where you take your stand. I must now enjoin you to go with me on a stretch of rigorous dialectics. The following emerges from thinking through Heidegger's position with a view to the subject matter of theology.

Beings are occasions for the experiencing of being; God is a being: thus God, when encountered, is an occasion for the experiencing of being. Being is experienced in beings as amazement at their being (existing), i.e., amazement that they are at all: thus the experience of being in God is amazement at his existing at all. Amazement at something being at all is to think with its being its not-being or its contingency: thus the experiencing of being in the encounter with God is the thinking of the not-being and the contingency of God.[14] Since being is not the being of this or that being, but *qua* being-itself transcends all particular being, the thinking of being in any particular being is a thinking away from that particular being—toward being as such and toward all other beings: thus the primal thinking of God is a thinking away from God or a thinking beyond God. Finally, since a thing, each thing, is a meeting or assembling of the four sides of the ontic "square" (*Geviert*), earth, heaven, the divine, the mortals, each thing properly encountered provides a complete revelation of the

---

14. This point has been made in a different form by James Robinson as follows: "If amazement at the being of beings corresponds to numinous awareness that their being is God's creation [as suggested by Ott], then awareness of God would seem to be latent in awareness of a being's being. When this correlation is applied to God as himself a being . . . confusion emerges. If awe-inspired awareness of a being's being corresponds to sensing a being as a creature, is then God a creature? If such awe at a being's being is ultimately reverence for a being's Creator, does God, as a being, have a Creator?" *Robinson-Cobb,* p. 42.

structure of being in all its dimensions—a more complete one than God who presumably represents only the divine. An evangelical theologian can welcome this thus: "In Heidegger's interpretation of the 'thing' the fatal idea of a closed immanence is no longer felt: the real, concrete world is structurally opened towards possible transcendence. . . . The relation to the 'divine ones' as the counterpart (vis-à-vis: *Gegenüber*) of men belongs to the essential structure of the 'thing' as such" (Ott, *op. cit.,* p. 224). This, it is true, (as the author is careful to add) does not imply an a priori revealedness of the living God: but on a priori revealedness of "the divine" in all things makes the revelation of a living God a redundancy. At this point I turn rather to Zen where I find the doctrine of the revelatory and saving function of each and every thing at first hand and on native ground. I sense a certain recalcitrance in the Christian substance to this kind of thing. But I may of course be wrong.

However that may be, the whole preceding argument was based on the supposition that "Being" is understood as strictly ontological and not ontic, not as something itself being (which, among other things, would involve an infinite regress). In other words, I have abided by the injunction that being not be hypostasized, while God, of course, must be a being. Under this dispensation there cannot obtain an *analogy* between the being of Heidegger's philosophy and the God of Christian theology, but instead there must follow all the consequences of the ontological difference which I have just developed. However, Ott, apparently with the backing of Heidegger, does precisely claim the analogy which the "ontological difference" precludes: "As philosophical thinking is related to being, when being speaks to thinking, so faith's thinking is related to God, when God is revealed in his word" (*Robinson-Cobb,* p. 43). Or, in Heidegger's own succinct formulation "philosophical thinking is to being as theological thinking is to the self-revealing God." This is oral tradition.[15] If correct, then, I must say, it lets the cat out of the bag and shows that we must not take Heidegger too strictly at his own word. For the claim to analogy,

---

15. Both statements are reported, as made at the 1960 Meeting of "Old Marburgers," in *Robinson-Cobb,* pp. 43 and 190. I was told in Germany by participants of that meeting that at least Heidegger's share in the formulation was hypothetical and for argument's sake, rather than as a statement of his own position.

since there just *cannot* be one between the ontological and the ontic, makes it clear that Heidegger's statements about being are really, at least in part, ontic, not ontological, whatever his protestations—and that is to say, that they are metaphysical. This is in my book not a bad word, and so no insult is intended. But it clarifies matters considerably. Indeed, what I have just merely postulated from the asserted analogy is fully borne out by the evidence of the eminently ontic, objectifying, and thus metaphysical, language of Heidegger's statements themselves. For surely, a "being" that acts must be; that which takes the initiative must exist; what unveils itself had a before when it kept hidden, and thus has a being beyond the act of revealing; what can give itself differs from that to which—and differs not by way of the ontological difference, but ontically, as here and there, as vis-à-vis. Indeed how can one speak of being's activity and man's receptivity, of the former's having and being a fate, being event, not only making possible thought but giving thought, clearing or obscuring itself in such thought, having voice, calling to man, happening upon man, sending man, entrusting itself to man's care, appropriating him into its own care, favoring him, enlisting his loyalty, summoning his gratitude, but also needing him—how can one attribute all this to it unless one understands it as an agency and a power, as some sort of subject? Certainly the language of the later Heidegger, in contrast to the rigorously ontological one of *Sein und Zeit,* has become increasingly and obtrusively ontic, and however figurative or poetical such language is meant to be (and poetic it is, even if bad poetry), its ontic meaning is inalienable from it on pain of its becoming empty sound. Let us then not be intimidated by the frown of the "ontological difference" and acknowledge that, of course, "being" is hypostasized in Heidegger, as was "the good" in Plato and the *"causa sui"* in Spinoza, only, to be sure, not in the category of substance. That there *are* alternatives to the being of substance *this* side of the ontological difference, Whitehead has impressively shown.[16] But if we

---

16. A study of Whitehead is urgently recommended to Heideggerians. *Inter alia,* it may inject a modicum of qualification into the unquestioningly accepted thesis of the "end of metaphysics." On the other hand, they would find there, in the rigor of concept, much of what they welcome in Heidegger's innovations: the break with "substance," the event-character of being, the reduction of entity to actual occasion, the inwardness of

grant the ontic or metaphysical meaning of Being in those aspects we have noted—letting infinite regress take care of itself—then we can also grant the analogy disputed before. Thus, on the new hypothesis, we can scrap the previous argument that landed theology in Zen, and we are free to appraise the reinstated analogy, viz., "as philosophical thinking is to being so theological thinking is to the self-revealing God." Let us see where that leaves the theologian. Not better off, I am afraid.

Of course, lest the analogy state a mere truism, we must rephrase it thus: "As philosophical thinking *according to Heidegger* is to self-unveiling being, so theological thinking should be to the self-revealing God." But since according to Heidegger what matters is not so much philosophical but primal thinking of being, of which philosophy is only one mode and poetry another, we must once more rephrase and say "As *primal* thinking is to being, so theological thinking should be to God" (here I can omit "unveiling" and "revealing" because it is included in "primal"); or: *theology should be primal thinking concerning God.* But since, again, the very conception of "primal thinking" is already a function of the particular concept of that which it is to think about, viz., of *"being"* (let me ignore the circle) and involves it and has no meaning without it, the analogy—now that theology itself is to be primal thinking—comes down to the proposition: Heidegger's thinking about being, in the twofold sense of *how* and *what* he thinks about it, should be the model for theology's thinking about God; and thus, if the model for the conception of him, then also the model for the conception of his self-revealing. And still one last step remains to be taken: since thinking, namely, primal thinking in response to the call of being, is man's most adequate relation to being, and thus the highest or truest mode of man's existence (formally the axiom of philosophy since Parmenides!), the former analogy finally becomes this: Heidegger's view of thinking as man's true avocation and as his adequate response to the call of being—not, e.g., action, brotherly love, resistance to evil, promotion of the good —I say, *thinking* as seen by Heidegger should be the model for

occasion as experience, the context of occasions as prehensions, and so on. But in Whitehead, all this is on the objectifying, ontic level. *Process and Reality* is "An Essay in Cosmology." No philosophy of nature can issue from Heidegger's thought.

theology's conception of man's perfection under God in adequate response to the call of God, and therefore for its conception of the content of this call itself.

V

I am fully aware that nobody wishes to go that far and that Professor Ott's intentions stop somewhere along the line I have traced. I believe that this cannot be done, that you must take or leave the whole, and that by buying a part you have willy-nilly bought the whole. But as there is no time for me to show this now, I will for argument's sake go with the eclectic approach and treat single themes as if they were isolable from the rest.

1. First, then, the very least you buy is a doctrine of *permanent revelation*. For it is really inseparable from the analogy of the unveiling of being as being's own history, etc., that its religious analogue too is an ever-renewed event, in happening and content determined by fate. Doctrinally this might be expressed, e.g., in an Adamitic prophetology of the kind we have in certain Gnostic speculations, or in the idea of a constant revelatory activity of the Holy Ghost. Perhaps this will not frighten the theologian who speaks so confidently of the *communio sanctorum*. Further implications the trained theologian can easily work out for himself, and it is for him to decide whether he wants what he finds—implications such as these: that the revelation is unfinished and has an entirely open horizon for future advents of the word; that future revelations are not prejudged by past revelations, and no one revelation supplies an authoritative criterion by which others are to be judged. This does away with the possibility of, but equally with the need for, distinguishing between true doctrine and heresy—the very idea of a true doctrine disappears. But it also, I am afraid, makes it impossible to distinguish between the inspirations of the Holy Ghost and the demons (I hope you agree with me that there are demons). Another consequence is that the whole Biblical revelation including the Christ event is only a phase in the ongoing process of divine self-revealing through events of language. And on those terms you can indeed not have a theology of saving facts, but only a theology of events of language (strangely enough itself an event of language), and its criterion is not the truth of God's actions,

i.e., the correct meaning of those saving facts, but the authenticity of speech about those actions.

2. This brings me to the second item you are buying from Heidegger, and at the same time back to our theme, the problem of nonobjectifying speech: the item, namely, that theology must be pneumatic theology or as you might say, glossolaly ("speaking in tongues"). This consequence is implicit in the claim that theology is, or should be, a species of primal thinking. Here it is not I that tell theologians what theology might unwittingly contract from an alliance with Heidegger, but this point is the declared choice of a theologian and the hub of his whole enterprise: viz., to transfer Heidegger's concept of "primal" or "essential" thinking to theology; and to set its thinking, as itself primal and essential in common with that of poetry, apart from the secondary, subjectivist-objectifying thought of metaphysics and science (cf. Ott, *op. cit.,* p. 45). When word reached me that theology is henceforth to be primal thinking, my first thought was: God forbid!—and my second: poor theologians!—in short, the classical reaction to tragedy—fear and pity. For primal thinking, as we have learned, is not at the thinker's command, but happens to him by the grace of being. And so the theologian is a man professionally committed to being continually granted that happening for the doing of his day's work; or a man who claims to dwell permanently that close to the source: a life's calling I would not care to choose. In fairness to Heidegger it must be said that what is here asked of theology does not follow from his philosophy and his doctrine of thinking as such. On the contrary, his unpublished lecture of 1928 on "Theology and Philosophy," which I recently had occasion to read, expressly terms theology a positive science, since it deals with a *positum,* God—*a* being, therefore an ontic discipline, as distinct from philosophy, which is nonpositive, ontological, dealing with being purely. And as a science that thinks about its object, theology is of course secondary and not primary thinking. This was before the famous "turn," when Heidegger was still a rational thinker (reason and profundity do not necessarily exclude each other). But even in terms of his later thought it is not at all plausible, let alone necessary, that theology must be or even can be primal thinking. It seems that only as an afterthought, heeding the plea of theologians who wished their discipline freed from the odor of science, after science had been

found out to be forgetfulness of being,[17] did Heidegger (at least orally) permit theology to be added to poetry and philosophy as possible modes of primal thinking. The ontological havoc that results from the analogy thus established has just been considered: the linguistic is not less. That theology must become pneumatic and its speech glossolaly, follows from the desired analogy to Heidegger's thinking about being, which must include his manner of speaking about being—the two things are inseparable. Where language coïncides with the self-unveiling of being, language rather than man becomes the speaker: "language speaks."[18] What kind of language is this? Robinson (*op. cit.,* p. 24) speaks of the "hauntingly suggestive rather than conceptually explicit style of the later Heidegger." May I, a mere nonsaved, but sympathetically caring child of the world, be permitted to pray: God protect theology from the temptation of resorting to haunting language! It is not merely that I find many of the linguistic offerings of the prototype exceedingly *kitschig* (I cannot translate that) rather than haunting: and that I shudder to think of what might happen when people begin to decide to be poets. More important than such considerations of taste is the specter of arbitrariness and anarchy that thus appears. You can no longer prove anything there—this you may disdain anyway—but neither can you refute, nay even reject anything there: as indeed the speaking in question cannot say "No" to the voice of being to which it responds. The only criterion that remains is authenticity of language. But of authenticity, I believe, one should not speak. Each one for himself should unremittingly strive for it in his own work, but not give marks on its score to the work of others. What yardstick would you have anyway?

But do I really need to dwell on this? The dangers of charismatic speech are familiar to the theologian versed in the history of his creed. But on another angle of this issue I must speak, because it leads us to the heart of our problem. Apart from the dubiousness of the potential products of the linguistic stance I have remarked on, what presumption, what arrogance, in the stance itself! As what do I

----

17. "Science does not think," cf. Heidegger, *Was heisst Denken?* (Tübingen, 1961), p. 4 and *passim.*
18. M. Heidegger, *Unterwegs zur Sprache* (Pfullingen, 1959), *passim.*

set myself and my speaking up there? But, it will be objected, isn't primal thinking and speaking just the opposite of self-assertion and thus of arrogance? Leaving the initiative to being, listening to what being speaks, responding to its call, letting oneself be grasped by its power, most of all: giving up the whole attitude of subjectity and of overmastering the object by my conceptualizing—isn't that reverence? isn't that humility? Here I must say something about the seeming, false humility of Heidegger's shifting the initiative to Being, so seductive to Christian theologians, but in fact the most enormous hybris in the whole history of thought. For it is nothing less than the thinker's claiming that through him speaks the essence of things itself, and thus the claim to an authority which no thinker should ever claim. And moreover it is the claim that in principle the basic human condition, that of being at a distance to things which we must bridge by the reaching-out of our mind, the so-called subject-object split, can be remitted, avoided, overcome. The claim, that is, to a possible immediacy that perhaps has a place in the person-to-person relation, but not in the relation to impersonal being and things and the world. There is really no precedent for this in the whole of Western philosophy. Closest to it comes, in one respect—Schopenhauer: a parallel hardly welcome to Heidegger, which for lack of time I cannot pursue here intriguing as it is,[19] except for one pointer: to Schopenhauer music, the only nonobjective art, is the direct voice of the thing-in-itself, of the universal Will. This, in Nietzsche's phrase, made the musician the ventriloquist of the Absolute. In the spirit of Nietzsche's witticism (it is well to remember that Nietzsche had wit) Heidegger's primal thinker would be the ventriloquist of being, ventriloquy then

---

19. Consider, for example, the following points. The world is the objectification of the universal Will. Will is the thing-in-itself, the individual forms are its appearance. Their boundedness and staticness hide the ceaseless driving of the Will. They can be seen and defined in concepts: this is the world as *Vorstellung:* representation. The Will is experienced within. But it can also be made to appear—to hearing; not however as call, but as music. Music is the art form in which the voice of the Will speaks directly, because it is nonobjective, nonspatial, and pure movement of time. All other arts, and language, and theory, are wedded to appearance, to representation, to objectivity. Nietzsche continued the theme in a new direction with his distinction of the Dionysian and the Apollinian. Heidegger represents the ultimate repudiation of the Apollinian.

denoting the secular equivalent of glossolaly. Schopenhauer's fantasy
was innocent, for music is nonresponsible and cannot suffer from the
misconception of a duty it does not have. But thinking is not indifferent to the conception of its task and nature. As responsible, it cru-
cially depends on the conception of its responsibility. Here the apparent humility and actual pride of the conception of primal thinking
may altogether ruin thought. Man's thought: the event of the self-
clearing of being, not his own erring bid for truth! Man: the shepherd of being—not, mind you, of beings! Apart from the blas-
phemous ring which this use of the hallowed title must have to Jewish
and Christian ears: it is hard to hear man hailed as the shepherd of
being when he has just so dismally failed to be his brother's keeper.
The latter he is meant to be in the Bible. But the terrible anonymity
of Heidegger's "being," illicitly decked out with personal characters,
blocks out the personal call. Not by the being of another person am I
grasped, but just by "being"! And my responsive thought is being's
own event. But called as person by person—fellow beings or God—
my response will not primarily be thinking but action (though this
involves thinking), and the action may be one of love, responsibility,
pity; also of wrath, indignation, hate, even fight to the death: it is him
or me. . . . In this sense indeed also Hitler was a call. *Such calls are
drowned in the voice of being to which one cannot say No;* as is also,
we are told, the separation of subject from object.

This is the final claim of pride, and the betrayal of man's task
growing from the acceptance of his lot. For let this be said now: the
subject-object *relation,* which presupposes, holds open, and stands
through the duality, is not a lapse but the privilege, burden, and duty
of man. Not Plato is responsible for it but the human condition, its
limits and nobility under the order of creation. For far from being a
deviation from Biblical truth, this setting of man over against the sum
total of things, his subject-status and the object-status and mutual
externality of things themselves, are posited in the very idea of creation and of man's position vis-à-vis nature determined by it: it is the
condition of man *meant* in the Bible, imposed by his createdness, to
be accepted, acted through—and transcended only in certain encounters with fellow beings and God, i.e., in existential relations of a very
special kind. The philosopher's respect for the Biblical tradition rests
precisely on the acknowledgment of the role it has played in impress-

ing this ontological scheme with its great and exacting tension upon the Western mind—more so, perhaps, because more unambiguously, than even the Greek tradition. The origin of the rift, whether deplored or hailed, is in Moses no less than in Plato. And if you must lay technology at somebody's door, don't forget, over the scapegoat of metaphysics, the Judaeo-Christian tradition.

V I

Where does all this leave the linguistic problem of theology? That there is a problem, that the issue troubling the theologian is a genuine one, has been granted at the very opening of this address. That the conceptualization and objective language of theory do not do justice, to some extent do violence, to the primary content committed to theology's care, on this there is agreement. Also on this: that there *is* nonobjectifying thought and speech. We find it in the prophets and the psalmists, in the language of prayer and confession and preaching, also in lyrical poetry; and in the life of the dialogue: much of what Buber has said about the "I-thou" relation and its language, as distinct from third person "I-it" relation and its language, falls squarely into the area of our problem. But the theologian, *when* he attends to theology (which he does not do all the time), is neither prophet nor psalmist nor preacher nor poet, nor in the I-thou situation, but under the yoke of theoretical discourse and therefore beholden to objective thought and language. This burden theology has to shoulder, and not even the later Heidegger offers legitimate release from it. Nor should such release be sought. On this point I agree completely with Rudolf Bultmann and with what has been said in his vein in the American discussion, notably in the excellent essays of Come and Ogden.[20] Nevertheless, and this is precisely the Bultmannian position, there can be a more or less adequate style of conceptuality and language in theology, or: a less or more inadequate one, since inadequacy will still be our lot. In short, there are degrees of objectification. And indeed—to give now at the end my own tentative view on the matter, which up to a point coincides with Bultmann's, but beyond that point diverges from his—the question is not

---

20. *Robinson-Cobb*, Nos. 3 and 5.

how to devise an adequate language for theology, but how to keep its necessary inadequacy *transparent* for what is to be indicated by it: its lesser or greater opaqueness is a matter about which something can be done.

My own early grapplings with the problem of objectification and its hermeneutical aspects made me stumble on the concept of "demythologizing."[21] I conceived this as one move in the process of deobjectifying for which the interpretation of certain ancient texts seemed to call. The translation—a retranslation as it were—of mythical terms into concepts of existential philosophy would return the *logos* into closer proximity to the substance from which it had originated, to wit, the dynamics and self-experience of human existence. Thus the demythologizing meant the retrieving of this substance from the most compact, most unyielding, most extreme form of objectification in which it was locked up, and here indeed the categories evolved in Heidegger's analysis of existence in *Sein und Zeit* offered a superior means of bringing to light the ground from which the projections of doctrine had risen and which contains their truth.[22] And the dialectical character of the concepts affords some protection against the kind of objective fixation to which the concepts of the philosophy of substance are prone. Thus they are less opaque, more transparent, more *appropriate* to the "subject matter of theology."

So far, I think, I am in complete agreement with my friend and teacher Bultmann. A possible difference lurks in the question: How far can the "translation" legitimately extend? Up to what sphere in the universe of religious discourse? The danger of "appropriateness" of a conceptual scheme is that it may blunt the sense of paradox and create a familiarity where none is permitted. The dividing line, the line whose crossing by the demythologized concept would have that

---

21. In a study on the hermeneutics of Church dogma, appended to my *Augustin und das paulinische Freiheitsproblem: Eine philosophische Studie zum pelagianischen Streit* (*Forschungen zur Religion und Literatur des Alten und Neuen Testaments* 44 [N. F. 27] (Göttingen, 1930; 2nd ed., revised and enlarged, 1965), *Anhang I: Über die hermeneutische Struktur des Dogmas;* cf. the Introduction by James M. Robinson to the second edition.

22. On the hermeneutical status of Heidegger's categories of existence compare the beginning of the Ninth Essay.

effect, can be clearly indicated. If it is said, on Bultmann's behalf, that "the concepts of Heidegger's existentialist analysis are better adapted to explicating the Christian understanding of man than the mythological concepts employed by the writers of the New Testament" (*Robinson-Cobb,* p. 167), we add: yes—precisely with respect to man: no—with respect to God or the divine. There, symbolic speech must begin. On pain of immanentism or mere anthropologism, the understanding of God is not to be reduced to the self-understanding of man. The domain of the existential concept extends as far as phenomenology, the sphere of its verification, extends: over the self-experience of man *"before"* God, *coram deo,* not *in* God; or: *homo sub lege,* not *homo sub gratia.* Where the divine itself is said to enter, the outpouring of the spirit, "God's love . . . poured into our hearts through the Holy Spirit" (Rom. 5:5), "the healing of the soul from the blemish of sin" (Augustine), phenomenology ceases to have a say; and with it the verifiable concepts of existentialist knowledge; and thus: demythologizing! And all the more for the sphere of divinity itself. The final paradox is better protected by the symbols of myth than by the concepts of thought. Where the mystery is rightfully at home, "we see in a glass darkly." What does "in a glass darkly" mean? In the shapes of myth. To keep the *manifest opaqueness* of myth transparent for the ineffable is in a way easier than to keep the seeming transparency of the concept transparent for that to which it is in fact as opaque as any language must be.

Myth taken *literally* is crudest objectification.

Myth taken *allegorically* is sophisticated objectification.

Myth taken *symbolically* is the glass through which we darkly see.

Immortality and the Modern Temper

For H. A.

In the following reflections[1] I shall start from what I consider an undeniable fact, namely, that the modern temper is uncongenial to the idea of immortality. It is that over and above the objections which the modern intellect entertains against it on theoretical grounds. These—which for brevity I will simply grant *en bloc*—are by themselves indecisive. As transcendental, the object of the idea—immor-

---

1. Originally delivered as the Ingersoll Lecture of 1961 at Harvard University and subsequently published in the *Harvard Theological Review,* 55 (1962), 1-20, this essay has been the subject of penetrating discussion in the article "Death, Dying, and Immortality" by Philip Merlan, and in the counterthesis "The Dialectic of Death and Immortality" by Maurice Natanson, in the *Pacific Philosophy Forum,* 3, 1 (1964), pp. 3-45 and 70-79 respectively. To these public voices must be added extensive comment in numerous private communications. Among the latter were the searching comments by Rudolf Bultmann which have been included, together with my reply, as an Appendix in the German publication of the essay in: H. Jonas, *Zwischen Nichts und Ewigkeit* (Göttingen, 1963), 63-72.—The virtually unchanged reprinting of the essay here does not mean that I have closed my mind to the important issues raised, but merely that I have neither succeeded yet, with their help, to advance beyond its admittedly tentative position, nor felt constrained, under their pressure, to retreat from it.

tality itself—is beyond proof or disproof: it is not an object of knowledge. But the idea of it is. Therefore, the intrinsic merits of its meaning become the sole measure of its credibility, and the appeal of that meaning remains as the sole ground of possible belief—as certainly the lack of such an appeal is sufficient ground for actual disbelief. But since what is meaningful depends, beyond the mere condition of logical consistency, largely on the dispositions and insights of the mind that judges it, we must interrogate these for their prevalent unresponsiveness as well as for any possible hold which the idea, even in its present eclipse, may still have, or reclaim, on our secularized estate. Thus an examination of the problem at this hour will be as much an examination of ourselves as an examination of the issue of immortality; and even if it should throw no new light on the latter, on which in more than two thousand years probably everything has been said there is to say, it may yet throw some light on the present state of our mortal condition.

I

On the inhospitableness of the contemporary mind to the idea of immortality I can, indeed must, be very brief, since much has been said about it in our century, and the area of agreement is broad, and little disputed; whereas on the less noticed, and less obvious, opening which the modern mind does offer to the idea in one of its possible meanings, and does so precisely by its "modern" turn, I shall have to dwell at some length. This "opening," however, stands forth essentially from the negative background without which the modern temper would not be what it is.

First, then, a look at the negative side. Let me start with the oldest and most empirical concept of immortality: survival by immortal fame. This was most prized in antiquity and considered not only the just reward of noble deeds but a prime incentive to them.[2] The deeds

2. Throughout Greek letters, from Homer to Plato, who marks the philosophic overcoming of the ideal but gives it eloquent expression in the words of Diotima: "Think only of the ambition of men, and you will wonder at the senselessness of their ways, unless you consider how they are stirred by the love of an immortality of fame. They are ready to run all risks greater far than they would have run for their children, and to

must be visible, that is, public, to be noted and remembered as great. The dimension of this living-on is the dimension itself in which it is earned: the body politic. Immortal fame is thus public honor in perpetuity, as the body politic is human life in perpetuity. Now, already Aristotle pointed out that honor is worth just as much as the judgment of those who bestow it.[3] But then, the desire for it, and *a fortiori* the desire for its extension into posthumous fame, and ultimately the estimation of this form of immortality in principle, are justified only by the trust we can reasonably place in the integrity of

---

spend money and undergo any sort of toil, and even to die, for the sake of leaving behind them a name which shall be eternal. Do you imagine that Alcestis would have died to save Admetus, or Achilles to avenge Patroclus, or your own Codrus in order to preserve the kingdom for his sons, if they had not imagined that the memory of their virtues, which still survives among us, would be immortal? Nay, I am persuaded that all men do all things, and the better they are the more they do them, in hope of the glorious fame of immortal virtue; for they desire the immortal" (Symposium 208 c-d; tr. B. Jowett). Perhaps the loftiest statement of the ideal occurs in Pericles' Funeral Oration on the Athenian dead in the first year of the Peloponnesian war: "They received, each for his own memory, praise that will never die, and with it the grandest of all sepulchres, not that in which their mortal bones are laid, but a home in the minds of men, where their glory remains fresh to stir to speech or action as the occasion comes by. For the whole earth is the sepulchre of famous men, and their story is not graven only in stone over their native earth, but lives far away, without visible symbol, woven into the stuff of other men's lives" (Thucydides, II 43; tr. A. Zimmern, *The Greek Commonwealth*, p. 207).—Not long ago, I encountered the ancient sentiment unalloyed in (of all places) television when one of our astronauts-in-training, asked what had made him volunteer for the task, answered, "Frankly, the chance of immortality; for this, I would willingly give my life." Given with engaging simplicity, there was no doubting the candor of the reply. Events in the meantime may have caused some reflections on how much, besides the merits of dedication and ability, also opportunity and luck—and not only our own, but that of unknown others—rule over this kind of immortality.

3. In discussing why honor cannot be "the good": it rests in those who bestow it rather than in him who receives it, whereas the good must be one's inalienable own; further, we seek it, i.e., the reputation of being good, as a confirmation of our being good, therefore from people who have good judgment, and adequate knowledge of us, and who accord honor to virtue—which on this admission stands as the primary good: *Eth. Nic.* 1095 b 22-30.

its trustee and master, namely, public opinion: in its enlightenment now, its faithfulness in the future—and, of course, in its own unceasing continuity, that is the indefinite survival of the commonwealth. Now on all these counts the modern temper cannot permit itself the innocent confidence of the Greeks. The selectiveness as such of this "immortality": that it admits few and excludes most, we might accept if only we could believe in the justice of the selection. But for that we know too much of how reputations are made, how fame is fabricated, public opinion engineered, the record of history remade, and even premade, to the order of interest and power. In the age of the party lines, and, for that matter, of Madison Avenue, in the age of the universal corruption of the word, we are sadly aware that speech, the vehicle of this immortality, is the medium of lies as well as of truth, and more often the former than the latter in the public sphere—with a busily fostered growth between them of unmeaningness, not even fit for either, eating away into both; and the older suspicion whether we are not dealing with a tale told by an idiot is overshadowed by the worse that it might be a tale concocted by knaves.

We have also learned that even superhuman heroism can be so effectively shut off from all public knowledge and testimony that in mundane terms it is as if it had never been. Further, if generally the premium put on the spectacular at the expense of the hidden provokes our disdain, the great evildoers we moderns have had the fortune to know face us with the wholly repugnant perspective that the famous and the infamous come to stand on a par: for let no one deceive himself on the fact that to the perversity of those agents, and to that of a posterity responding to theirs, their evil fame is an achievement and not a penalty: and so the Hitlers and Stalins of our era would have succeeded to extract immortality from the extinction of their nameless victims.

Shall we add that only the vain craves immortality of name, while the truly proud and good can do with anonymous survival of his work? This leads to another version of the empirical concept: immortality of influence—to some extent the hope of every earnest effort in the service of higher purpose. But, alas, there again we are too worldly wise to trust in the worldly causality of things as a faithful repository of acts, since we can credit it neither with adequate discrimination of worth nor with its conservation in the shifts of time.

This much, sober judgment could always have known. But we know something more and never known before: that the repository itself, namely human civilization, is perishable. This new knowledge invalidates both concepts, immortality of name and of influence—even that of great works of art and thought, which most of all resist obliteration by time: for what is itself mortal cannot well be the vehicle of immortality. With the dramatic sharpening which the generally modern awareness of the passing nature of cultures and societies has undergone more recently—to the point where the survival of the human race itself seems in jeopardy—our presumptive immortality, as that of all the immortals before us, appears suddenly at the mercy of a moment's miscalculation, failure, or folly by a handful of fallible men.

II

Let us, then, turn to the non-empirical and really substantive concept of immortality: survival of the person in an hereafter. This finds itself at even greater odds with the modern temper. I do not concern myself with the persuasive inference from the indubitable organic basis of "person" to its essential non-separableness therefrom. But, do at least the non-empirical reasonings behind the *postulate* still have our ear? The serious ones, if we dismiss the mere creaturely recoil from death, fall roughly under two heads: justice, and the distinction between appearance and reality, of which the idea of the mere phenomenality of time is a case. Both have this in common that they accord to man the metaphysical status of moral subject and, as such, of belonging to a moral or "intelligible" order besides the sensible one. This should not be lightly dismissed. But the principle of justice, be it retributive or compensatory justice, does by its own criterion not support the claim to immortality. For temporal merit or guilt calls for temporal, not eternal retribution, and justice thus requires at most a finite afterlife for settling accounts, not an infinity of existence. And as to compensation for undeserved suffering, or denied chances, or missed happiness here, there applies the additional consideration that a *claim* to happiness as such (how much of it?) is questionable to begin with; and that missed *fulfillment* could only be made up for *in its original terms,* that is, in the terms of effort and obstacles and uncertainty and fallibility and unique occasion and limited time—in short: in terms of non-guaranteed attainment and possible miss. These are the very terms of *self*-fulfillment, and they are precisely the terms of the world. To try in them our being, and to experience the vicissitudes of our try, not knowing the outcome in advance—this is our genuine claim. Without those terms, without the anxiousness of chance and the zest of challenge and the sweetness of achievement under such terms, no bliss gratuitously granted can be anything but a counterfeit coin for what has been missed. It also would lack all moral worth. Indeed the here cannot be traded for a there—such is our present stance.

This also contains the modern temper's response to the distinction of appearance and reality. I have always felt that the idealistic philosophers who profess it may have been too sheltered from the shock of the external, so that they could regard it as a spectacle, a representation on a stage. They certainly do less than honor to what they demote to mere appearance. We hard-pressed children of the now insist on taking it seriously. Where we find it deceptive we take a harder look at it to make its truth more truly appear. The starkness of a barren mountainside, the beauty of an animated face, are the direct language of reality. And when in horror we look at the pictures from Buchenwald, at the wasted bodies and distorted faces, at the utter defilement of humanity in the flesh—we reject the consolation that this is appearance and the truth is something else: we face the terrible truth that the appearance *is* the reality, and that there is nothing more real than what here appears.

Most unsympathetic, perhaps, is modern philosophy to the view that *time* is not ultimately real but only the phenomenal form under which a timeless, noumenal reality appears to a subject which "in itself" is of that noumenal world. This was the tenuous theoretical link to possible personal immortality left by Kant's critical idealism, and it has withered away in the climate of the modern mind. From the discovery of Man's basic historicity to the ontological elaboration of the innermost temporality of his being, it has been borne in upon us that time, far from being a mere form of phenomena, is of the essence of such things as selves, and that its finitude for each is integral to the very authenticity of his existing. Rather than dissemble, we claim our perishability: we do not wish to forego the pang and poignancy of finitude: we insist on facing nothingness and on

having the strength to live with it. Thus, without a secret life-line for
reassurance, existentialism, this extreme offspring of the modern
temper or distemper, throws itself into the waters of mortality. And
we, whether of its doctrine or not, share enough of its spirit to have
taken our lonely stand in time between the twofold nothing of before
and after.

III

And yet—we feel, temporality cannot be the whole story, because in
man it has an inherently self-surpassing quality, of which the very
fact and fumbling of our idea of eternity is a cryptic signal. If ever-
lastingness is a wrong concept, "eternity" may have other meanings
—and a reference to the temporal of which our mortal experience,
transcending its mere transience in the stream of events, may sometimes bear witness. The opaqueness of the here and now clears at
times as if by sudden precipitation at the critical point: if there is any
such transparency of the temporal for the eternal, however rare and
brief, then the moments and modes in which it comes to pass can give
us a clue as to what of our being, if not the substance of our selves,
may be said to reach into the deathless and, therefore, to be our stake
in immortality. In what situations and in what forms do we encounter
the eternal? When do we feel the wings of timelessness touch our
heart and immortalize the now? In what manner does the absolute
enter the relativities of our everyday existence?

I shall not invoke the testimony of mystical experiences that are
not mine and, if they were, would find their claim come under the
invincible suspicion of the psychologizing modern mind. Nor should
the unsolicitable encounters of love or of beauty, which we might
grant to be flashes of eternity, be summoned as evidence in discourse
as if they were at our call, to the complacence of him who can claim
them, and the discomfiture of him who cannot. Rather, in keeping
with the modern temper, I turn to the one kind of evidence that
depends on ourselves because we are active there, not receptive,
wholly subject and in no way object.

In moments of decision, when our whole being is involved, we feel
as if acting under the eyes of eternity. What can we mean by it—nay,
by our willing that it be so? We may express our feeling in different

symbols according to articulate beliefs which we hold or to the images we cherish. We may say, for instance, that what we do now will make an indelible entry in the "Book of Life," or leave an indelible mark in a transcendent order; that it will affect that order, if not our own destiny, for good or for evil; that we shall be accountable for it before a timeless seat of justice, or—if we are not there for the accounting, because we have flowed down the river of time—that our eternal image is determined by our present deed, and that through what we do to that image of ours here and now, we are responsible for the spiritual totality of images that evergrowingly sums up the record of being and will be different for our deed. Or, less metaphysically, we may say that we wish to act so that, whatever the outcome here in the incalculable course of mundane causality—whether success or miscarriage—we can live with the spirit of our act through an eternity to come, or die with it the instant after this. Or, that we are ready to see ourselves, in an eternal recurrence of all things, when our turn comes round, and again we stand poised as now, blind as now, unaided as now—to see ourselves making the same decision again, and ever again, always passing the same imaginary test, endlessly reaffirming what is yet each time only once. Or, failing that certainty of affirmation, that at least the agony of infinite risk may be rightfully ours. And in this, eternity and nothingness meet in one: that the "now" justifies its absolute status by exposing itself to the criterion of being the last moment granted of time. To act as if in the face of the end is to act as if in the face of eternity, if either is taken as a summons to unhedging truth of selfhood. But to understand the end in this way is really to understand it in a light from beyond time.

I V

What shall we make of these feelings and metaphors, and what, if anything, do they contribute, what hints do they furnish towards the issue of immortality? It will be noted that the symbols referred to speak, not of immortality, but of eternity—which, to be sure, is deathlessness but not necessarily mine, yet must have such a relation to my mortality that with something in or of my being I can, even must, share in it. What can that be? Let us further note that in all those symbols it was not the realm of feeling but that of acting, not the matter of bliss and pain but the spirit of decision and deed, in short, not our passive but our active nature, which came to stand in a relation to eternity. Let us take that hint. It seems a paradox at first. For is it not feeling which has duration, which spreads over time and, as a time-filling content, can at least be thought spread out indefinitely? whereas decision is of all the most transient occupant of time, an infinitesimal magnitude in extension, entirely lodged in the moment and irretrievably carried off with its fleeting now? And is it not feeling which craves immortality, which wishes to last, which tells to the moment "O stop and stay!"—while the act presses on, self-liquidating, looking beyond itself, not even wishing to stay, nay, wishing to end? The paradox is that in what is self-negating, not in what is self-affirming with respect to lastingness, we should look for the relation—as yet undefined—to eternity. But perhaps the paradox contains its own hint. For that which has extension may have more or less of it, but must have an end: duration feeds on the boon of quantity, but is also enclosed in its limits: its benefit from the largess of a sensible continuum is at the same time its confinement—the confinement to its own immanence. Lasting as long as it does, it cannot outlast itself. On the other hand, the critical divide of the existential now, in which free action is born, has dimension only by accident and is not measured by it. The evanescence as much as the protraction of its sensible span is defied by a transcendence of meaning which is indifferent to the long or the short of duration. Thus it may well be that the point of the moment, not the expanse of the flux, is our link to eternity: and the "moment" not as the *nunc stans,* the "standing now," in which the mystic tastes release from the movement of time, but moment as the momentum-giving motor of that very movement. On the threshold of deed holding time in suspense, but not a respite from time, it exposes our being to the timeless and with the turn of decision speeds us into action and time. Swiftly reclaimed by the movement it actuates, it marks man's openness to transcendence in the very act of committing him to the transience of situation, and in this double exposure, which compounds the nature of total concern, the "moment" places the responsible agent between time and eternity. From this place-between springs ever new the chance of new beginning, which ever means the plunge into the here and now.

Thus, to say it again, not what lasts longest in our experience, but what lasts shortest and is intrinsically most adverse to lastingness, may turn out to be that which binds the mortal to the immortal. From its testimony, then, we can perhaps extract a better meaning of what, inadequately, is called the "immortality of man," than the literal ones we have found wanting. Let us at least proceed on that expectation and by that hint.

To look in this direction for a tenable concept of immortality is in keeping with the modern temper which we found so keenly conscious of the essential temporality of our being, of its intrinsic reference to finite situation, and so suspicious of the possibility and the very sense of endless self-persistence. And it is also in keeping with the most meaningful, if misapplied, aspects in traditional ideas of immortality. It was the meteoric flash of deed and daring which was to be immortalized by worldly fame; the life-sum of purpose, acts, and failure to act, on which retribution in an afterlife was to be visited; our moral being, from which alone Kant held immortality of the person to be arguable—as a postulate of "practical" (not an inference of theoretical) reason. Dubious as the vehicle of fame has been found, faulty as the correlation of temporal merit with eternal reward or punishment; and invalid as the argument of infinite perfectibility and the supposed right thereto is—the aspect of justice as such in these ideas of immortality, as against the wholly untenable argument from indestructible substance, still commands in us a stirring of acknowledgment by the transcendent dignity it confers on the realm of decision and deed. Let us then follow the intimations of our acting experience, of our freedom and responsibility, and take the tentative term of an "immortality of deeds" for our lead in interrogating some of the quoted metaphors which must themselves have sprung from intimations of just that kind. I wish to choose two of those we encountered: the "Book of Life," and the transcendent "Image."

V

What can the symbol of the Book of Life tell us? In Jewish tradition it means a kind of heavenly ledger wherein our "names" shall be inscribed according to our deserts: we shall qualify by our deeds to be inscribed "for life," namely ours. And this, of course, implies individual immortality. But instead of seeing deeds in the light of deserts, to be accounted to the agent, we can choose to see them as counting in themselves—and then adopt a different concept of the Book whereby it fills with deeds rather than names. We are, in other words, speaking of the possibility that deeds inscribe *themselves* in an eternal memoir of time; that whatever is here enacted somehow registers—beyond its registering and eventual dissipating in the causal patterns of time—in a transcendent realm by rules of effect quite different from those of the world, ever swelling the unfinished record of being and forever shifting the anxious balance of its reckoning. Might it not even be, to venture yet a step further, that what we thus add to the record is of surpassing import—not indeed for a future destiny of ours, but for the concern of that spiritual account itself kept by the unified memory of things? and that, although we mortal agents have no further stake in the immortality which our acts go to join, these acts of ours, and what through them we make of our lives, may just be the stake which an undetermined and vulnerable eternity has in us? And with our freedom, what a precarious stake!—Are we, then, perhaps an experiment of eternity? our very mortality—a venture of the immortal ground with itself? our freedom—the summit of the venture's chance and risk?

We turn for further advice to another simile, that of the transcendent "Image" filled in, feature by feature, by our temporal deeds. We encounter it in gnostic literature, especially of the Iranian branch, in several versions.

One is the conception of a celestial double of the terrestrial self, which the departing soul will meet after death: "I go to meet my image and my image comes to meet me: it caresses and embraces me as if I were returning from captivity"—thus a Mandaean source.[4] And in the beautiful Hymn of the Pearl, this "double" (first described as a "raiment"), when meeting the returning "prince," is recognized

---

4. Ginza, left, 31 (end): M. Lidzbarski (tr.), *Ginzā. Der Schatz oder Das Grosse Buch der Mandäer* (Göttingen, 1925), p. 559, 29-32. In an Avestic source, this image addresses the soul thus: "I am, O youth of good thoughts, good words, good deeds, good conscience, none other than thine own personal conscience . . . Thou hast loved me . . . in this sublimity, goodness, beauty . . . in which I now appear unto thee" (Hādōkht Nask 2.9 ff.).

by him as the image of his own self, and in turn acknowledges him as the one "for whom I was reared in my Father's house, and I perceived in myself how my stature grew in accordance with his labors."[5] According to this version, then, everyone seems to have his alter ego, "kept safe" in the upper world while he labors down below, yet as to its state ultimately entrusted to his responsibility: symbolizing the eternal self of the person, it grows with his trials and deeds, and its form is perfected by his toils—perfected or else, we must add, remembering *The Picture of Dorian Gray,* spoiled and defiled by them. In the salvational turn of our texts this sinister but logically necessary alternative is regularly omitted. There, the encounter as such marks the successful conclusion of the soul's earthly journey and results in a consummating fusion of the two, a mutual absorption, a reuniting of what was temporarily parted. Again, this symbolism expresses immortality of the individual self.

However, beside this individualized there is a collective version of the image symbolism, which connects our deeds not with a perpetuity of our separate selves but with the consummation of the divine self. I quote from one of Mani's writings, discovered about 1930 in a Coptic translation in Egypt. "At the end, when the cosmos is being dissolved, the Thought of Life shall gather himself in and shall form his Self in the shape of the Last Image.[6] . . . With his Living Spirit he shall catch the Light and the Life that is in all things, and build it onto his body." . . . "He gathers in his own Soul unto himself and forms himself in the shape of this Last Image. And thou shalt find him as he sweeps out of himself and casts out the impurity which is alien to him, but gathers in to himself the Life and the Light that is in all things and builds it onto his body. Then, when this Last Image is perfected in all its members, then it shall . . . be lifted out of the great struggle through the Living Spirit . . . who comes and . . . fetches the members out of . . . the dissolution and the end of all things."[7]

---

5. The Hymn of the Pearl (or Hymn of the Soul) is a gnostic poem included in the apocryphal Acts of the Apostle Thomas: on text and interpretation cf. H. Jonas, *The Gnostic Religion.* Boston: Beacon Press, 1958, ch. 5, pp. 112-129; for bibliography cf. *ibid.,* p. 296.

6. Or: the Last Statue: the Coptic uses of Greek work *andrias.*

7. Kephalaia V. 29, 1-6; XVI. 54, 14-24: *Manichäische Handschriften der Staatlichen Museen Berlin, Bd. I: Kephalaia, 1. Hälfte* (Stuttgart, 1940).

It would take us far beyond our present purpose to expound the precise dogmatic meaning of this symbolism. It must suffice to say that what is here called "the last image," emerging at the end of time, is according to Manichaean doctrine built up progressively over and through the world process as a whole: all history, of life in general and of man in particular, incessantly works at it and, in the "final image," restores to its pristine fullness that immortal but passible deity, an emanation from the First God (called "Primal Man"), whose initial self-surrender to the darkness and danger of becoming made the material universe possible—and necessary at the same time. —Now, neither the reasons which Mani gives for this initial divine surrender, nor their more sophisticated alternatives in other gnostic speculations, nor, in general, the denigration of corporeal nature as such common to all these versions, will be acceptable to the modern mind in its resolutely antidualistic temper. Nor will the finite eschatology, positing a determinate goal and end of time, suit our conviction of indefinite continuation of cosmic change and our profound disbelief that the mechanics of it would provide for any ending within or of it to coincide with consummation. Yet the motif of the total "image" can speak to us across these barriers of doctrine and mood. Let us note what in it is potentially significant for us.

I for one would note these features. In the temporal transactions of the world, whose fleeting now is ever swallowed by the past, an eternal presence grows, its countenance slowly defining itself as it is traced with the joys and sufferings, the triumphs and defeats of divinity in the experiences of time, which thus immortally survive. Not the agents, which must ever pass, but their acts enter into the becoming godhead and indelibly form his never decided image. God's own destiny, his doing or undoing, is at stake in this universe to whose unknowing dealings he committed his substance, and man has become the eminent repository of this supreme and every betrayable trust. In a sense, he holds the fate of deity in his hands.

This, I contend, makes sense and as a hypothetical background of metaphysical fact can validate those subjective feelings about an eternal issue which we experience in the call of conscience, in the moments of supreme decision, in the total commitment of deed, and even in the agony of remorse—and these may well be the only empirical signs of an immortal side to our being which our present critical consciousness will still be ready to consider in evidence.

V I

But into what complete metaphysics would such a hypothetical fragment fit?

If, as one sometimes cannot resist doing, I permit myself the license of ignorance, which in these matters is our lot, and the vehicle of myth or likely imagination, which Plato allowed for it, I am tempted to thoughts like these.

In the beginning, for unknowable reasons, the ground of being, or the Divine, chose to give itself over to the chance and risk and endless variety of becoming. And wholly so: entering into the adventure of space and time, the deity held back nothing of itself: no uncommitted or unimpaired part remained to direct, correct, and ultimately guarantee the devious working-out of its destiny in creation. On this unconditional immanence the modern temper insists. It is its courage or despair, in any case its bitter honesty, to take our being-in-the-world seriously: to view the world as left to itself, its laws as brooking no interference, and the rigor of our belonging to it as not softened by extramundane providence. The same our myth postulates for God's being in the world. Not, however, in the sense of pantheistic immanence: if world and God are simply the same, the world at each moment and in each state represents his fullness, and God can neither lose nor gain. Rather, in order that the world might be, and be for itself, God renounced his own being, divesting himself of his deity—to receive it back from the Odyssey of time weighted with the chance harvest of unforeseeable temporal experience: transfigured or possibly even disfigured by it. In such self-forfeiture of divine integrity for the sake of unprejudiced becoming, no other foreknowledge can be admitted than that of *possibilities* which cosmic being offers in its own terms: to these, God committed his cause in effacing himself for the world.

And for aeons his cause is safe in the slow hands of cosmic chance and probability—while all the time we may surmise a patient memory of the gyrations of matter to accumulate into an ever more expectant accompaniment of eternity to the labors of time—a hesitant emergence of transcendence from the opaqueness of immanence.

And then the first stirring of life—a new language of the world: and with it a tremendous quickening of concern in the eternal realm and a sudden leap in its growth toward recovery of its plenitude. It is the world-accident for which becoming deity had waited and with which its prodigal stake begins to show signs of being redeemed. From the infinite swell of feeling, sensing, striving, and acting, which ever more varied and intense rises above the mute eddyings of matter, eternity gains strength, filling with content after content of self-affirmation, and the awakening God can first pronounce creation to be good.

But note that with life together came death, and that mortality is the price which the new possibility of being called "life" had to pay for itself. If permanence were the point, life should not have started out in the first place, for in no possible form can it match the durability of inorganic bodies. It is essentially precarious and corruptible being, an adventure in mortality, obtaining from long-lasting matter on its terms—the short terms of metabolizing organism—the borrowed, finite careers of individual selves. Yet it is precisely through the briefly snatched self-feeling, doing, and suffering of *finite* individuals, with the pitch of awareness heightened by the very press of finitude, that the divine landscape bursts into color and the deity comes to experience itself. If, then, mortality is the very condition of the separate selfhood which in the instinct of self-preservation shows itself so highly prized throughout the organic world, and if the yield of this mortality is the food of eternity, it is unreasonable to demand for its appointed executants, the self-affirming selves—immortality. The instinct of self-preservation indeed acknowledges this, for it implies the premise of extinction in its straining each time to ward it off for the nonce.

Note also this that with life's innocence before the advent of knowledge God's cause cannot go wrong. Whatever variety evolution brings forth adds to the possibilities of feeling and acting, and thus enriches the self-experiencing of the ground of being. Every new dimension of world-response opened up in its course means another modality for God's trying out his hidden essence and discovering himself through the surprises of the world-adventure. And all its harvest of anxious toil, whether bright or dark, swells the transcendent treasure of temporally lived eternity. If this is true for the broadening spectrum of diversity as such, it is even truer for the heightening pitch and passion of life that go with the twin rise of perception and motility in animals. The ever more sharpened keenness of appetite and fear, pleasure and pain, triumph and anguish, love and even cruelty—their very edge is the deity's gain. Their countless, yet never blunted incidence—hence the necessity of death and new birth —supplies the tempered essence from which the Godhead reconstitutes itself. All this, evolution provides in the mere lavishness of its play and the sternness of its spur. Its creatures, by merely fulfilling themselves in pursuit of their lives, vindicate the divine venture. Even their suffering deepens the fullness of the symphony. Thus, this side of good and evil, God cannot lose in the great evolutionary game.

Nor yet can he fully win in the shelter of its innocence, and a new expectancy grows in him in answer to the direction which the unconscious drift of immanence gradually takes.

And then he trembles as the thrust of evolution, carried by its own momentum, passes the threshold where innocence ceases and an entirely new criterion of success and failure takes hold of the divine stake. The advent of man means the advent of knowledge and freedom, and with this supremely double-edged gift the innocence of the mere subject of self-fulfilling life has given way to the charge of responsibility under the disjunction of good and evil. To the promise and risk of this agency the divine cause, revealed at last, henceforth finds itself committed; and its issue trembles in the balance. The image of God, haltingly begun by the universe, for so long worked upon—and left undecided—in the wide and then narrowing spirals of pre-human life, passes with this last twist, and with a dramatic quickening of the movement, into man's precarious trust, to be completed, saved, or spoiled by what he will do to himself and the world. And in this awesome impact of his deeds on God's destiny, on the very complexion of eternal being, lies the immortality of man.

With the appearance of man, transcendence awakened to itself and henceforth accompanies his doings with the bated breath of suspense, hoping and beckoning, rejoicing and grieving, approving and frowning—and, I daresay, making itself felt to him even while not intervening in the dynamics of his worldly scene: for can it not be that by the reflection of its own state as it wavers with the record of man, the transcendent casts light and shadow over the human landscape?

V I I

Such is the tentative myth which I would like to believe "true"—in the sense in which myth may happen to adumbrate a truth which of necessity is unknowable and even, in direct concepts, ineffable, yet which, by intimations to our deepest experience, lays claim upon our powers of giving indirect account of it in revocable, anthropomorphic images. In the great pause of metaphysics in which we are, and before it has found its own speech again, we must entrust ourselves to this, admittedly treacherous, medium at our risk. The myth, if only it is conscious of its experimental and provisional nature and does not pose as doctrine, can from the necessity of that pause bridge the vacuum with its fleeting span. I at any rate felt driven to it for once under the constraint of a task which philosophy even in its helplessness must not deny.

To continue, then, in the same speculative vein, there follow certain ethical conclusions from the metaphysics which my myth has adumbrated. The first is the transcendent importance of our deeds, of how we live our lives. If man, as our tale has it, was created "for" the image of God, rather than "in" his image—if our lives become lines in the divine countenance: then our responsibility is not defined in mundane terms alone, by which often it is inconsequential enough, but registers in a dimension where efficacy follows transcausal norms of inner essence. Further, as transcendence grows with the terribly ambiguous harvest of deeds, our impact on eternity is for good *and* for evil: we can build and we can destroy, we can heal and we can hurt, we can nourish and we can starve divinity, we can perfect and we can disfigure its image: and the scars of one are as enduring as the lustre of the other. Thus the immortality of our deeds is no cause for vain rejoicing—what most often ought to be wished for is rather their leaving no trace. But this is not granted: they have traced their line. Not, however, as the individual's destiny. The individual is by nature temporal, not eternal; and the person in particular, mortal trustee of an immortal cause, has the enjoyment of selfhood for the moment of time as the means by which eternity lays itself open to the decisions of time. *As* enacted in the medium of becoming, that is, as transient, are personal selves eternity's stake. Thus it is that in the irrepeatable occasions of finite lives the issue must be decided time and again:

infinite duration would blunt the point of the issue and rob occasion of its urgent call.

Nor, apart from this ontological consideration, does man have a moral claim to the gift of immortality. Availing himself of the enjoyment of selfhood, he has endorsed the terms on which it is offered, and rather than having it is a title for more he owes thanks for the grant of existence as such—and for that which made it possible. For *there is no necessity of there being a world at all.* Why there is something rather than nothing—this unanswerable question of metaphysics should protect us from taking existence for an axiom, and its finiteness for a blemish on it or a curtailment of its right. Rather is the fact of existence the mystery of mysteries—which our myth has tried to reflect in a symbol. By foregoing its own inviolateness the eternal ground allowed the world to be. To this self-denial all creature owes its existence, and with it has received all there is to receive from beyond. Having given himself whole to the becoming world, God has no more to give: it is man's now to give to him. And he may give by seeing to it in the ways of his life that it does not happen, or not happen too often, and not on his account, that "it repented the Lord"[8] to have made the world. This may well be the secret of the "thirty-six righteous ones" whom, according to Jewish tradition, the world shall never lack[9]: that with the superior valency of good over evil, which, we hope, obtains in the non-causal logic of things there, their hidden holiness can outweigh countless guilt, redress the balance of a generation and secure the serenity of the invisible realm.

But does that serenity, or its contrary, matter to our life on earth? Does it touch it? Let me join this question with another one, in conclusion of my groping journey. What about those who never could inscribe themselves in the Book of Life with deeds either good or evil, great or small, because their lives were cut off before they had their chance, or their humanity was destroyed in degradations most cruel and most thorough such as no humanity can survive? I am thinking of the gassed and burnt children of Auschwitz, of the defaced, dehumanized phantoms of the camps, and of all the other, numberless victims of the other man-made holocausts of our time. Among men,

---

8. Gen. 6:6-7.
9. Sanhedrin 97 b; Sukkah 45 b.

their sufferings will soon be forgotten, and their names even sooner. Another chance is not given them, and eternity has no compensation for what has been missed in time. Are they, then, debarred from an immortality which even their tormentors and murderers obtain because they could *act*—abominably, yet accountably, thus leaving their sinister mark on eternity's face? This I refuse to believe. And this I like to believe: that there was weeping in the heights at the waste and despoilment of humanity; that a groan answered the rising shout of ignoble suffering, and wrath—the terrible wrong done to the reality and possibility of each life thus wantonly victimized, each one a thwarted attempt of God. "The voice of thy brother's blood cries unto me from the ground": should we not believe that the immense chorus of such cries that has risen up in our lifetime now hangs over our world as a dark and accusing cloud? that eternity looks down upon us with a frown, wounded itself and perturbed in its depths?

And might we not even feel it? I think it possible, in spite of what I have said about the closed immanence of the worldly realm. For the secret sympathy that connects our being with the transcendent condition and makes the latter depend on our deeds, must somehow work both ways—or else there would not even be that inward testimony for us to invoke on which our whole case for the eternal was grounded. If so, the state of transcendence, as *we* have let it become, will in turn have a resonance in ours—sometimes felt, though mostly not, and presently felt, perhaps, in a general malaise, in the profound distemper of the contemporary mind. Things human do not prosper under our hands. Happiness eludes our pursuit, and meaning mocks our desperate need. Could it be that, superinduced upon the many-layered, but never completely explaining causes from within our historical existence, also the disturbance of the transcendent order which we have caused by the monstrous crimes of our time, thus reacts on the spiritual mood of men—and thus the modern temper paradoxically might itself reflect the immortality which it disowns? It would be fitting—more I dare not say—if the slaughtered had that share in immortality, and on their account a great effort were asked of those alive to lift the shadow from our brow and gain for those after us a new chance of serenity by restoring it to the invisible world.

But even if not their shadow, certainly the shadow of the Bomb is there to remind us that the image of God is in danger as never before, and on most unequivocal, terrestrial terms. That in these terms an eternal issue is at stake together with the temporal one—this aspect of our responsibility can be our guard against the temptation of fatalistic acquiescence or the worse treason of *après nous le deluge*. We literally hold in our faltering hands the future of the divine adventure and must not fail Him, even if we would fail ourselves.

Thus in the dim light at the end of our wandering we may discern a twofold responsibility of man: one in terms of worldly causality, by which the effect of his deed extends for some greater or shorter length into a future where it eventually dissipates; and a simultaneous one in terms of its impact on the eternal realm, where it never dissipates. The one, with our limited foresight and the complexity of worldly things, is much at the mercy of luck and chance; the other goes by knowable norms which, in the Bible's words,[10] are not far from our hearts. There might even be, as I indicated, a third dimension to our responsibility in terms of the impalpably reciprocal way in which Eternity, without intervening in the physical course of things, will communicate its spiritual state as a pervading mood to a generation which will have to live with it.

But the first two are more than enough to summon us to our task. Although the hereafter is not ours, nor eternal recurrence of the here, we can have immortality at heart when in our brief span we serve our threatened mortal affairs and help the suffering immortal God.

---

10. Deut. 30:14.

Epilogue
Nature and Ethics

We opened this volume with the proposition that the philosophy of life comprises the philosophy of organism and the philosophy of mind. At its end, and in the light of what we have learned, we may add a further proposition, implied in that first one but setting a new task: a philosophy of mind comprises ethics—and through the continuity of mind with organism and of organism with nature, ethics becomes part of the philosophy of nature. This again is out of tune with modern belief. Is not man alone? Does not the seeming call to our moral being originate in ourselves and merely come back to us from the putative scheme of things as our reflected voice? Has not that scheme been endowed by us with whatever meaning it may have for us? For man alone, so we have been taught for some centuries now, is the source of all demand, command, and call with which he finds himself addressed, and their imputation to a nature barren of mind is no more than an anthropomorphic liberty. We mirror being, but in doing so we mirror ourselves in it, and recognizing our image there at last for what it is we find pride in our cosmic solitude. Whatever moral quality enters the relation of self and world can have its origin nowhere but in the self.

[282]

Here, two different propositions are mixed into a dubious half-truth. True it is that obligation cannot be without the idea of obligation, and true that within the known world the capacity for that or any idea appears in man alone: but it does not follow that the idea must therefore be an invention, and cannot be a discovery. Nor does it follow that the rest of existence is indifferent to that discovery: it may have a stake in it, and in virtue of that stake may even be the ground of the obligation which man acknowledges for himself. He would then be the executor of a trust which only he can see, but did not create. At any rate, the contention—almost axiomatic in the modern climate of thought—that something like an "ought" can issue only from man and is alien to everything outside him, is more than a descriptive statement: it is part of a metaphysical position, which has never given full account of itself. To ask for such account is to reopen the ontological question of human within total existence. Ontology may yet relocate the foundation of "ought" from the ego of man, to which it has been relegated, to the nature of being in general. It may have been premature despair which denied the doctrine of being the power to yield a ground of obligation—for beings, of course, that are pervious to obligation, and who must be there so that obligation can find its respondent.

Ontology as the ground of ethics was the original tenet of philosophy. Their divorce, which is the divorce of the "objective" and "subjective" realms, is the modern destiny. Their reunion can be effected, if at all, only from the "objective" end, that is to say, through a revision of the idea of nature. And it is becoming rather than abiding nature which would hold out any such promise. From the immanent direction of its total evolution there may be elicited a destination of man by whose terms the person, in the act of fulfilling himself, would at the same time realize a concern of universal substance. Hence would result a principle of ethics which is ultimately grounded neither in the autonomy of the self nor in the needs of the community, but in an objective assignment by the nature of things (what theology used to call the *ordo creationis*)—such as could still be kept faith with by the last of a dying mankind in his final solitude. The fact that by cosmic scales man is but an atom is a quantitative irrelevancy: his inner width can make him an event of cosmic importance. The reflection of being in knowledge may be more than a human event: it may be an event for being itself and affect its metaphysical condition. In Hegelian language: a "coming to itself" of original substance.

However that may be (and the idea is frankly speculative), only an ethics which is grounded in the breadth of being, not merely in the singularity or oddness of man, can have significance in the scheme of things. It has it, if man has such significance; and whether he has it we must learn from an interpretation of reality as a whole, at least from an interpretation of life as a whole. But even without any such claim of transhuman significance for human conduct, an ethics no longer founded on divine authority must be founded on a principle discoverable in the nature of things, lest it fall victim to subjectivism or other forms of relativity. However far, therefore, the ontological quest may have carried us outside man, into the general theory of being and of life, it did not really move away from ethics, but searched for its possible foundation.

Index

absolute   257, 268

abstract   148, 199

abstraction   24, 30, 32, 91, 147, 149, 162, 168, 170, 174, 184

acceleration   116, 132

accident(al)   48, 49, 51, 52, 80, 213, 214, 233

acosmic, acosmism   216, 221, 224, 225

acoustic   30, 137, 138, 139, 142, 146

act   82, 91, 269, 270, 271, 272, 274, 280

action, acting   2 f., 20, 22, 23, 24, 25, 26, 27, 29, 31, 32, 33, 40, 60 n.3, 62 n.4, 104, 105, 116, 119, 122, 127, 137, 141, 146, 148, 151, 153, 155, 183, 184, 190, 198, 204, 269, 276

active, activity   22, 23, 24, 26, 30, 31, 76 n., 82, 85, 104, 105, 112, 114, 140, 143, 144, 145, 153, 155, 156, 191, 204, 206, 268, 270
  life   194, 206

adaequatio   172, 181

Adam   173, 247

adaptation, adaptive   46, 50, 103, 116, 117

adventure, -ous   45, 106, 275, 276, 281

affection, affective, affectivity   29, 84, 85, 168

affirmation   177, 179, 208

agent   27 n.2, 31, 76 n., 140, 156 n., 272, 274

aggregate   75, 78, 79, 201

agility   105

a-lēthēs, a-lētheuein   181

algebra   67, 68, 69 n.

alien   218, 219, 220, 224

alienated   231

alienation   220, 221

amoeba   46, 51, 65

analogy   111, 251, 252, 253, 256

analysis   35, 40 n., 54, 56, 67, 69, 69 n., 77, 78, 87, 88, 90, 95, 132, 200, 202

Anaxagoras   14 n.

animal   47, 51, 55, 57, 59, 60, 63, 70, 74, 76 n., 90, *99-107,* 116, 125, 126, 127, 145, 155, 158, 166, 167, 175, 177, 178, 179, 183, 184, 186, 227, 276
  life   33
  nisus   33
  rationale   47

animality   57, 102, 104, 107, 126, 185, 227

animate   ix, 4, 96

animism, animistic   7, 9, 15, 22, 25, 36 f., 72

Anselm of Canterbury   242

answer   246, 247

anthropocentric   ix, 34, 60

anthropomorphism, -ic   10, 23, *33-37,* 91, 117, 122, 233, 278, 282

[285]